GERRY ADAMS

SELECTED WRITINGS

BRANDON

This new, expanded edition first published in 1997;
first edition published in 1994

Brandon Book Publishers Ltd,
Dingle, Co. Kerry, Ireland

British Library Cataloguing in Publication Data is available for this book.

ISBN 0 86322 233 1

Typeset by Brandon
Cover design by The Public Communications Centre, Dublin
Cover photograph by Derek Speirs/Report
Printed by The Guernsey Press Co. Ltd., Guernsey, Channel Islands.

For all the people who have opened their homes
and their hearts to me, and others like me.
xoxoxo

Contents

Introduction

Successive governments in Dublin and London have over much of the last twenty-five years banned the voice of Gerry Adams from radio and television. Even the advertising of his short stories has been banned in Ireland. However, these acts of suppression tell us more about the governments and the qualities of our democracies than they do about the writings of an author whose first book, a work of local history and reminiscence, was published in 1982.

My attention was drawn to his writing in late 1981 when I read in *An Phoblacht*, the Sinn Féin newspaper, an account by Gerry Adams of growing up on the Falls Road in Belfast. It was particularly well written, showing that its author had a finely tuned ear for the dialogue of the streets in which he had been reared. I wrote and asked him if he had any more material in a similar vein, and he replied that he had, in fact, been thinking of putting a pamphlet together about the Falls Road area.

"See," I said, "if you can make it book-length."

He was somewhat daunted when I spelled out how much he would need to write, but we met in Dublin and agreed the outlines of the proposed book. I knew Adams to possess considerable intellect combined with an intense feeling for the people amongst whom he lived and from whom he sprang. As a writer he possessed a fine sense of humour, especially of irony, and he seemed to have an admirable lack of ego; his interest in the lives of the people around him was not an affectation, nor the tactical manoeuvre of a conventional politician; rather, he was genuinely self-effacing. He also possessed the kind of feeling which can transform raw material, rendering it compelling reading.

We published *Falls Memories* in November 1982, quickly sold out the first printing, and published a new, revised edition. Reviewers for a wide range of newspapers praised the book, remarking upon its "light-hearted humour" and describing it as "an excellent example of the urban folklorist at work". A couple of Dublin columnists sought to denigrate Brandon for publishing Adams at all, but response to the writing itself was generally very positive.

The qualities of the writing in *Falls Memories* were in some respects the qualities of fiction. While parts of the book included relatively dry recitations of historical facts, the heart of it showed imagination allied to a sensitive ear and eye. I was therefore very interested when Gerry Adams mentioned that he had written a couple of short stories, one of which he had submitted under an assumed name for a competition, which it had won. I asked him to send me whatever he had in the way of stories and some months later I received a small bundle, certainly not sufficient to make a book. A number of them concerned his experience of internment in Long Kesh and I advised him that he might like to work up a book-length manuscript offering a portrait of internment.

We had published *Falls Memories* in 1982 and in the following year he had been elected both President of Sinn Féin and MP for West Belfast. His schedule had been busy before, but now his life was even less his own, and so I understood that the Long Kesh book was a long-term prospect. Meanwhile, however, I was well aware that what a great many readers wanted was a book outlining his political philosophy. Recognising that himself, he had written in a note at the front of *Falls Memories*: "I trust that those readers who buy this book expecting something else will not be too disappointed".

I raised with him the possibility of publishing a book which would constitute a direct personal political statement, but he raised two major problems: firstly, he was extremely reluctant to present himself as a "leader", in the sense of someone above and beyond the general membership of the republican movement; secondly, there was no question of him being able to give the necessary time to the project. I countered that, while I did not wish to commission a party political document, I did feel that there was a broad public need and demand for an exposition of Irish republicanism as it stood now. He, I knew, was saying that important changes were in train within the movement; it was time, I suggested, that this be properly exposed to public view. After a certain amount of gentle badgering and a lot of exchanges of chapter drafts over many months, we finally had a manuscript and were able to publish *The Politics of Irish Freedom* in December 1986.

British Labour MP Ken Livingstone welcomed the book's publication and a *New Statesman* reviewer wrote that "Adams's 'personal statement' must rank as the most considerable one to date from a leading member of the republican movement clarifying and defending its aims and methods. It thus has a role to play as one corrective among others to the flow of misinformation ... that passes for journalistic analysis of affairs in the North of Ireland". It sold very well in both Ireland and Britain, was reprinted several times, was published in Spanish in 1991 and in a new, revised American edition in 1994 under the title of *Free Ireland: Towards a Lasting Peace*.

Following the success of *The Politics of Irish Freedom* I again discussed his short stories with him, and I felt that he was closest to being able to complete the collection of pieces about internment we had discussed before. Revision, expansion and development were needed, and this he did in 1989, and in 1990 we published it under the title of *Cage Eleven*. Benefiting from a considerable amount of work in rewriting and revision, many of the stories in *Cage Eleven*, which hovered between fact and fiction, showed a literary quality which surprised some reviewers. *Books Ireland* described it as "Quite brilliant", while the *Listener* described him as "a natural storyteller, with a warm and agile wit". The *Sunday Press* suggested that "When the work of most of the participants in literature's yearly orgy of hype has been consigned to history, Adams's slim volume will be alive and well". In the Introduction to the US edition, published in 1993 by Sheridan Square Press, the veteran civil rights lawyer Paul O'Dwyer wrote of the stories that they were "by turns humorous and soul-wrenching, satirical and compassionate, witty and entertaining". In 1994 a French edition was published.

Encouraged by the response to *Cage Eleven*, Gerry Adams

managed to steal the time to develop and add to his other short stories, and in 1992 we were able to publish a collection of stories which were more decidedly fictional. *The Street and other stories* also elicited a positive response from reviewers. The *Times Literary Supplement* praised their "elegiac quality", while the *Sunday Press* found them "well written and authentic in form and tone". Published in the US in 1993 with an introduction by Jimmy Breslin, *The Street and other stories* was also published in Italian and Spanish editions in 1994.

Governments, the courts, broadcasting authorities, politicians of various parties, and many commentators have sought to silence the author of this book. Some do so on the grounds of the content of his writings, some on the basis simply of their authorship. They even seek to prevent people from knowing that Gerry Adams is an author. However, readers of this book can make up their own minds; can form their own opinions about the qualities of the writing and about the views expressed; can decide for themselves what they make of the author.

I wrote in the introduction to another book by the same author that "The publication of this book will do nothing either to promote or to end violence. It may, however, promote and increase knowledge and understanding, and these are valuable commodities irrespective of any degree of sympathy or antipathy". I think now that I was perhaps understating the case, for one of the most vital ingredients in building any lasting peace must be a growth of understanding. The truth of any situation is likely to be made up of contradictory elements, to be expressed by contrasting and conflicting voices. Suppress one of those voices, exclude one of those elements, and you prevent access to the truth.

Steve MacDonogh
Editorial Director, Brandon
9 August 1994

THE LOWER WACK

For since the civil modern world began
What's Irish history? Walks the child a man?
William Allingham

E ARLY ONE BRIGHT Monday morning, I dandered along
Sorella Street in the direction of the Falls Road. I
hadn't been along this way in a good while but now, on
impulse, I decided to venture into the area, curious to see how
much the district had changed at the hands of planners. So instead of heading up Dunville Street, I strolled towards
Abercorn Street North.

Here I used to live, spending an uneventful childhood playing rally-oh, kick-the-tin, handball and football, sprinkled
with occasional forays against the Getty Street lads who were
foolhardy enough to venture into our territory. It appeared to
me at the time that our gang had a fearsome reputation,
though I suppose that by today's standards we weren't really
at all fearsome.

"I must be getting old," I said to your man.

"And sentimental," he retorted. "You'll be saying next that
the weather was always warm, the food more wholesome and
the football better."

"And so it was. Well, I mean to say, we had less distractions in those days. Look at the park, not a sinner in it. I remember when the place would have been black with people."

"At ten o'clock on a Monday morning! The kids are at school," your man interrupted me scornfully as I gazed forlornly across a deserted Dunville Park.

"I suppose you're right," I admitted as I passed the wee gate of the park. Maybe I am getting old, I mused. I recalled older people telling me the same thing about their childhoods; and thought that such recollections must be coloured, not by any generation's monopoly on good weather and all that goes with it, but more likely by one's increasing and self-inflicted inability to participate in simple pleasures associated with childhood.

"No use getting philosophical at this hour of the morning," I muttered aloud.

"There's wiser locked up," your man suggested, leaving me to my own devices at the corner. I walked by Getty Street entry and then, stunned, I stopped and stared as I entered a new world – a waste land. On my left, behind hoardings, new houses were rising, while on my right – emptiness. Gone was the rag store and Patsy's corner shop. All the old neighbours' houses had vanished, leaving a view, obstructed only by an occasional remnant of the past, right down to the Long Bar; while across from me in the distance stood the twin spires of St Peter's where Divis Flats raised their tower blocks to the heavens.

I stopped outside where Begleys had lived. Just an empty space. No wee girls swinging on the lamp-post now. Not even a lamp-post; just a broken pavement. But what of the neighbours? Scattered far and wide, no doubt; some dead, the younger ones married and living up the road, with a few lucky enough to win a house back in the old area, thus escaping the transport costs that a regular visit to the "broo" demands. In a short while the district will have vanished, and those returning from exile in America or Long Kesh may well wonder at the changes as they pass through what is now a strange, alien landscape.

16

I passed Harbinson's corner and memories came flooding back. Of Sundays spent tickling trout in Kansas Glen, only to have our catch devoured by a great-uncle in Gibson Street whose greatness was measured not least by his relish for fresh trout. Of double-decker candy apples with coconut on top. Of being slapped on my first day at St Finian's. Of pig's feet and matinées in Clonard picture house. Hopping the carts in Leeson Street. The "reg" men and the wee man selling coal brick. The happy horse man and the refuse man.

Ghost stories told at gable ends and re-enacted on bedroom walls with nightmarish results. Over towards Raglan Street we played handball and heard occasional stories of Pig Meneely or Paddy-Me-Arse, two peelers well known to older people in the area. Or the Durango Kid, our nickname for their contemporary, an RUC motorcyclist who scattered softball games of football or rounders with his forays down Balaclava Street into our part of the district.

Whispers about "the boys" or an occasional witness to meetings of pale-faced earnest young men who, we gathered disinterestedly, had just "got out". Being chased by "the wackey" while fleeing gleefully after hours from Dunville Park or after disturbing old men playing marleys at the shelter. Later still, but with less glee, being pursued by RUC riot squads and, later again, by the British Army.

The rubble-filled waste land filled with ghosts as I headed along Ross Street. Years ago it had echoed to the clatter of millworkers crowding the pavement as they linked their way to and from work.

You'll easy know a doffer
As she comes into town
With her long yellow hair
And her ringlets hanging down
With her rubber tied before her
And her picker in her hand
You'll easy know a doffer
For she'll always get her man.

I headed across Albert Street and towards the Loney. Or at least towards where the Loney used to be. A few years ago when asked where you lived it was always "down the Falls" as distinct from the area from Springfield Road upwards which, although on the Falls Road, isn't really "the Falls". It's "up the road". You see, we were from "down the road", a clearly defined territory wedged between the Grosvenor, the Falls and Durham Street. Part of our district was called Leeson Street, a term which covered the streets from Leeson Street itself to the Grosvenor.

The Loney would have to have had flexible boundaries to accommodate all those who claim the status of former residence. The extent of its territory is thus often much disputed. Bingo Campbell, for example, swears that it was the streets bounded by Divis Street, Albert Street and Durham Street, though others, myself included, disagree.

In the early seventies the entire area became known as "the Lower Wack", a local jibe at the British Army spokesmen's habit of talking grandiosely about "the Lower Falls". That is, when they weren't talking about some place on the other side of town known to everybody else as Ardoyne but which they persisted in calling "the Ardoyne". Later the Lower Wack became known in contemporary republican jargon as "the Dogs", after the local IRA's famous D Company, which a local wit christened "D for Dog" during a period when their tenacity brought the area repeatedly to the headlines.

Since then, of course, the Falls has become a household name, and television coverage of riots, curfews and pogroms has made its small streets known to many who never had the privilege of experiencing them, their back entries, yard walls and the hospitality of their people.

Now, only that hospitality and the people's resistance remain, and as I stopped at St Peter's and reflected on the passing of a community, a wee woman approached me.

"You'd better watch yourself, son; there's Brits down at the Flats."

"Thanks, missus," I replied as, startled out of my musings and brought back to reality by her warning, I retraced my steps and hurried, more carefully now, towards the crowded and relatively safer Falls Road.

My short walk had filled my head with memories. Stories of IRA volunteers like Charlie Hughes, Paddy Maguire and Squire Maguire or Jimmy Quigley. I passed Alma Street and looked down to where Garnett Street used to be. Remember the day that Mundo O'Rawe was shot there? Remember hearing about the girl volunteer, her face streaming with tears and her body wracked with sobs as she tried to exact vengeance on a hovering helicopter with an aged .303 rifle which was too big for her to shoulder properly? I never found out who she was. Maybe she never existed. Just another story? You never know. I heard it said she stood there, on her own, firing away and all the time muttering "You bastards, you bastards" to an implacable sky and a whitewashed wall, which had probably seen it all before. You see, they shot Mundo after he had been arrested. But then, I suppose that's the way it goes.

And what about local characters like Bunny Rice and Paddy-with-the-glass-eye? We had some crack with Paddy, God forgive us; but to tell the truth I was a wee bit scared of him. Remember getting called for supper: the long-drawn-out chant of "Gerry, you're awanted for your dinner". But life goes on. Still, it's strange to see the gardens facing the Baths, though maybe there were gardens there in the first place. As I passed by McLarnon's shop I wondered what it was all like years and years ago.

"Somebody should write a book about what it was like here," I said to your man. "Right from the very beginnings. Maybe I'll do it, if I get a chance."

"Well, you'd better do it quick or nobody'll know where you're talking about," said your man back to me. "It'll be like all the things you say you're going to do. The district will be completely gone and you'll still be spoofing about doing something about it. You'd wonder you never catch yourself on."

"Oh yeah," said I. "Well, we'll see about that. ..."

DÉJÀ VU

For this Edward Fitzgerald died,
And Robert Emmet and Wolfe Tone
All that delirium of the brave?
W.B. Yeats

THE OLD MAN drew heavily on his Park Drive and settled back on the settee.

"So you want to know about the twenties," he declared, gazing past potted geraniums through lace curtains at the grey half-demolished street. It was a Thursday evening. He was due to shift on Monday. "They wanted me to go on Saturday, but I told them I'd go in my own good time. A Saturday flit is a short sit. So I'm going on Monday. My next stop after that will be Milltown. There's not many of us left, you know. I was born here. Thought I'd be buried from here as well."

He sighed and reflected in silence. Then, decided, he deftly poked the dying fire into life, flicked the Park Drive butt into the newly born flames and handed me a battered photograph album.

"That's me and my mates. We worked just around the corner from here in the stables. There was stables all around here, you know. Nearly any wee court or yard you see was a stable. I recall a herd of cows in the ones in Leeson Street and pigs round in Cyprus Street. A lot of people kept chickens as well. That's Jimmy there; he worked for a street hawker, kept his horse in Balaclava Street; I was in Sevastopol Street, cleaned the stables night and morning; and that's Paddy," a stubby finger identified Paddy. "I haven't seen Jimmy since Paddy's funeral. He's up in Twinbrook now with his daughter; says he'd rather be down the road. Paddy minded the horses in Ross Street and then he worked in Kinahan's. That's our Seán. He went to the States. He wouldn't know the place now if he came back. You know, when me, Jimmy, Paddy and Seán were wee bucks the Falls was a great place. People nowadays don't know they're living. We had our troubles, same as today, but the neighbours were good. We looked after our own, be they sick or old, drunk or sober. No need for meals on wheels in them days."

He thumbed through faded photographs, stopping only to light another cigarette. "I used to know your grandfather, you know. He was the first of the Adamses to turn republican. Him and the Elliots and the Begleys – Paddy Begley, your granny's brother, was a handy boxer. Fought under the name of Boyd. That's why everybody called him Boyd Begley. Though you wouldn't recall that. I remember him fighting Kenny Webb, the Irish champion.

"That's my mother there. She reared nine of us in this house. I'm the only one left. She always told me she wouldn't be happy till I was married and settled. Well, I settled okay," he smiled, "but I never did get round to marrying. Ach, we had good times then. There was big stones, you know, outside every door and on summer nights the women would sit outside their doors and play housey. The streets were cobbled then; no motor cars. The coalman – we bought coal by the stone – the milkman, hawkers and the like all had horses and carts. The milkman ladled out the milk into jugs with a big measure. Many a time I got a jug of milk and a pitcher of buttermilk. Real buttermilk with dollops of cream and butter floating on top.

"All the womenfolk baked: like, we got a ticket of shop bread or a Barney Hughes bap every so often, but mostly me ma baked on the griddle. Treacle farls and soda farls, and bannocks or wheaten and potato bread. Potato apple or bread pudding would be a special treat. I'm making myself hungry with all this talk of food! Go on in there like a good man and stick us on a cup of tea. You'll find bread in the cupboard. And don't mind the mess: this place is like Maggie Marley's with me shifting. I couldn't be annoyed doing anything with it. Sure, what's the point?"

He fell silent again as I rummaged in the tiny scullery, rinsing cups in the jawbox – the big stone sink – and wetting the tea.

"You know," he shouted in to me, "there was none of these so-called modern amenities in those days. No wirelesses, well very few anyway, only crystal sets in the beginning and all of them tuned in, round here anyway, to Radio Éireann. And no TVs. TV is a curse. We made our own fun. No, things were simpler then. See this?"

I returned with tea and a plate of bread and butter.

"See this?" he pointed to the coffee table. "Well, we had a white scrubbed table and four scrubbed chairs. Me da had an armchair, the only one in the house: it sat here, where I am now, at the fire. All the houses had ranges and a gas ring on the hob. No electric lights: two gas mantles; we used candles up the stairs and in the scullery. A cupboard for food and sometimes bits of clothing and that was that. Big double beds upstairs and in the back room. We slept head to foot, five in the back and two in the front with me ma and da. Our Kathleen and Ena slept down the street in their granny's. There was a gas lamp outside the front door – you can still see the mark – they tuk it down a couple of years ago. Used to be able to read by it. And the floors were tiled: great fuss here with the mother and sisters every week, scrubbing the tiles and the furniture, doing the brasses and black-leading the grate. But I suppose you don't want to hear all this. You'd think my head was cut the way I'm going on. No visitors, you see. Though I read a lot. What was it exactly you wanted to hear about?"

He gazed at me, supping his tea and chewing one of the pieces of bread.

"You want to know about the troubles in the twenties? Ah, now," he chuckled, "I hope you've plenty of time for listening. There's many a story I cud tell: make your teeth curl, but," he paused mischievously, "you never know who you're talking to. Can't be too careful nowadays." Then, laughing at my discomfort, "I'm only having you on. To tell you the truth, I consider myself a bit of a historian. Once I get my thoughts in order I'll give you your fill of facts and figures. You're in no rush you said? Well, you know that the United Irishmen was founded in Belfast, in Sugar House Entry? All sorts of famous people came to Belfast. John Mitchel, Daniel O'Connell, Thomas Francis Meagher, Michael Davitt. I used to read about them all. Henry Joy, Russell – he's 'the man from God knows where' – Jemmy Hope, Orr, Harry Munro and the rest of them used to meet in Sugar House Entry. Henry Joy's family, the McCrackens, owned some of the cotton and linen mills in Belfast. He was hanged in Corn Market. Was interned for a while in Dublin, if my memory serves me right. They were all hanged in the end or deported. Mostly Presbyterians. Funny how people change. Things never change, you know, only people."

He poked at the fire again, then satisfied with the result settled back and continued. "Anyway, when I was a young fellah, we had our troubles as well, not as bad as nowadays but rough enough just the same. I recall my mother talking about the Fenians, sitting here at night at this very hearth. Some of them's commemorated in the monument in Milltown, at the old Republican plot. Now wait till we see: there's William Harbinson, a great man altogether. He was a colour-sergeant in the Antrim Militia stationed in the barracks in North Queen Street. The Fenians infiltrated the British Army, you know. No chance of that nowadays. Anyway, Harbinson died in Belfast Prison; he was only forty-four. Buried up in County Antrim, I think in Ballinderry. The first monument in Milltown was erected in his memory; it was blew up in 1937. It also commemorated about seventy other ones including over twenty Protestant Fenians – that's a contradiction, people would say nowadays: ignorance is a great man – and some Yanks who came over as part of an expeditionary force from the States. They ended up in Belfast Prison as well. Does a great trade does 'the Crum'. It was built in 1846 you know."

He lit another cigarette. "I remember, in 1919, with all the talk of home rule, that there was a great strike for a forty-four hour week. The gas department and the electricity – that didn't effect us – the trams were laid up and the bakeries, even the mills were idle. We used to sing 'We'll work no more till we get the forty-four, on the good ship *Lullabell'*. Then Carson started to rouse up the Orangemen. This state was born in trouble and has caused trouble ever since.

"Did you ever hear of Ned Trodden? Well, Ned had a barber's shop on the Falls: number 68. He was prominent in the IRB and in the twenties Sinn Féin and the IRA held meetings in Ned's shop. One night towards the end of 1920, two peelers were shot dead up the road at Broadway. The Specials used the Beehive Bar as a billet in them days. Anyway, in the early hours of the morning Ned's door knocked and when Ned called out 'Who's that?' he received the reply 'Military to raid'. Now, then like now, that wasn't an unusual occurrence so young Eddie, the son, went down and opened the door and outside what do you think but weren't there four men with the faces all blackened and rifles in their hands. Eddie tried to slam the door but they forced their way in and fired a shot at him as he charged up the stairs. Then they poured petrol all over the kitchen and threatened to burn the family out. Eventually, they made their way up and took Ned down and into the backyard where they shot him dead. They also broke his arms in two places. They murdered two other men the same way that night. Seán Gaynor, he was a volunteer as well, played for O'Connell's hurling club, and Seán McFadden. The two of them lived on the Springfield Road. It was the peelers done it. Volunteer Don Duffin and his brother Pat from Clonard Gardens suffered the same fate. It wasn't long after that, and I wasn't long left school, that I became connected. I remember well the day they were buried. We hardly went over the door that week. With reprisals and the like, people were cowed to some extent, afraid of the knock on the door, waiting for the B men or the peelers to call. An old invalid man was shot dead like that in Varna Street. Of course, the IRA did a good deal of shooting as well but they were so outnumbered and partition had cut off the nationalists so much that the IRA spent most of its time defending areas or trying to reassure people."

He paused for a minute unravelling a piece of fluff from a cushion beside him. Then with a smile he said, "The ambush in Raglan Street was an exception, of course. A cage-car was lured into Raglan Street and ambushed. I don't recall it clearly myself; just heard the shooting and then the talk around the area. You know, I couldn't even tell you what casualties, if any, there were. My head's away. I do remember long afterwards that Hughie McMenamy, he was in charge of issuing Free State pensions, he told me that if all those who applied for a pension because they were involved in the Raglan Street ambush had really been there then they could have ate up the cage-car, peelers and all.

"All the areas had to have stand-bys, against the Orangemen, especially in places like Ballymacarrett. That wee district came under attack a good few times. I recall the funeral of an IRA volunteer, Murtagh McAstocker. He was shot dead during the pogroms and his funeral was massive. The British military drove armoured cars through the ranks of marching mourners to try to break up the funeral cortège. They didn't succeed, though. There was an IRA firing party at the graveside and shots were fired over the grave at Milltown. We used to lie all night around Clonard Chapel on stand-by against the Orangemen just like at the start of these troubles.

"There were men from here fought in the South as well, you know. Seán O'Carroll lived in Gibson Street: his family came originally from Celbridge in Kildare and as he grew up here he became involved with the volunteers. He became OC of D Company. A great man with the Irish language. He went to Ardee to teach the language there and he was shot dead in a reprisal shooting by the Black and Tans. He's buried in Milltown and in Ardee they've a street named after him. And then there was Seán MacCartney from Norfolk Street. He was on active service with a Belfast flying column in County Cavan. He was shot dead in the Lappinduff mountains during a fierce engagement with the British Army."

Outside, the rain threw itself in handfuls against the window, forcing our attention to the grey sky beyond our warm room. The old man was undeterred. "Don't you know that Joe McKelvey was from Cyprus Street, just around the corner from here. Joe's da was a sergeant in the RIC and the family came to live here when the da was stationed at Springfield Road. When the da died Joe became active in the Fianna and then in the IRA, eventually becoming OC of the 3rd Northern Division. After the split over the treaty in 1921 he was appointed Assistant Chief of Staff to Liam Lynch, and for a time he acted as Chief of Staff. He was arrested in the Four Courts when the English lent the Free Staters the guns to attack the IRA garrison there. And well you know what happened then. Rory, Liam, Dick and Joe were shot dead by the Staters in the prison yard of Mountjoy, without charge or trial on the Feast of the Immaculate Conception, 1922. We brought Joe's body home two years later. The four men executed were from each province of Ireland. That was a black day in Irish history; and not too long ago either. Then things started to settle a bit after the Civil War; on the surface at least. There were men in jail for years after, interned and sentenced, and great poverty everywhere. The curfews that went on for about four-and-a-half years were lifted in 1924. We were beaten but not defeated and they knew it, so they gave no quarter, and man, woman and child from the areas lived as displaced persons, oppressed by the Northern government and deserted by Dublin. And that, son," he looked at me for a long quiet minute, "was the twenties. Nowadays, the crowd in Dublin think Ireland stops at Dundalk. Whatever freedom they have, and I don't think it's that much the way they kowtow to Thatcher, they would have less if it wasn't for the people of the North." He smiled weakly. "The North began, the North held on, God bless the Northern land."

"What about the thirties and forties?" I asked.

"The thirties and the forties? You come round to see me in my new house and I'll tell you about them times. We've stirred up too many memories today for an oul' man. Not that I didn't enjoy my life. I've had a long innings and I regret none of it. But I'm not used to talking so much. Come round next Wednesday. You've got my address, haven't you? Well, I'll be settled in then and I'll dig out some oul' papers for you. Okay? You'll see yourself out? Thinking of shifting out of this oul' house has me near destroyed. G'wan on now, *a mhic,* and don't be heeding an oul' man's gurnings."

I left him in his chair by the fire and pulled the front door after me. His was the last house left occupied in the street. I rapped the window at him on my way past and he grinned at me and waved a cheery goodbye.

That's the way the removal men found him on Monday, sitting in his chair by a dead fire, gazing with lifeless eyes past potted geraniums through lace curtains at the grey half-demolished street he was born in.

(1982)

Falls Memories

BUNKING IN

A little child
Kicking a stone
Going to the pictures
All alone.

The years have flown
And all alone
A man is left
Kicking a stone.
(with apologies to) Nora Hill

THE TROLLEY BUSES whirred their way past us as we
queued in a long straggling line for the matinée in
Clonard picture house.

"Do youse think we cud bunk our way in, when your man's
not lukin'?" asked Josie McMenamy, nudging my attention towards the usher who stood Horatio-like in the foyer.

"You've two hopes," said Jamesie Magee casting an experi-
enced eye along the line, "Bob Hope and no hope. Your man
knollered two wee bucks last week and barred the two of
them, so he did."

"Awh, they walked right into it!" Josie scoffed. "I stud here and I knew they were going to get knollered the way they were going about it. Your man was blimping right at them when they made their move. Stands to reason, doesn't it, that you'll get caught trying stupid things. Now, I reckon if his attention was distracted two of us cud sneaky-beaky in past him."

"And how could you distract his attention?"

"Well, when the line gets down close to him and when me and him is talking, youse two can nip in."

"Do you think we came up the Lagan in a bubble?" I retorted. "You're dead fly, Josie: me and Jamesie's the ones who'll get caught."

"You'll not get caught," said Josie. "Your man is nuts about pigeons, and if I ask him about that new tumbler me da's got he'll be so mesmerised telling me the whole ins and outs of it that you'll be in before he knows what's hit him."

"I'm not too keen on it," said Jamesie. "I wudn't like to miss the big picture."

"Ah, stop your whingeing," Josie interrupted. "We'll be able to split the spondooliks between us – a three-way split. Okay? And you'll see the big picture, and the wee one, for nothing."

"I don't see why it has to be in a three-way split," Jamesie grumbled. "I mean to say, we're taking all the risks, you shud only be getting a wing."

"Ah, be a brick, Jamesie, don't be gurning now. We'll work it out after. Sure we're nearly there now. Are youse game?"

"Aye," we agreed as the crowd jostled its way past the gateway and towards the ticket box. Minutes later me and Jamesie stood in the rain at the corner of Leeson Street. We glared at the spot where Josie McMenamy had disappeared into the friendly innards of Clonard.

"I'll knock his pan in when I see him," scowled Jamesie as he gingerly touched his backside. "Your man nearly ruined my marriage prospects. Wait till I get that wee gett Josie, him and his 'What do you think my da should feed his new pigeon on, mister?' I thought your man was going to murder us."

"Awh well," said I, "sure it wasn't a very good picture anyway. I saw the coming attractions and it looked desperate.

Let's go for a wee dander. Next time we'll make Josie sneak in and we'll talk to your man."

"It's always the same with me," Jamesie complained as we dandered up Dunlewey Street to Mrs Rooney's. "I knew things weren't going to work out and yet Josie talked me into it, so he did. I'm as thick as champ, so I am. Our Paddy says if I had any sense I'd be a half-wit."

"Ach, it's not as bad as all that," I said. "I mean to say, like, it cud have been worse. I mean your man cud have barred us altogether. Like, he caught us fair and square and he just give us a good boot, and that was that. Like, I thought my tonsils were going to come out my throat." I laughed in a feeble effort to cheer Jamesie up.

"Oh, I don't know," he persisted. "You'll be laughing at the other side of your face next Sunday when your man shows us the road home."

"Well if you're going to be gurning all day I'm getting some honeycomb and some mixed-ups and I'm going home right this minute."

"Okay, okay," Jamesie conceded, "don't be getting your knickers in a twist. I was only saying, like, here we are out here in the rain and Josie McMenamy, the fly wee slabber, is in watching the pictures. But if you're going to take it out on me, well, we'd be better forgetting the whole episode so we wud."

"All right," I said as we went into Mrs Rooney's to spend our picture money, "just put it down to experience."

Later, as me and Jamesie divided our sweeties in the summer house of a deserted and rain-swept Dunville Park, we pondered on the part that fate and Josie McMenamy had played in our lives.

"It seems to me," said Jamesie, "that me and you always come off the worst."

"Ach, not all the times," I countered, "I mean to say, Josie's not the worst and he did save you from that wee tin gang from Getty Street a couple of times."

"Aye, but that was only because he wanted to cog my ecker. If he thinks he's going to so that again he's another think coming."

"And what about the way he always gets us the buns off his uncle who works in Hughes's?"

"Aye, well, that's true enough," said Jamesie wistfully, "I wudn't mind one of them snowballs and a Paris bun right now."

"Or a diamond and a sorehead," I added moving up on the damp wooden seat. "C'mon and we'll go on home. I'm starving."

"Me too. My belly thinks my throat's cut. But we'd better wait till the pictures gets out. I hope your man doesn't tell me da the score. He'll kill me. We better wait for a wee while yet."

"It must be nearly tea-time now. I'm looking forward to a big fry – a dipped soda and a fried egg would be smashing."

"Don't think about it," Jamesie suggested. "If you think about it, it only makes you worse. Let's take a dander down the road and by that time they shud be out."

"Dead on," said I, glad to be out of the summer house now that the sweets were done. "C'mon and we'll have a race to the gate."

Down at the Clonard as we arrived the matinée crowds were beginning to stream out into the light drizzling rain. Jamesie and I took shelter at the corner of Spinner Street as we watched for Josie McMenamy to come our way.

"Remember," said Jamesie, his murderous mood returning, "remember the time he wanted us to rob the orchie up the Glen Road. He nearly got us killed that time as well."

"So he did," said I, "thon big dog nearly ate me."

"I know," said Jamesie. "I'm never going to listen to one word Josie ever says again. He's far too sleekit. Remember that time: 'Just give us a wee scoutsie up the tree and I'll shake off a pile of apples,' he said. Aye, dead on. He was safe up the tree when the dog made a go at us. Well, this is me finished with his wee schemes."

At that Josie approached us, cheerfully splashing his way through a puddle of rainwater. "Bully, Jamesie," he said. "Okay our kid," he greeted me, "youse made a right mess of that. Youse are two chancers. If I knew youse weren't serious I wudn't have made the effort."

"What do you mean?" we both exploded indignantly. "It's you that messed it up. We never had a chance."

"You're supposed to run," said Josie. "Once you get in he never gets you and he can't leave his place long enough to try. I mean to say, youse were like two oul' dolls at a funeral."

"We'll soon see whose funeral it is if you keep on like that, Josie McMenamy," said Jamesie darkly, taking a pace forward.

"Ah, catch yourself on, wee buck," said Josie. "I'm only slegging. You can't even take a geg now. Well, have it your own way. It was a desperate picture anyway. I'm away on home. Youse coming? C'mon and we'll call in and see our Tommy. He told me to call for a few buns."

We glared at him sullenly. "All right," he said. "It's your own funeral, it's all the same difference to me."

"Okay," I said, "sure it's on our way home; c'mon, Jamesie."

We set off together, Jamesie reluctantly bringing up the rear and glaring at Josie.

"Wait till you see the size of the gravy rings you get on a Saturday," Josie enthused.

"You'd think you were the only one ever got gravy rings," said Jamesie sourly.

"Well, one sure thing. I'm the only one here has the picture money left," said Josie, "and the way you're carrying on I don't know whether to split it or not."

We stopped dead in our tracks. "What do you mean?" I asked. "You haven't still got the picture money, have you?"

"Aye," said Josie with a grin. "When your man was busy kicking youse two out I just dandered on in."

"Well, you dirty rat," said I in amazement. "You're dead lucky."

"Let's see it," said Jamesie grudgingly.

"Disbelieving Thomas," returned Josie, "you'll see it in the shop."

"Three-way split, Josie," we shouted charging after him.

"Last one in's a dodo!" he yelled over his shoulder and we dashed across the road. Later, strolling down Leeson Street, with our bellies full of buns and poke full of sweets, just in time for our tea, Jamesie stopped at the corner of Cairns Street.

"You know," he reflected, "it wasn't such a bad day after all. Was the big picture really stinking?" he asked Josie.

"Desperate altogether," said Josie. "I'll see youse after tea and tell youse all about it. Youse'll be glad youse didn't get in when youse hear the score. The fella got killed in the end," he added as we arrived at the corner.

"See youse in half an hour," said Jamesie.

"Okay," we replied.

"Hould on a wee minute. Do you fancy sneaking up into me da's pigeon shed?" asked Josie. "He'll never hear us if we go over Ma Delaney's yard wall."

"I don't know," said Jamesie.

"It's a dead cinch," said Josie. "Oul' Ma Delaney's stone deaf and we'd be nice and dry."

"It's still a wee bit dodgy."

"No problem," interrupted Josie, "and I'll get some mineral to bring with us. Are youse game?"

"Okay," I said, "what about you Jamesie?"

"Aye, I suppose so," said Jamesie reluctantly. "Mind you, I'm not going first."

"Sure, we'll see about that later," replied Josie.

"See you."

"See youse," concluded Jamesie, "and Josie, don't be forgetting about the mineral, will you?"

(1982)

Falls Memories

COCKER AND COMPANY

I am a wee falourie man, a rattling roving
Irishman
I can do all that ever you can for I am a wee
falourie man.
Belfast street song

LOCAL LEGEND HAS it that some of the kidney pavers which covered the streets of the Falls Road were used to decorate the courtyards in Divis Flats – surely the only claim which that monstrosity has to architectural nicety. Today the flagstones which replaced them are vanishing also, victims of twelve years of street fighting, and pavements are so uneven now that one has to step carefully through the dark streets at night.

Now, what this has to do with Cocker and Company will come out in a minute. The system of macadamising road surfaces was named after its inventor John L. MacAdam. Another MacAdam, Robert S., was one of the owners of the Soho foundry in Townsend Street. He and I share the same family name, Mac Adaimh. He was a collector of anecdotes and, more importantly, a man greatly interested in the Irish language. He brought to Belfast, for the purpose of translating

34

Irish manuscripts, a number of Gaelic scribes including Hugh MacDonnell and Peter Galligan, who lived in the Millfield area. MacAdam also published over five hundred Ulster Gaelic proverbs and the very interesting narrative of the wars of 1641 by Friar O'Mellan, chaplain to Phelim O'Neill, which MacAdam had translated from the Irish. His efforts to preserve some record of our Gaelic heritage are well chronicled in Breandán Ó Buachalla's splendid book *I mBéal Feirste Cois Cuan*.

Belfast has always had its share of local characters and wits, and as far back as 1837 Robert MacAdam recorded in his notes stories of the railway stoker who described slow-burning anthracite coal as "damned antichrist", of the bookseller who ordered as a medical work Delolme's *On the Constitution* and of bed-warming pans being exported by accident by a Belfast merchant to the West Indies where they were sold at a great profit after being modified for use as skimmers for sugar pans.

In the 1820s street musicians included Cocky Bendy, a very small bow-legged man who knew the tune to play at every house he visited. "Garryowen", "Patrick's Day" and the "Boyne Water" were his best paying airs.

Black Sam, another street character, was a black man who had highly popular performing dogs, and William Scott or Tantra Barbus was a notorious and eccentric street pedlar and hawker. He was born in Ballynahinch in 1778 but never visited County Down after the '98 rebellion because of an accusation that he acted as a spy during that period. So famous was he that after his death in 1833, a small book was published, *The Life of William Scott alias Tantra Barbus with numerous anecdotes connected with that eccentric character together with an elegy written on his death by a Gentleman in Belfast, printed for the Hawkers 1833*.

Cathal O'Byrne records in *As I Roved Out* how earlier, at the turn of this century, Belfast street-singers Alex McNicholl and Arthur Quinn, who used to perform regularly in North Street, and other unnamed ballad makers interchanged homespun verses with "The Rose of Tralee", "The Bard of Armagh" and "The Garden Where the Praties Grow". He also recalls the woman ballad singer who would change the words and the mood of "Dobbin's Flowery Vale" to suit her own mood, ending:

An' to hell with you, an' Armagh too,
An' Dobbin's flowery vale.

In the streets of the Falls at the time wandered Nicholas Ward, a blind singer who specialised in "The Smashing of the Van", "Clare's Dragoons", "The West's Awake" and "The Felons of Our Land". Through these streets came the hurdy-gurdy man, and small groups of musicians, and tap dancers who carried their own dancing boards. People sat at their doors, all the better to enjoy such entertainment and whole streets joined in community singing and crack, often sitting up late into the night.

In more recent times I recall a street singer, cap in hand, knocking on doors and filling Abercorn Street with the air of many a patriotic tune. I was much surprised therefore, while cutting with my granny through the back streets of the Shankill Road, to spy the man putting on the same performance for the benefit of the residents there. My granny, suffice to say, wasn't at all taken aback and as we drew within earshot I realised why. Instead of "Seán South of Garryowen" our enterprising balladeer was giving forth "Abide with Me" and other religious offerings. I think he winked at me as we passed by and he certainly jingled his capful of coppers towards us in a decidedly cavalier fashion as he rendered his version of "Nearer my God to Thee".

Street singers, of course, weren't the only entertainers to thread our back streets. My Uncle Paddy recalls Oiney Boike, whose name lives on yet in local jargon. He used to sit the children along the kerb stone – the pavements were higher affairs in those days – where they swayed slowly from side to side while chanting "Oiney Boike, Oiney Boike" as he conducted them and danced to their accompaniment. My Uncle Paddy reckons that Oiney Boike is a Belfast bastardisation of the Irish *Eoinín beag*, and he's probably right.

Another uncle of mine, Alfie, remembers a character of that period with illusions of grandeur known as the "Duke of

Millfield" who used, like an early John Cleese, to walk with great loping strides while holding a small soap container before him, for all the world like some noble personage bearing a valuable casket. Then there was John Donnelly of Cinnamond Street, alias Dr McNab, who sang with great fervour and a lisp "St Tewesa of de Woses" and "Bootiful Dwema". John, who hated his other nickname, "Vinegar Bottle", was prone to attack those who dared to tease him and on more than one occasion actually threw his accordion at such tormentors. The queue at the old Ritz cinema on the Grosvenor Road was one of his more lucrative pitches, when he wasn't playing around the pubs, and he and Harry Tully, another street musician, used to do battle to get playing there.

Willie John McCorry recollects following Jimmy Madden for a blow on his tin whistle. Jimmy played on Friday nights, when the mill workers were paid, and Willie John's music lessons were always interrupted by Jimmy's impatient "Hurry up, there's people coming". An equally well-known figure was blind Dan McAuley, who was so tormented by local youngsters that he developed the painful habit of striking out at any passerby unlucky enough to come within the swing of his walking stick. He lived at the corner of Abyssinia Street, and he must have been equal only to Bunny Rice, who boxed with shadows, and with any available pedestrian, on street corners throughout the Falls. Egged on by locals, Bunny was a daunting adversary as I found out to my embarrassment on more than one occasion at the corner of Sultan Street.

Big Joe Walsh, living yet, was in regular attendance at all Falls Road funerals. Weeping real tears and slobbering profusely into a large handkerchief, he accompanied most corpses from the area on their last journey to Milltown and was so much a local institution that attendance by anyone at a number of funerals was invariably described as being "like Joe Walsh". Afterwards Joe would retire to a local public house where he proceeded to get "drunk" on a pint of lemonade. Joe, like all true Falls Road characters, was a "harmless cratur", a source of innocent amusement who was well liked by people of the area.

Paddy-with-the-glass-eye, in my childhood days, used to beseech us while we taunted him to "say a prayer for our mothers". Once when mine was ill he told me he was praying for her. I held Paddy in some awe ever afterwards when my mother not only got better but produced a new baby into the bargain. In answer to the catechism question "Who made the world?" Paddy, his glass eye peering blankly at the heavens, would reply: "God made the world but me da carried the bricks for him."

The area also boasted a number of strong men – mostly quiet hard-working individuals like Paul Jones from Scotch Street who was employed in the docks. Paul was well known for his unorthodox method of docking dogs' tails. Most dog owners nowadays have their dogs' tails cut by a vet or a doggie man, but Paul Jones performed this task by simply biting off the offending item. He featured once in a weight-lifting contest in Diamond's pub in Millford Street – later in the sixties the venue, as Terry's Bar, for a revival of traditional music in Belfast. Paul was the only contestant to succeed in lifting a barrel of porter with two fingers from a bar room floor up to the bar counter.

John James Hagens was a quiet man who became fiercely hostile towards peelers when he had a few pints. Stripped to the waist, he fought off many an RIC man and continued to practice when that force became the RUC. On one historic occasion the peelers suffered such a heavy defeat and John James was going at them with so much success that they only overwhelmed him when one peeler, Billy Pepper, thought of handcuffing him to a handcart. And that's the way that John James was taken, surrounded by battered peelers, to the barracks.

From Baker Street came Porky Flynn, another strong man, known to wheel a handcart with five or six hundredweight of scrap on it. Porky set off at four-thirty every morning to tour the city centre for scrap metal. He never owned a clock or watch but arose punctually with the aid of a candle which he had measured to go out at the time he wished to get up. Porky and his colleagues, rag men, refuse men and the like, could have exchanged their handcarts, at the cost of thirty shillings a week, for a horse and cart from Horsey Hughes at his yard in Servia Street. Horsey, well known also for his great strength, used, after midnight on New Year's Eve, to lead or ride a horse into neighbours' houses. In more recent years another member of the family, Yako Hughes, continued this custom, using a donkey on occasions instead of a horse, until his death in tragic circumstances in 1980.

Before Yako's time Jimmy Duffin could be seen and heard making his way from Seán McKeown's public house in Lemon Street. Jimmy, a quiet enough chap while in the pub, commenced singing, his hand cupped *sean nós* style over his ear, as soon as he hit the street. Between songs he argued loudly with himself or shouted and guldered, oblivious of strangers' stares or the knowing smiles of local people. At times he would inform onlookers "you're inconjudical" before continuing with his singing.

Paky and Maggie McCoo, a brother and sister, lived rough or in a flat above Kivlahan's bar in Cinnamon Street and were institutions around the locality. Maggie sometimes pushed an old pram and was accompanied occasionally by another chap. He was an Irish speaker and reputedly a competent organist from County Armagh, and Maggie and he often shared tuppence-worth of chips in Malachy Morgan's. Today people like Maggie and Paky would be called dipsos or winos. Perhaps they were so-called in those days also, but if so it was only by those who didn't know them. The Falls Road people treated them as friends, and Paky, who was in and out of prison for short periods on begging charges, was always looked after by the political prisoners. He and his colleagues lived similar life styles in the Loney area, surfacing after the night's sleep from beneath an old van or lorry to get breakfast in some friendly house.

One story told about Paky concerns his considerable gymnastic ability. One morning he got a bowl of cold black tea from Mrs McGinn at the corner of Curry Street. Paky topped up the tea with a touch of meths or wine and drained the bowl. Then, putting both his hands on the lamp-post outside

Mrs McGinn's, he pushed himself straight out until he was at right angles to the lamp-post, three or four foot high and parallel to the ground. Then, with a wink to Mrs McGinn and a word of thanks for the tea, he proceeded on his way.

In more recent times another street character, a hawker who used to live rough, was Frank McCaul. Frank made a small fortune and got his nickname "Fr Peyton" by selling photographs of the highly popular rosary crusade priest, Fr Peyton, as well as handkerchiefs and other knick-knacks. Frank's sales of handkerchiefs boomed during internment when they were much in demand by prisoners' relatives, who dispatched them to Long Kesh where the internees converted them into small hand-painted wall hangings.

Frank was to die in his sleep behind St Peter's Church in the black taxi in which he was sheltering for the night. Winter, as so often, took its toll.

Most of the street characters, hawkers and drop-outs frequented the many pubs along the Cullingtree Road fringe of the Loney. So relaxed, and illegal, were their Sunday drinking hours that this part of the area was known locally as Omeath. In the early seventies, with a temporary boom in shebeens, the same sense of dry humour echoed in the names of these drinking establishments. In Leeson Street we had "The Cracked Cup", so called because it was situated in Eddie McGuigan's old shop from which Eddie used to sell delph to the ragmen. "The Frying Pan" at the corner of Balaclava Street and Raglan Street got its name from the owner's eagerness to supply a bowl of stew or a fry at seven o'clock in the morning for those remaining on the premises. "Doctor Hook's", a former dentist's surgery, had similar drinking hours, opening at six-thirty in the morning and a definite port-of-call for those seeking a cure. In McDonnell Street "The Nail Bomb", so called for obvious reasons, did an equally heavy trade.

Shebeens to one side, the street characters of old have their contemporaries today: Fonsie Conway, Neddie Doherty, Starrs Kelly and all those unknowns who enrich life in every generation – like the anonymous scribe who was moved to write in large gable-size letters, "F... 1690, WE WANT A REPLAY", or the woman who admonished a black British soldier with the words: "To think I spent years giving the priest money for the black babies and now you have the cheek to come over here and torture the life out of us." Or the lady who chided a British Army major for sending troops into a back entry after a group of youngsters. "He hasn't enough sense to order his own dinner. Sending youse out to do his dirty work." Then to the major: "Come on out of that jeep and fight your own battles." When he ignored her challenge, telling her to "Fuck off", she retorted, "Yiz are all the same, yiz think you know everything. I cudn't like ye even if I rared yeh. Hell's gates and somebody blows yiz up. Then youse'll get some sense. Annoying people with your oul' carry on. Lads can't even stand at their own corner. Someday the shoe'll be on the other fut, then ye'll know what side your bread's buttered on. Go away on home and leave us in peace. And take lappy lugs (the major) with youse. God help his poor wife. My heart goes out to her. At least with my Paddy if I've nothing to eat I've something to luk at. Imagine that poor woman waking up in the morning with your big watery gub in the bed beside her. Ya big long drink of water, giving your orders there. You think you're the fellah in the big picture. If I was a man I'd go through you like a dose of salts. You cudn't fight your way out of a wet paper bag." And then, as the Brits left without their intended captives, she concluded, "God forgive youse for making me make an exhibition of myself in the street. Them wee bucks showed youse the road home. There's better men in the Children's Hospital. You cudn't catch a cold."

Another British Army foot patrol had a similar experience in Marquis Street when they chanced to stumble upon Neddy Doherty and Starrs Kelly. The senior Brit commenced to conduct an ID check on our two heroes and having established their names he proceeded to ascertain their addresses.

"Roight, moite," he addressed Neddy, "what's your 'ome haddress?"

"I live everywhere and anywhere," replied Neddy.

"I must 'ave a proper haddress."

"Well, put down the summer house in the Dunville Park."

The Brit in exasperation scribbled furiously in his notebook and turned to Starrs, who despite his fondness, along with Neddy, for an occasional snort of vino, was always tidily dressed in yellow boots, Paddy hat and check suit.

"Where do you live?" asked the Brit.

"None of your business," answered Starrs with considerable dignity.

"I must have an address!" the Brit declared impatiently.

"What have you down for him?" queried Starrs.

"No fixed abode," replied the Brit.

"Well, put down the same for me," said Starrs with a straight face. "I live up his stairs."

As we would say down our way, Starrs is as stupid as a fox. Such Belfast parlance, not restricted to any particular district or sect, had a famous son in Cocker Murray from Leeson Street. Our dog, Cocker, is so called in his memory, and Falls Road republicans or ex-internees have loads of stories of Cocker's rather unique turns of speech. One describes a period when Cocker worked on the construction of Ballymurphy's Corpus Christi Church. (Joe Cahill, incidentally, was the foreman on that job and myself and two compatriots put up the railings. Never did get paid, but that's another story.) Anyway Cocker had gathered, as was common practice, scrap pieces of wood for some household purpose. He returned to find that the nipper had used his blocks to kindle the fire to brew up the day's tea. In exasperation Cocker exclaimed, "What the bloody hell do you think you're doing. You've burned up all my wood. Do you think the bloody stuff grows on trees?"

Another time, during a coal shortage, Cocker borrowed his brother-in-law's electric fire. In the bar that night his friend advised him against using such a device. "You're mad, Cocker," he reasoned, "that thing's dead expensive. It'll ate up your electricity."

"Ach, I'm not worried about that," replied Cocker. "It's not my fire. It's the brother-in-law's."

Or, witnessing an incident in which a cat only narrowly escaped being knocked down by a passing motor vehicle,

Cocker observed, "Did youse see that? If that cat had been a dog it would have been a dead duck." On one memorable occasion Cocker drew the attention of two local republican activists to a hovering helicopter: "That's very fishy looking, you know. It's been stuck up there for twenty minutes in the same place. It must be broke down."

Not that Cocker was stupid. Far from it. He was a kind man who delighted in making people laugh at life. Once in returning from Casement Park he meditated while passing Milltown Cemetery, "If God spares us, it won't be long till we're all in there." And that seems a fitting note on which to end this brief look back on local characters and local crack. Long may their memory last.

(1982)

Falls Memories

PAWN SHOPS AND POLITICS

Time has triumphed, the wind has scattered all,
Alexander, Caesar, empires, cities are lost,
Tara and Troy flourished a while and fell
And even England itself, maybe, will bite the
dust.
Anon. Translated from the Irish by Brendan Kennelly

IN 1960 OR thereabouts I transferred from St Finian's
School, via St Gabriel's, to St Mary's in Barrack Street. On
our way home from school we walked along Divis Street
and up the Falls, spending our bus fares in one of the many
shops which littered our route. On brisk autumn evenings,
with leaves carpeting the pavement and the road bustling with
people, the great linen and flax mills made a formidable backdrop while, facing them, cheek to cheek, the rows of small
shops served the miscellaneous needs of local customers.
There were a couple of stretches of the road which I particularly favoured. From Northumberland Street up as far as the
Baths, along the convent wall by St Dominic's or alongside
Riddell's field.

Paddy Lavery's pawn shop at Panton Street did a roaring
trade in those days, its windows coming down with family

heirlooms, bric-à-brac, clocks, boots, even fishing rods, and inside, rows and rows of Sunday-morning-going-to-Mass-suits, pledged between Masses to feed the family or pay the rent. There was a horse trough at Alma Street and an old green Victorian lavatory facing it, beside the baths. In Dunville Park the fountain occasionally worked, cascading water around those who defied the wackey to paddle in the huge outer pool.

In Divis Street a woman sold us hot home-made soda farls and pancakes plastered with jam. Br Beausang packed us into the *Ard Scoil* for oral exams to win a place in the Donegal Gaeltacht; Ducky Mallon taught us our sevens; and lunch breaks were spent playing football beside the glass factory and afterwards seeing who could pee the highest in the school bog. Handball at gable walls in St Mary's, or cards and cigarettes for the big lads, were normal lunchtime diversions.

We were all part of a new generation of working class Taigs, winning scholarships to grammar schools and "getting chances" which, as our parents and grandparents frequently reminded us, they never had. We wore school uniforms – a fairly new and expensive luxury – and were slightly bemused to see our mirror reflections in Austin's, the school outfitters, just below Dover Street. I always noticed that the shop facing Austin's had its name sign painted in Irish. You could buy hurling sticks in another shop just below that, while almost opposite our school Wordie's kept their great shire horses in unique multi-storied stables.

Summer evenings were spent in the Falls Park playing hurling and football with infrequent formal handball sessions at the handball alley in St Malachy's. During the winter we cadged money for the Clonard, Broadway or Diamond picturehouses or for the baths and, exams to one side, life was pleasant and uneventful. Divis Flats weren't there then; instead a flour mill dominated the landscape. Victor's ice-cream parlour sold smokies, and Raffo's on the opposite side of the street offered scallops – one for a penny. Gerry Begley and Paddy Elliot, stalwarts of Dwyers Gaelic Athletic Club, became my local heroes as they established themselves as experts on the hurling and football pitches of MacRory, Corrigan and the Falls Parks.

Men walked greyhounds up the road or further afield and pigeon fanciers admired their birds tumbling, free from backyard sheds, into the early dusk, while the street pigeons or hokers quarrelled with sparrows and starlings over their evening meal. Jim McCourt from Leeson Street delighted us all by winning an Olympic medal while John Caldwell, who hailed from Cyprus Street, boxed his way to a world championship title. We learned little of local or national history at school and had no sense of history as we passed through streets as historic as any in Ireland.

From the school at Barrack Street we passed by the Farset, which one teacher by name of "Dirty Dick" Dynan told us could be seen from behind the houses in Durham Street. The houses are now gone, replaced by a car park, but the Farset can be seen still the same. We regularly dandered up Pound Street, knowing nothing of its history or even the old barracks which gives Barrack Street its name.

There were three RUC barracks in our day: one at Hastings Street, one at Springfield Road and another at Roden Street, flanking the area on its three sides. A fourth, at Cullingtree Road, had only recently been replaced. Not that we were worried or even interested in such places. Nowadays, of course, with heavily fortified British Army and RUC barracks and forts dotted strategically throughout West Belfast, it is difficult to remain disinterested or neutral about their existence. It is especially so, in wet wintry times, when the Falls Road, washed grey by drizzling rain and suffering from the ravages of war and redevelopment, appears bleak and shabby, with the omnipresent foot patrols of British soldiers treading carefully through back streets a threatening intrusion into an area hostile to their presence.

Not that British soldiers were a new feature of the scenery in West Belfast. Since its days as a country lane raids and harassment have been occupational hazards suffered by residents of the Falls Road.

The Belfast *Newsletter* of 23 May 1797 records, for example:

At four o'clock in the evening Lieutenant General Lake directed Colonel Barber and Mr Fox (town mayor) to proceed with as much expedition as possible to the cotton manufactory of Robert Armstrong on the Falls Road. Arriving there before two persons, who were on the watch, could give an alarm, they caught a smith and his assistant forging pikes and, on threatening them with immediate death, they produced sixteen they had secreted in an adjacent house, newly forged. A detachment from the Monaghan militia, and some yeomanry who followed, were so incensed at seeing those implements of destruction that they smashed the forge and levelled it to the ground. The pikes were then hung around the villains who were marched prisoners to the town.

A better known testimony of such raids is an expression which is often used even today by older Belfast people when unexpected visitors arrive: "They're in on us and not a stone gathered." It harks back to the days when cobblestones, locally known as kidney pavers or pickers, were used against British Army and RIC raiding parties.

My first personal recollection of such raids was in 1964 when carefree and sleepy-headed I noticed on the way to school a tricolour displayed in a shop in Divis Street, just down from Percy Street opposite St Comgall's School. That evening a character, better known now than then, by name of Paisley threatened to march on Divis Street and remove the offending flag. Our curiosity, further aroused by a warning from our Christian Brother teachers to go straight home and not dilly-dally in Divis Street, led dozens of us to gather and peer into the window of what we were to discover was a Sinn Féin election office. Further encouragement was supplied by the RUC who sledge-hammered their way into the premises and seized the flag. It was with some satisfaction, therefore, the following day that we witnessed a large crowd replacing it, an occasion for a most defiant rendering of *Amhrán na bhFian* and the subject of some schoolboy speculation upon what would happen next.

What happened next, of course, was the Divis Street riots, an exercise which we found most educational, though in truth it wasn't much of a spectator sport, with the RUC being unable or unwilling to distinguish between curious scholars and full-blooded rioters. Some of us learned quickly that it was as well to be hanged for a stone as a stare and thus I found myself after homework had been cogged, folding election manifestos in the Felons Club, above Hector's shop in Linden Street. The republican candidate, Liam McMillan, lost his deposit – as did all the Sinn Féin candidates – but I suspect with hindsight that the electioneering was geared more to canvassing recruits than votes and in that it undoubtedly succeeded.

In the months afterwards children playing in the streets parodied the then current Perry Como song, "Catch a Falling Star", to rhyme during hopscotch and skipping games:

Catch a falling bomb and put it in your pocket,
Never let it fade away.
Catch a falling bomb and put it in your pocket,
Keep it for the IRA.
For a peeler may come and tap you on the shoulder
Some starry night,
And just in case he's getting any bolder
You'll have a pocket full of gelignite.

For those old enough to recall Perry Como, it sounds better if you sing it. And if you're moved to go that far you might as well get a bit of rope and skip. That way you'll get the mood of the whole thing. Of course, youngsters are still parodying popular songs and turning them into their own little songs of resistance. In back streets and schoolyards throughout the Six Counties you'll hear rhymes which instruct British soldiers on how to dispose of their plastic bullets, and popular IRA actions are committed to verse with a speed which amazes many adults.

In the build-up and aftermath of the Divis Street riots there was some awakening of national consciousness and a few of us began to query, with candid curiosity, the state of the nation. We were puzzled by our description in official forms as British subjects and wondered as we passed the customs posts on our way to Bun Beag for a summer in the Gaeltacht what exactly the border was. We were beginning to get a sense of our own essential Irishness, and events on the Falls Road served to whet our political appetites. Before the sixties were over we would be canvassing the streets of the Loney for support for our efforts in opposing the building of Divis Flats. "Low rents not high flats" would be the cry as we picketed the corporation and all others directly or indirectly involved; for this we would be publicly chastised by the parish priest of St Peter's. From that agitation would arise the West Belfast Housing Action Committee, under whose auspices we squatted families from condemned houses, particularly in Mary Street, in newly built flats. We would receive many summonses from the RUC and occupy many city centre offices in the process, escaping imprisonment only because of the "Paisley Amnesty". So, too, would emerge temporarily the West Belfast Unemployment Action Committee, and by that time we were in the Civil Rights Association and later the Central Citizens' Defence Committee and all that grew from it, from barricades to today. But that was all in front of us.

By the end of 1964 I was merely an interested part of a small group which gathered in a dingy room in a Cyprus Street GAA Club to learn about Fenians and Fenianism, colonialism, neo-colonialism, partition and British imperialism. Sinn Féin, then an illegal organisation, was beginning to expand once again and I was happy to be part of this new expansion. The Special Powers Act, the ban on Sinn Féin and on the *United Irishman* newspaper, the lack of adult suffrage, discrimination in jobs and housing, the gerrymandering of local government boundaries and the sectarian divisions which were built into the Stormont structures all became real and deeply felt grievances.

"Do you know," I remarked to Jamesie Magee as we stood at the corner of Leeson Street and Getty Street, "that you can be imprisoned for singing a rebel song?"

"Sure, everybody knows that," he replied with indifference, "sure, me da got six months once for burning a Union Jack."

"I didn't know that."

"Ah, you see," he retorted, "you don't know everything, do you?"

"I never said I did, did I?" Mortified at his suggestion, I glared down towards the Varna Gap.

"Well, if I ever get time it'll be for more than burning a Union Jack," he continued. "Josie had the right idea: he's in Canada. If I don't get a job soon I'm going to Australia. There's nothing in this place for anyone. If you had to pay for a living we'd all be dead."

"Ach, it's not as bad as that," I asserted. "A few changes here and there and we'd all be happy."

"It's okay for you, still at St Mary's learning to be whatever you're learning to be. I've left school six months now and still no sign of work. If your ma or your granny weren't keeping you, you'd soon know your master. You jack in school and you'll see the difference."

"You're putting the scud on me, Josie. C'mon and we'll go for a wee dander. Did you know that you can be whipped with a cat-o'-nine-tails under the Special Powers Act?"

"And you want me to stay here? Your head's a marley. If me da can raise the money I'm taking myself off out of it."

And so he did. And shortly afterwards I jacked in school, and from then on *mar a deirtear, is é sin scéal eile* (as they say, that's another story). In the meantime, by some unnoticed, the Loney, Leeson Street and all that they meant have been erased and the likes of it, as Tomás Ó Criomhthain wrote in *An tOileánach*, will not be seen again.

(1982)

Falls Memories

POLITICAL ORIGINS

*The development of democracy in Ireland has been
smothered by the Union.*
James Connolly

IN 1961, THE last of the republicans interned during the
IRA's border campaign of the fifties were released. For
most of them it was a time for counting the cost and for
adjusting to life outside. There were no fanfares as they returned home: imprisonment then, unlike today, evoked little
active community support or popularity. There were no coherent support organisations and the internees and their families were isolated.

I was thirteen years old and blissfully unaware of internment, the IRA campaign and political matters in general. For
me it was a time of school exams – I had recently passed my
"Eleven Plus" – of hurling matches and long summer holidays.
My father had just returned from working in England and he
and my mother were contemplating emigrating to Australia;
uncles and aunts were already scattered in Canada, Dublin
and England.

A few of the released internees set about picking up the
pieces of a scattered and demoralised organisation; in 1961

the total strength of the Belfast IRA was twenty-four, their total armaments were two short-arms. Republicanism had not died, but it had suffered a substantial defeat, and, amongst those who remained active, a process of reassessment was begun while a low level of political organisation commenced.

Wolfe Tone committees were established by republicans throughout Ireland to mark the 200th anniversary, in June 1963, of Tone's birth. Theobald Wolfe Tone, the founder of Irish republicanism, was a Protestant barrister who, influenced by the American and French revolutions, set up the Society of United Irishmen in 1791 to unite "Protestant, Catholic and Dissenter" in the cause of Irish independence, and was secretary to the Catholic Committee which campaigned for civil rights for Catholics. He attempted to gain French military support for the fight for independence, but was captured in 1798 and sentenced to death. He cheated his captors by killing himself before the sentence could be carried out.

At the commemoration in Belfast, an internal controversy provoked a local leadership crisis in the republican movement. It was the practice of republicans to carry the Irish tricolour on parades, despite the fact that the flag, as the symbol of Irish nationalism, was banned under the Flags and Emblems Act (1954). The failure to carry it in June 1963 in defiance of the ban sparked off a period of infighting, at the end of which a Belfast leadership supportive of Cathal Goulding, Chief of Staff of the IRA since the previous year, was firmly in control.

The tricolour played a role too in bringing me into politics. During the Westminster elections in October 1964, rioting occurred after a tricolour was displayed in the window of Sinn Féin's election office in Divis Street in Belfast. Ian Paisley objected loudly to the display of the flag and threatened to march on Divis Street and remove it within two days if it hadn't been removed by then. The next day a force of RUC men broke down the door of the office and removed the flag. Two days of intense rioting followed and the republicans, accompanied by a large crowd of local people, replaced the flag, only to have it removed again by RUC men wielding pickaxes. Three hundred and fifty RUC men, using armoured cars and water-cannons and wearing military helmets, launched an attack on the Falls, and fifty civilians and twenty-one RUC ended up in hospital. The government had responded to pressure from Paisley and had provoked a violent reaction from the Catholic working class. It was a stark reminder of where the balance of power lay in the Six Counties.

I was in school at the time, but the Divis Street events concentrated my mind on politics. I already possessed a vague sense of discontent, and the naked display of state violence against the people of the Falls made me feel I did not want merely to stand by looking on. I found myself spending a few evenings in the Felons Association rooms on the Falls Road folding election material for Liam McMillan, the Sinn Féin candidate. Despite, or maybe because of, all the republican candidates losing their election deposits, within a few months I joined Sinn Féin.

I suppose I was a member for about eighteen months before I realised what I was in at all. I had, after all, joined as a reaction to what had happened in Divis Street. This had had the effect of reawakening a sense of national consciousness which whetted my political appetite. I was eager to find out why things were as they were, and as I read those history books which were not on our school curriculum I became increasingly aware of the nature of the relationship between Ireland and Britain. Having reached the conclusion that this relationship was a colonial one, and having decided that it must be ended, I began with youthful innocence the task of ending it. My new-found knowledge dictated the logic that the British government had no right to govern any part of Ireland, that that right belonged to the Irish people and that we could surely govern ourselves in our own interests more efficiently than anyone else. All we had to do was to get rid of the British. With that I was, I felt, starting off on the right foot. I was to discover that I was a long way from fully understanding how we might get there.

I had a republican family background. My maternal grandfather, a prominent full-time trade union organiser on personal terms with both James Connolly and James Larkin, had worked for de Valera in the 1918 election; my paternal grand-father and his in-laws traced their republican involvement back to the Irish Republican Brotherhood (IRB). They reared republican sons and daughters who included my mother and my father, who was shot and wounded by the RUC and imprisoned in the 1940s. In spite of all this, I was no more politically conscious than many of my contemporaries, but the everyday aspects of our situation were obvious enough: bad housing, poverty, political structures with which we could not identify and, above all, the endemic, structural unemployment. Many of my contemporaries left, complaining that the sectarian state where everything was rigged against them from the start was no place for a decent life; others reckoned they would stick it out and see if maybe they couldn't bring about some improvements.

I decided to stick it out. I was never in any doubt that I would. I loved the city of Belfast, its streets, its hills, its people; it was the world I knew and I had no intention of being forced out of my own place. I was also naive, like most of my generation, and thought that a few rational, sensible changes could easily be made which would improve the quality of life and bring about equal opportunities for all.

That sense of possibility was what lay behind my decision to become involved in political activism. The options were clear: you could emigrate; you could stay and adopt an attitude of passivity which would hopefully get you by; or you could get involved in trying to change things. Of course, I had absolutely no idea then where this would lead me or how events in the Six Counties would develop; none of us did. We were certain only of one thing: the injustice of the system could not go unchallenged. It was wrong. Irish national self-determination was the only solution.

Sinn Féin was a very small organisation then. It was also illegal. You could almost describe it as an incestuous association, made up as it was of members of a few spinal republican families, some of whom could trace their involvement right back through the fifties, forties, thirties and twenties to the Fenians and the Irish Republican Brotherhood (IRB) and perhaps even beyond. There was a small number of young people – mostly from republican backgrounds like myself – a larger number of much older people, and a middle group of people who had been active in the 1950s; that is, people who had been imprisoned then.

The mid-sixties was a period of turmoil in the republican movement. Following the failure of the fifties campaign, there was a major rethink. The impetus for debate came from the leadership, but the need for reassessment was naturally apparent in the organisation as a whole. In Belfast, we were picking up an outer ripple of a wave which was centered at national leadership level in Dublin. Accordingly, several developments were taking place more or less simultaneously, both inside and outside the movement.

The Wolfe Tone Societies, formed in 1963, had become a meeting point for republicans and socialists, for Irish language enthusiasts and communists. They held occasional seminars and, while little actual work was done, the societies in Dublin, Cork and Belfast provided a platform for ideas and an important gathering point for anti-imperialist opinion makers.

This was set against a political background in the Six Counties which was characterised, on the nationalist side, by low-level social justice campaigning by individuals and small groups, most notably the Dungannon-based Campaign for Social Justice. The Dungannon people documented instances of discrimination and briefed the London-based Connolly Association, its Irish Democrat newspaper and a minority element in the British Labour Party, based around Kevin McNamara MP.

Despite this, the unionists ran the Six County state exactly as they wished. And as long as British interests were safeguarded there was no British interference. Apart from some of the more obvious features, "Northern Ireland" was a police state similar to South Africa's apartheid system. It was a one-party state, "a Protestant parliament for a Protestant people". Efforts to change this by physical force activity, by publicising the injustices or by the development of a party political alternative had failed. There were none of the usual manifestations of normal class politics; partition and sectarianism ensured that this was the case. Indeed, I came into politics just as the Northern Ireland Labour Party (NILP), which had enjoyed some popularity with electoral gains in 1958 and 1962, was poised to commit political suicide on the issue of whether swings in public parks should be chained up on Sundays.

Nationalist opinion was represented by the conservative Nationalist Party, though in Belfast and Derry there were more radical tendencies which were to come to the surface again in the years ahead. The Nationalist Party was occasionally abstentionist, totally ineffectual and politically amateur. It did not satisfy the needs of the emerging, better-educated Catholic middle class, a section of whom were committed to working for social and economic reforms within the Six County state. After some attempts to ginger-up and democratise the Nationalist Party through a National Unity association which was established by a group of Catholic graduates, the rival National Democratic Party was formed. This development, and Dublin premier Sean Lemass's acceptance of an invitation by Terence O'Neill, the new Prime Minister, to visit him at Stormont, led to the Nationalist Party entering the Stormont parliament and becoming the official opposition.

The Lemass/O'Neill meeting was probably the first step by Fianna Fáil towards recognising the Six County state. It flowed naturally from the North–South collaboration against the 1950s IRA campaign. This, together with the acceptance by the Nationalist Party of the institutions of the state and the emergence of a politicised Catholic middle class in the National Democratic Party, pointed the direction for the possible rehabilitation of the Six Counties. Those who sought such a reformation took succour from O'Neill's apparent willingness to apply to the state the democratic veneer necessary for the demands of the twentieth century. But, even at that stage, it was too little too late. "No Surrender" unionism would not be so easily brought to heel, and already in the opposite camp, within the radical anti-unionist ranks, the disparate ingredients involved in the slow fermentation of agitation activity were coming together.

In 1965, the first Republican Club was set up in Belfast in an attempt to break the ban on Sinn Féin. In the same year, republicans attempted to set up "one man, one vote" committees. However, largely because of their lack of political acumen, allied to the hostility of the NILP, that initiative floundered, but only temporarily. Within the Wolfe Tone Societies, the question of civil rights in the Six Counties had become a recurring theme. In August 1966, they hosted a conference on civil rights in Maghera, County Derry, and another in November in Belfast, where republicans were enjoying a rise in local support. In 1963 they had been badly fragmented over the question of whether to carry the tricolour or not, in 1964 the flag was seized and rioting resulted, but, in 1966, West Belfast saw a massive display of tricolours and banners in the parade to celebrate the fiftieth anniversary of the Easter Rising.

This Easter commemoration received very widespread support from nationalists and involved cultural associations, trade unionists and social groups, and there were organisations, almost street committees, for the making of flags, bunting and banners. There was a one-day pageant at Casement Park in Andersonstown and a week of events including concerts and the like, and for the parade itself about 20,000 people turned out.

In the unionist press there were scare stories about the IRA, and the B Specials were put on stand-by. Two or three Belfast republicans received prison sentences for organising the parade, which was illegal, and in Newry a local republican was charged under the Flags and Emblems Act. At this time also, a major influence in moulding the political character of my generation of republicans was the popularisation of the writings of the leaders of the 1916 Rising, in particular the writings of James Connolly. The process of political education within the republican ranks was enhanced by the availability of a flood of publications, and we began to develop a view of the class nature of the struggle and of the relationship between its social and national dimensions.

The slight raising of the political temperature at this time led to a number of small but dangerous developments. In the months before Easter, there were petrol bomb attacks on Catholic homes, shops and schools. In May, a Protestant woman died in a petrol bomb attack on the Catholic-owned public house next door to her home.

The following month Paisley led a demonstration against the General Assembly of the Presbyterian Church. What is sometimes forgotten is that he marched to that demonstration through Cromac Square, a Catholic area. The residents who attempted to block the road were very brutally dispersed by the RUC, who returned the following night and renewed the assault. The IRA played a small part in organising people against these RUC incursions, and one local republican activist received a prison sentence. A few weeks later, Peter Ward was killed and two other Catholics were wounded outside the Malvern Arms public house on the Protestant Shankill Road. On the same night, a loyalist gang had attempted to enter the home of Leo Martin, a prominent republican. It was also discovered that a Catholic man, John Scullion, who died on 11 June, had been shot on 27 May in Clonard Street by a loyalist terror gang. On 23 July, Paisleyite marchers rioted in Belfast city centre, attacking the Catholic-owned International Hotel and attempting to burn down a bookmaker's in Sandy Row which employed Catholics.

These incidents offered examples of the politico-religious relationship within loyalism. The crisis of loyalism, as always, was finding its expression in attacks on Catholic property and in the assassination of Catholic people. At the trial of three UVF members for the murder of Peter Ward, the RUC stated that Hugh McClean, one of the defendants, had said when charged, "I am terribly sorry I ever heard of that man Paisley or decided to follow him."

In the midst of the growing tensions, republicans were trying to come to terms with the needs of the struggle, the needs of the people and the relevance of the struggle to the people and to the Ireland of the 1960s. There have always been three tendencies within the republican movement: a militaristic and fairly apolitical tendency, a revolutionary tendency, and a constitutional tendency. Throughout the history of the movement, one or other of these has been in the ascendancy. Since partition, however, there had been no dominant tendency capable of giving proper and relevant leadership to the mass of Irish people.

By the mid-sixties, the movement had shed most of its militaristic leanings and a small, politically conscious organisation was developing and beginning to examine critically the role of republicanism and the task of finding a strategy towards the goal of an independent republic.

As part of a major review of strategy, the whole relationship between revolutionary struggle, armed struggle and mobilization of the masses – all of those now tired jargon phrases – was discussed at length. A very thorough and useful analysis was presented, which went right back to the days of agrarian struggle and the Fenians. Various questions were examined in a historical sense: why, for example, had Fintan Lalor failed, why had the Fenians failed, and so on. The republican movement had long been a conspiratorial movement which manifested itself almost exclusively in physical force actions. Since Connolly, Pearse and Mellows and the Republican Congress of the 1930s, there had been no real effort to put any meat on the ideas of what type of a republic was aimed at.

The impact of this major review was that Sinn Féin began to define its politics more, to the extent of talking about a "workers' republic", "a workers' and small farmers' republic" and a "socialist republic" or a "democratic socialist republic". But what came most clearly from these discussions was a recognition that republicans needed to identify their philosophy as being relevant not to the vision of a future Ireland but to the actual Ireland of today, and that they needed to enlist mass support, or at least the maximum support possible, for the republican cause. As we immersed ourselves in the business of political education, that truth became of paramount importance. We could not free the Irish people. We could only, with their support, create conditions in which they would free themselves.

These kinds of conclusions resulted in people like myself becoming involved in housing action and the other agitation activities which the movement had begun to promote. In the Twenty-six Counties, republicans became involved in the Waters Restoration Committee, a campaign for the restoration of inland waters to the Irish people. There were campaigns against absentee landlordism and against foreign investors; in one case, at least, this took the form of military action. An IRA volunteer from Cork was killed and Cathal Goulding was tried for incitement over his speech at the funeral.

There was a realisation that one could not organise politically as an illegal organisation; the party newspaper could not be sold, the Special Powers Act could be used against the organisation and its members at the whim of an RUC inspector, and so on. So, that led to making a priority of the attempt to fight the ban on Sinn Féin, and this was a conscious decision to leave the back-room conspiracies and come out into the open.

The IRA in Belfast occasionally came into public prominence itself. Towards the end of 1966, a British army recruiting class at St Gabriel's School was broken up by Volunteers armed with hurling sticks and, in 1967, there were three attacks on British army training centres – two in Belfast and one in Lisburn. By this time there were five Republican Clubs in Belfast and I had graduated to being the PRO of the Andersonstown one. Contrary to its title, our small membership covered Ballymurphy, Turf Lodge and part of the Falls as well.

Our relatively low-level agitation in Belfast, the rising political temperature and the new openness of the republicans was bringing us into contact with various elements: members of the Communist Party, the NILP, the Republican Labour Party, Young Socialists and people who had long records of working against discrimination. We were meeting through the Wolfe Tone Society, through debates in St Malachy's Old Boys' Club, and through the beginning of the revival of Irish music. The sessions and fleadhs provided gathering points – in the docks, in the city centre, in the Falls – and, over a pint, people who might otherwise not have met were discussing the politics of the day. I worked in a pub, the Duke of York, at that time. It was close to the head office of the NILP and a number of trade union offices, as well as the *Newsletter*, and there you got a mingling of NILP and CP members, republicans, trade union officials and journalists discussing issues of the day.

The Vietnam war was one of those issues and I was one of many who went along to rallies against the war. Similarly, the black civil rights campaign in the United States not only had its obvious influence in terms of the anthem of "We Shall Overcome" but also in terms of its affinity with what was happening in the Six Counties. Courtesy of television, we were able to see an example of the fact that you didn't just have to take it, you could fight back.

People did not live their lives in isolation from the changes going on in the world outside. They identified to a greater or lesser extent with the music, the politics, the whole undefined movement of ideas and changes of style. Bob Dylan, the Beatles and the Rolling Stones, long hair and beads, the "alternative society", music and fashion were all markers put down by a new generation against the complacency of the previous one, and one of the most important messages to come across was that one could change the world. This was the promise of the sixties, that the world was changing anyway and the tide of change was with the young generation. This produced a sense of impatience with the status quo allied to a young, enthusiastic and euphoric confidence.

The public declaration of their existence by the Republican Clubs brought this mingling of elements into a new focus, and a great deal of attention became centered on the demand for the lifting of the ban which had been slapped on them almost immediately. There was a meeting in Chapel Lane at which republicans demanded that they be recognised and Liam Mulholland announced publicly that he was the Chairman of the Six County Executive of the Republican Clubs. Next day a newspaper had a huge photo of Liam and the headline: this man is head of an illegal organisation. When the Republican Clubs were banned, students at Queen's University Belfast immediately announced themselves as a Republican Club, and from this small start young radicals like Michael Farrell, Tom McGurk, Bowes Egan and others came into a certain prominence and also came into contact with other political influences. Shortly after this, a colleague and myself were arrested for selling the *United Irishman* in what was a planned defiance of the ban on that newspaper. We were released, however, without being charged. While we were thus robbed of the opportunity of fighting a political case in the courts, one of the pickets who had retired patiently to a nearby pub while waiting for our arrest was so incensed and inebriated when the RUC eventually frogmarched us to the barracks that he found himself, contrary to instructions, attacking the arresting party and getting heavily assaulted and subsequently fined. We, of course, had to organise a collection to defray his court costs and pay the fine.

In Derry, Eamonn McCann (of the Derry Labour Party) and Finbar O'Doherty (of the local Republican Club) and others were busy exposing and opposing the appalling housing situation arising from the specific forms of discrimination there. In Dublin, Cork and Waterford, Housing Action Committees were also active and occasionally a number of us would travel to Dublin to attend housing marches and protests. The success of these activities led a few of us in Belfast to get together on the same issue, and we set up the West Belfast Housing Action Committee.

An example of the kind of activity we became involved in was a case when I was approached by people called Sherlock who were living off the Falls Road in Mary Street, which was a very small street of two-bedroomed houses in very bad condition indeed. We brought them along to the Housing Trust and tried to get them rehoused, and when no movement was forthcoming we simply took over a flat in what was then the beginning of the Divis Flats complex. In Derry and in Caledon similar squats had already taken place with some success. The Caledon instance, which had been organised by the local Republican Club, had received considerable media attention when Austin Currie, then a Nationalist MP, became involved. The Sherlock case was the first instance in Belfast; it received some media attention and was successful in the end because the family was allocated a new house. And that experience and success provided us with a major impetus: it was proof that direct action could work and it was something that enjoyed popular support in the area. After the years and years of atrocious housing, here, at last, some break seemed to have been made. The Housing Action Committee was a very ad hoc creation, called into existence on the second day of the occupation. From this start we embarked on a campaign of occupying and picketing the Housing Trust's offices, and we found that other people came to us looking for help. Earlier we had attempted to agitate against the building of the Divis Flats complex, but without evoking popular support. Now we found we were able to organise in a much more coherent way, with much more support, and the residents of the Loney district marched against the tower blocks and in favour of the rebuilding of their own traditional houses.

There were only six or seven of us from the movement involved in the housing agitation and in the unemployment agitation which also developed, but when the Northern Ireland Civil Rights Association (NICRA) was formed, following an initiative by the Belfast Wolfe Tone Society with the assistance of the Campaign for Social Justice, the small groups active around such issues fitted naturally into the wider civil rights struggle. The meeting to establish NICRA was well attended and was packed by republicans, who wielded the biggest bloc vote.

Contrary to later claims by the unionists that republicans took over the civil rights movement, we were there from the very beginning. Republicans were actually central to the formation of NICRA and, far from using it as a front organisation, those of us who attended the inaugural meeting were directed to elect only two of our membership to the executive. NICRA went through a low-key period of citizen advice activity at first. It held protest rallies in Newry and Armagh in 1968, after the banning of an Easter Commemoration parade in Armagh, but it turned down a republican proposal for a Belfast march.

The first NICRA march took place in August 1968, from Coalisland to Dungannon. It was barred from the centre of the town; a rally was held in front of an RUC blockade and the crowd dispersed following some confusion between the republicans and the others as to whether they should sing the Irish national anthem or the American black civil rights anthem. It was unimportant. The civil rights struggle had begun and the Coalisland-Dungannon march was the beginning of a broad-based, if uneasy and sporadic alliance between all the anti-unionist elements in the Six Counties. October 5 in Derry was to accelerate the process.

The organisers of this Derry march sought sponsorship from NICRA and from prominent people in the local community, including John Hume, who refused. NICRA very reluctantly and belatedly endorsed the march and Stormont banned it; the scene was set for confrontation. The republicans decided that, if there was going to be trouble, the people who should get hit should be the visiting MPs who had been invited to attend as observers. As the late Liam McMillan recalled in a pamphlet:

The Belfast republicans had been instructed in the event of the parade being halted by police cordons to push leading nationalist politicians or any other dignitaries who were sure to be at the head of the parade into police ranks. This they did to such effect that one became the first casualty of the day of violence, receiving a busted head. In the ensuing clash the RUC spared no one. A British MP, Mrs Anne Kerr, who had been invited over as an observer, said the savagery that day was worse than anything else she had seen during the Chicago riots a short time previously. And the television coverage of the RUC brutality exposed the fascist nature of the Orange-unionist domination and its ruthless denial of elementary democratic rights to a large section of its citizens.

A sizeable Belfast contingent went to the march. Unable to get yet another day off work, I watched the television coverage of the RUC smashing into the demonstrators who were only a few hundred strong. The following week a protest march against RUC brutality drew 15,000 people, and NICRA felt confident enough to state its demands clearly: universal franchise in local elections, an end to gerrymandered boundaries, the repeal of the Special Powers Act, an end to housing discrimination, disbandment of the B Specials and the withdrawal of the Public Order Bill which the unionists were pushing through Stormont to outlaw civil rights demonstrations.

These demands also became a focus for the emerging differences between the republican leadership and some rank and file activists. The leadership felt that a democratisation of the Six County statelet was necessary if republicans were to engage freely and legally in the social and economic struggle which affected both the unionist and anti-unionist working class. From involvement in these struggles would emerge, they argued, a united republican working class. For them the civil rights struggle was therefore a serious attempt to democratise the state. In the process the national question would be subordinated in order to allay unionist fears and, because the democratisation was going to be a lengthy one, the movement was to be demilitarised. This theory had one serious defect: it underestimated the reactionary nature of the state itself and the reluctance of the Westminster government and its management at Stormont to introduce reforms.

The contrary position was dawning slowly upon those of us who were deeply involved in grassroots agitation. We were beginning to realise that the Six County statelet could not be reformed, that by its very nature it was irreformable and that the major effects of the civil rights struggle would be to show clearly the contradictions within the state, its colonial nature and the responsibility of the British government for this situation. This position only became clear as the civil rights struggle and the state's backlash intensified and as the leadership's position clarified.

The leadership maintained that, following the democratisation of the state, there could be a coming together of Protestant and Catholic workers in support of progressive politics, and the way to achieve this was through a heavy involvement of republicans in the trade unions. Having accepted the desirability of finding common, neutral ground on which Catholic and Protestant could combine, the trade union movement was, on the British Communist Party model, identified as the organisation in which we should be involved and which provided that mutual ground.

The strategy flew in the face of James Connolly's analysis of the loyalist workers as "the aristocracy of labour". It also flew in the face of reality, not least the reality of Catholic working class employment and unemployment. The members of the republican movement in the Six Counties who were supposed to implement this strategy were mostly Catholics who, if they had jobs, had mostly unskilled ones, and who had little or no meaningful access to trade unions. The vast majority of members were either unemployed or were building workers; there were no professional people involved at all, and the few skilled workers were bricklayers and joiners on building sites, occupations with a notoriously low level of union organisation. With a ready labour market there was little motivation or opportunity to organise successfully.

Members of the Dublin leadership of the republican movement came to Belfast, and I was among those who went to the lectures they gave. I found them very interesting and instructive, but they failed to accord with my experience and opinions at that time. In my view, and to some degree with hindsight, the development of the "stages" theory of progressive democratisation was conditional in the first place on the state and its supporters being willing to redress the state's own injustices. This, it was rapidly becoming apparent, was hardly the case. In particular I felt that the analysis of the ways to unite the Protestant and Catholic working class ignored the very nature of the state and my own occasional personal and parochial encounters with loyalism.

Where I lived in Ballymurphy, the relationship between Protestant and Catholic was devoid of any sectarian difficulties. Neighbouring Moyard and New Barnsley were Protestant estates and there was a good level of social intercourse between people of my age. A crowd of us used to go regularly to Moyard and meet with young people there. We would hang around the corners, talk and take our chances with the local talent. We never discussed politics or religion except in a joking or bantering fashion. Then I became involved in a small campaign which involved both Catholics and Protestants.

On the Springfield Road, a child from New Barnsley had been knocked down at the junction with the Whiterock Road, and I went to New Barnsley and saw the parents and then went to Ballymurphy, which even in those days had a fairly energetic and well-organised tenants association. We organised a small campaign to have safety rails put up at the corner and also to have a pedestrian crossing near by. The campaign was successful and we were delighted. Not only was it a gain, albeit small, but it was Catholics and Protestants coming together – in a very parochial sense but nonetheless coming together – and agitating. News of this percolated upwards into the unionist establishment, and one of Paisley's people arrived on the scene, and for the first time, I heard serious talk about "papists" and "pope-heads" and "Fenians" and "Taigs". The Protestants in New Barnsley who had previously been involved with us just stopped their involvement like that.

What we were saying to the Dublin visitors was, "Look, you can talk about all this coming together of Protestant and Catholic working class, but here's yet another instance where the sectarian card was played and the people who had been united were effectively separated. Your notions just don't square with reality." If the state would not allow Catholics and Protestants to get a pedestrian crossing built together, it would hardly sit back and watch them organise the revolution together.

They also saw the trade unions as an important means of pursuing politics. But again my experience gave me doubts. I was working as a barman and was sacked for demanding the trade union rate for the Twelfth of July holiday, which was double time and a day off in lieu. I went to the trade union of which I was a member and wanted them to fight it, but they wouldn't. Although there were no sectarian overtones, it was characteristic of the fact that apprentices were a dime a dozen and in this context, even when one tried to look for something very simple through the trade unions, they just didn't respond.

My own experience was that the sectarian card could be invoked effectively and that there was little basis for making any progress on the national question through the trade union movement. And both of these experiences flew in the face of what the republican leadership was proposing.

The nature of the civil rights struggle added to these contradictions. For example, the directive to Belfast republicans to push visiting notables into the front line at Duke Street, on 5 October in Derry, was really a common sense instruction. But it also accepted that while attempting to democratise the state there was a need for dramatic confrontations in order to expose what was wrong. And these confrontations flatly contradicted the leadership's position of being non-provocative. Furthermore, the people who were making the running on the ground were developing their own thinking on the issues which confronted us. We were not at the centre of the policy-making process, but we were in the centre of what was happening on the ground, so that, for example, in January 1969, following the loyalist and RUC attacks on the Burntollet marchers, it was republican stewards who took the initiative, discarded their armbands, and turned with gusto on the RUC at a banned march in Newry.

The other important development was, of course, the emergence of People's Democracy after the 5 October march. They were to have the most unified approach of all the elements involved in the civil rights campaign. It was they, by their Burntollet march in January 1969, who showed that the reforms promised by O'Neill, in November 1968, and the public relations exercise which followed his "Ulster at the Crossroads" television appeal in December of that year were meaningless.

The Burntollet march showed that nothing had changed. The British state of Northern Ireland had certainly not made reforms gratuitously. It would never, of its own accord, have even moved towards a situation of doing away with some of the things which were disfiguring the state. In fact these things were quite consciously maintained and, once there was any movement towards removing them, the very foundations of the state became insecure. In hindsight it was inevitable, as we approached 1969, that we were headed for a major confrontation. Something had to give and it wasn't going to be us. At the moment that the RUC smashed their way into the crowd in Duke Street, it was as if all the small things that had been happening suddenly came together in a more coherent and a more ominous shape. The civil rights movement, the creation of the republican leadership, was out of their control. There would be no turning back. What had started as a campaign for civil rights was developing into the age-old struggle for national rights.

(1986)

The Politics of Irish Freedom

THE MOUNTAINS OF MOURNE

GEORDIE MAYNE LIVED in Urney Street, one of a net-work of narrow streets which stretched from Cupar Street, in the shadow of Clonard Monastery, to the Shankill Road. I don't know where Geordie is now or even if he's living or dead, but I think of him often. Though I knew him only for a short time many years ago, Geordie is one of those characters who might come into your life briefly but never really leave you afterwards.

Urney Street is probably gone now. I haven't been there in twenty years and all that side of the Shankill has disappeared since then as part of the redevelopment of the area. Part of the infamous Peace Line follows the route that Cupar Street used to take. Before the Peace Line was erected Lawnbrook Avenue joined Cupar Street to the Shankill Road. Cupar Street used to run from the Falls Road up until it met Lawnbrook Avenue, then it swung left and ran on to the Springfield Road. Only as I try to place the old streets do I realise how much the place has changed this last twenty years, and how little distance there really is between the Falls and the Shankill. For all that close-ness there might as well be a thousand miles between them.

When we were kids we used to take short-cuts up Cupar Street from the Falls to the Springfield Road. Catholics lived in the bottom end of Cupar Street nearest the Falls; there were one or two in the middle of Cupar Street, too, but the rest were mainly Protestants till you got up past Lawnbrook

70

Avenue, and from there to the Springfield Road was all Catholic again. The streets going up the Springfield Road on the right-hand side were Protestant and the ones on the left-hand side up as far as the Flush were Catholic. After that both sides were nearly all Protestant until you got to Ballymurphy.

When we were kids we paid no heed to these territorial niceties, though once or twice during the Orange marching season we'd get chased. Around about the Twelfth of July and at other appropriate dates the Orangemen marched through many of those streets, Catholic and Protestant alike. The Catholic ones got special attention, as did individual Catholic houses, with the marching bands and their followers, sometimes the worse for drink, exciting themselves with enthusiastic renderings of Orange tunes as they passed by. The Mackie's workers also passed that way twice daily, an especially large contingent making its way from the Shankill along Cupar Street to Mackie's Foundry. The largest engineering works in the city was surrounded by Catholic streets, but it employed very few Catholics.

Often bemused by expressions such as Catholic street and Protestant area, I find myself nonetheless using the very same expressions. How could a house be Catholic or Protestant? Yet when it comes to writing about the reality it's hard to find other words. Though loath to do so, I use the terms Catholic and Protestant here to encompass the various elements who make up the unionist and non-unionist citizens of this state.

It wasn't my intention to tell you all this. I could write a book about the *craic* I had as a child making my way in and out of all those wee streets on the way back and forth to school or the Boys' Confraternity in Clonard or even down at the Springfield Road dam fishing for spricks, but that's not what I set out to tell you about. I set out to tell you about Geordie Mayne of Urney Street. Geordie was an Orangeman, nominally at least. He never talked about it to me except on the occasion when he told me that he was one. His lodge was The Pride of the Shankill Loyal Orange Lodge, I think, though it's hard to be sure after all this time.

I only knew Geordie for a couple of weeks, but even though

that may seem too short a time to make a judgement I could never imagine him as a zealot or a bigot. You get so that you can tell, and by my reckoning Geordie wasn't the worst. He was a driver for a big drinks firm: that's how I met him. I was on the run at the time. It was almost Christmas 1969 and I had been running about like a blue-arsed fly since early summer. I hadn't worked since July, we weren't getting any money except a few bob every so often for smokes, so things were pretty rough. But it was an exciting time: I was only twenty-one and I was one of a dozen young men and women who were up to their necks in trying to sort things out.

To say that I was on the run is to exaggerate a little. I wasn't wanted for anything, but I wasn't taking any chances either. I hadn't slept at home since the end of May when the RUC had invaded Hooker Street in Ardoyne and there had been a night or two of sporadic rioting. Most of us who were politically active started to take precautions at that time. We were expecting internment or worse as the civil rights agitation and the reaction against it continued to escalate. Everything came to a head in August, including internment, and in Belfast the conflict had been particularly sharp around Cupar Street. This abated a little, but we thought it was only a temporary respite: with the British Army on the streets it couldn't be long till things hotted up again. In the meantime we were not making ourselves too available.

Conway Street, Cupar Street at the Falls Road end and all of Norfolk Street had been completely burned out on the first night of the August pogrom; further up, near the monastery, Bombay Street was gutted on the following night. These were all Catholic streets. Urney Street was just a stone's throw from Bombay Street; that is, if you were a stone thrower.

The drinks company Geordie worked for were taking on extra help to cope with the Christmas rush, and a few of us went up to the head office on the Glen Road on spec one morning; as luck would have it I got a start, together with Big Eamonn and two others. I was told to report to the store down in Cullingtree Road the next morning and it was there that I met Geordie.

He saw me before I saw him. I was standing in the big yard among all the vans and lorries and I heard this voice shouting: "Joe ... Joe Moody."

I paid no attention.

"Hi, boy! Is your name Joe Moody?" the voice repeated.

With a start I realised that that was indeed my name, or at least it was the bum name I'd given when I'd applied for the job.

"Sorry," I stammered.

"I thought you were corned beef. C'mon over here."

I did as instructed and found myself beside a well-built, red-haired man in his late thirties. He was standing at the back of a large empty van.

"Let's go, our kid. My name's Geordie Mayne. We'll be working together. We're late. Have you clocked in? Do it over there and then let's get this thing loaded up."

He handed me a sheaf of dockets.

"Pack them in that order. Start from the back. I'll only be a minute."

He disappeared into the back of the store. I had hardly started to load the van when he arrived back. Between the two of us we weren't long packing in the cartons and crates of wines and spirits and then we were off, Geordie cheerfully saluting the men on barricade duty at the end of the street as they waved us out of the Falls area and into the rest of the world.

Geordie and I spent most of our first day together delivering our load to off-licenses and public houses in the city centre. I was nervous of being recognised because I had worked in a bar there, but luckily it got its deliveries from a different firm. It was the first day I had been in the city centre since August; except for the one trip to Dublin and one up to Derry I had spent all my time behind the barricades. It was disconcerting to find that, apart from the unusual sight of British soldiers with their cheerful, arrogant voices, life in the centre of Belfast, or at least its licensed premises, appeared unaffected by the upheavals of the past few months. It was also strange as we made our deliveries to catch glimpses on television of news coverage

about the very areas and issues I was so involved in and familiar with..Looked at from outside through the television screen,
the familiar scenes might as well have been in another country.

Geordie and I said nothing of any of this to one another.
That was a strange experience for me, too. My life had been
so full of the cut-and-thrust of analysis, argument and counter-
argument about everything that affected the political situation
that I found it difficult to restrain myself from commenting on
events to this stranger. Indeed, emerging from the close cama-
raderie of my closed world, as I had done only that morning, I
found it unusual even to be with a stranger. Over a lunch of
soup and bread rolls in the Harp Bar in High Street I listened
to the midday news on the BBC's Radio Ulster while all the
time pretending indifference. The lead item was a story about
an IRA convention and media speculation about a republican
split. It would be nightfall before I would be able to check this
out for myself, though a few times during the day I almost left
Geordie in his world of cheerful pubs and publicans for the security of the ghettos.

The next few days followed a similar pattern. Each morning
started with Geordie absenting himself for a few minutes to
the back of the store while I started loading up the van. Then
we were off from within the no-go areas and into the city
centre. By the end of the first week the two of us were like old
friends. Our avoidance of political topics, even of the most
pressing nature, that unspoken and much-used form of political protection and survival developed through expediency,
had in its own way been a political indicator, a signal, that we
came from "different sides".

In the middle of the second week Geordie broke our mutual
and instinctive silence on this issue when with a laugh he
handed me that morning's dockets. "Well, our kid, this is your
lucky day. You're going to see how the other half lives. We're
for the Shankill."

My obvious alarm fuelled his amusement.

"Oh, aye," he guffawed. "It's all right for me to traipse up
and down the Falls every day, but my wee Fenian friend
doesn't want to return the favour."

I was going to tell him that nobody from the Falls went up the Shankill burning down houses, but I didn't. I didn't want to hurt his feelings, but I didn't want to go up the Shankill either. I was in a quandary and set about loading up our deliveries with a heavy heart. After I had only two of the cartons loaded I went to the back of the store to tell Geordie that I was jacking it in. He was in the wee office with oul' Harry the storeman. Each of them had a glass of spirits in his hand. Geordie saw me coming and offered his to me.

"Here, our kid, it's best Jamaicay rum. A bit of Dutch courage never did anyone any harm."

"Nawh thanks, Geordie, I don't drink spirits. I need to talk to you for a minute ..."

"If it's about today's deliveries, you've nothing to worry about. We've only one delivery up the Shankill and don't be thinking of not going 'cos you'll end up out on your arse. It's company policy that mixed crews deliver all over the town. Isn't that right, Harry?"

Harry nodded in agreement.

"C'mon, our kid. I'll do the delivery for you. Okay? You can sit in the van. How's that grab you? Can't be fairer than that, can I, Harry?"

"Nope," Harry grunted. They drained their glasses.

"I'll take a few beers for the child, Harry," Geordie said over his shoulder as he and I walked back to the van.

"You know where they are," said Harry.

"Let's go," said Geordie to me. "It's not every day a wee Fenian like you gets on to the best road in Belfast ..." he grabbed me around the neck "... and off it again in one piece. Hahaha."

That's how I ended up on the Shankill. It wasn't so bad but before I tell you about that, in case I forget, from then on, each morning when Geordie returned from the back of the store after getting his "wee drop of starting fuel" he always had a few bottles of beer for me.

Anyway, back to the job in hand. As Geordie said, we only had the one order on the Shankill. It was to the Long Bar. We drove up by Unity Flats and on to Peter's Hill. There were no signs of barricades like the ones on the Falls, and apart from a patrolling RUC landrover and two British Army jeeps the road was the same as it had always seemed to me. Busy and prosperous and coming awake in the early winter morning sunshine.

A few months earlier, in October, the place had erupted in protest at the news that the B Specials were to be disbanded. The protesters had killed one RUC man and wounded three others; thirteen British soldiers had been injured. In a night of heavy gun-fighting along the Shankill Road the British had killed two civilians and wounded twenty others. Since then there had been frequent protests here against the existence of no-go areas in Catholic parts of Belfast and Derry.

Mindful of all this, I perched uneasily in the front of the van, ready at a second's notice to spring into Geordie's seat and drive like the blazes back whence I came. I needn't have worried. Geordie was back in moments. As he climbed into the driver's seat he threw me a packet of cigarettes.

"There's your Christmas box, our kid. I told them I had a wee Fenian out here and that you were dying for a smoke."

Then he took me completely by surprise.

"Do y' fancy a fish supper? It's all right! We eat fish on Friday as well. Hold on!"

And before I could say anything he had left me again as he sprinted from the van into the Eagle Supper Saloon.

"I never got any breakfast," he explained on his return. "We'll go 'round to my house. There's nobody in."

I said nothing as we turned into Westmoreland Street and in through a myriad of backstreets till we arrived in Urney Street. Here the tension was palpable, for me at least. Geordie's house was no different from ours. A two-bedroomed house with a toilet in the backyard and a modernised scullery. Only for the picture of the British Queen, I could have been in my own street. I buttered rounds of plain white bread and we wolfed down our fish suppers with lashings of Geordie's tea.

Afterwards, my confidence restored slightly, while Geordie was turning the van in the narrow street I walked down to the corner and gazed along the desolation of Cupar Street up towards what remained of Bombay Street. A British soldier in a sandbagged emplacement greeted me in a John Lennon accent.

"'Lo, moite. How's about you?"

I ignored him and stood momentarily immersed in the bleak pitifulness of it all, from the charred remains of the small houses to where the world-weary slopes of Divis Mountain gazed benignly in their winter greenness down on us where we slunk, blighted, below the wise steeples of Clonard. It was Geordie's impatient honking of the horn that shook me out of my reverie. I nodded to the British soldier as I departed. This time he ignored me.

"Not a pretty sight," Geordie said as I climbed into the van beside him.

I said nothing. We made our way back through the side-streets on to the Shankill again in silence. As we turned into Royal Avenue at the corner of North Street he turned to me.

"By the way," he said, "I wasn't there that night."

There was just a hint of an edge in his voice.

"I'm sorry! I'm not blaming you," I replied. "It's not your fault."

"I know," he told me firmly.

That weekend, subsidised by my week's wages, I was immersed once more in subversion. That at least was how the unionist government viewed the flurry of political activity in the ghettos, and indeed a similar view was taken by those representatives of the Catholic middle class who had belatedly attached themselves to the various committees in which some of us had long been active. On Monday I was back delivering drink.

We spent the week before Christmas in County Down, seemingly a million miles from the troubles and the tension of Belfast town. For the first time in years I did no political work. It was late by the time we got back each night and I was too tired, so that by Wednesday I realised that I hadn't even seen, read or heard any news all that week. I smiled to myself at the thought that both I and the struggle appeared to be surviving without each other; in those days that was a big admission for me to make, even to myself.

In its place Geordie and I spent the week up and down

country roads, driving through beautiful landscapes, over and around hilltops and along rugged sea-shores and lough-sides as we ferried our liquid wares from village to town, from town to port and back to village again; from market town to fishing village, from remote hamlet to busy crossroads. Even yet the names have a magical sound for me, and at each one Geordie and I took the time for a stroll or a quick look at some local antiquity.

One memorable day we journeyed out to Comber and from there to Killyleagh and Downpatrick, to Crossgar and back again and along the Ballyhornan road and on out to Strangford where we ate our cooked ham baps and drank bottles of stout, hunkering down from the wind below the square tower of Strangford Castle, half-frozen with the cold as we looked over towards Portaferry on the opposite side, at the edge of the Ards Peninsula. We spent a day there as well, and by this time I had a guide book with me written by Richard Hayward, and I kept up a commentary as we toured the peninsula, from Millisle the whole way around the coastline and back to Newtownards. By the end of the week we had both seen where the Norsemen had settled and the spot where Thomas Russell, "the man from God knows where", was hanged, where Saint Patrick had lived and Cromwell and Betsy Grey and Shane O'Neill. We visited monastic settlements and stone circles, round towers, dolmens and holy wells. Up and down the basket-of-eggs county we walked old battle-sites like those of the faction fights at Dolly's Brae or Scarva, "wee buns" we learned compared to Saintfield where Munroe and 7,000 United Irishmen routed the English forces, or the unsuccessful three-year siege by the Great O'Neill, the Earl of Tyrone, of Jordan's Castle at Ardglass. And in between all this we delivered our cargoes of spirits and fine wines.

This was a new world to me, and to Geordie too. It was a marked contrast to the smoke and smell and claustrophobic closeness of our Belfast ghettos and the conflicting moods which gripped them in that winter of 1969. Here was the excitement of greenery and wildlife, of rushing water, of a lightness and heady clearness in the atmosphere and of strange magic around ancient pagan holy places. We planned our last few days' runs as tours and loaded the van accordingly so that whereas in the city we took the shortest route, now we steered according to Richard Hayward's guide book.

On Christmas Eve we went first to Newry where we unloaded over half our supplies in a series of drops at that town's licensed premises. By lunchtime we were ready for the run along the coast road to Newcastle, skirting the Mournes, and from there back home. At our last call on the way out to the Warrenpoint Road, the publican set us up two pints as a Christmas box. The pub was empty and as we sat there enjoying the sup a white-haired man in his late sixties came in. He was out of breath, weighed down with a box full of groceries.

"A bully, John," he greeted the publican. "Have I missed the bus?"

"Indeed and you have, Paddy, and he waited for you for as long as he could."

Paddy put his box down on the floor. His face was flushed.

"Well, God's curse on it anyway. I met Peadar Hartley and big MacCaughley up the town and the pair of them on the tear, and nothing would do them boys but we'd have a Christmas drink and then another till they put me off my whole way of going with their ceili-ing and oul' palavering. And now I've missed the bloody bus. God's curse on them two rogues. It'll be dark before there's another one."

He sighed resignedly and pulled a stool over to the bar, saluting the two of us as he did so.

"John, I might as well have a drink when I'm this far and give these two men one as well."

He over-ruled our protests.

"For the season that's in it. One more'll do yous no harm. It's Christmas. Isn't that right, John? And one for yourself and I'll have a wee Black Bush meself."

"Will you have anything in the Bush, Paddy?"

"Indeed and I'll not. Now John, if it was Scotch now I'd have to have water or ginger ale or something but that's only with Scotch. I take nothing in my whiskey!"

We all joined him in his delighted laughter.

"What way are yous going, boys? Did you say yous were going out towards Newcastle?" the publican asked us.

Geordie nodded.

"Could you ever drop oul' Paddy out that road? He has to go as far as Kilkeel and by the looks of him if he doesn't go soon he'll be here till the New Year."

"No problem," Geordie grinned. I could see he was enjoying the old man who was now lilting merrily away to himself.

"De euw did eh euw, did eh euw did del de."

"Paddy, these two men'll give you a wee lift home."

Paddy was delighted.

"Surely to God, boys, but yous is great men so yous are. Here, we'll have another wee one before we go. A wee *deoch don dorais*. All right, John?"

"Indeed and it isn't," John told him. "Kate'll be worrying about you and these two lads can't wait. Isn't that right, boys?"

"Well, let it never be said that I kept men from their work," Paddy compromised.

"A happy New Year to you, John." The three of us saluted our host and retreated into the crisp afternoon air.

"It'll snow the night," our new-found friend and passenger announced, sniffing the air. I was carrying his box.

He did a jig, to Geordie's great amusement, when he saw that we were travelling in a drinks van.

"It'll be the talk of the place!" he laughed as we settled him into the passenger seat while I wedged myself against the door. Geordie gave him a bottle of stout as we pulled away.

"Do you want a glass?" I asked. "There's some here."

"A glass? Sure yous are well organised. Yous must be from Belfast! No, son, I don't need a glass, thanks all the same. This is grand by the neck. By the way, my name's Paddy O'Brien."

We introduced ourselves.

"You'll never get a job in the shipyard with a name like that," Geordie slagged him.

"And I wouldn't want it. 'Tis an Orange hole, begging your pardon lads and no offence, but them that's there neither works nor wants."

To my relief Geordie guffawed loudly, winking at me as he did. For the rest of the journey Paddy regaled us with stories of his mishaps in black holes and other places.

"I wouldn't like to live in Belfast. I'll tell yous that for sure. I worked there often enough, in both quarters mind you, and I always found the people as decent as people anywhere else. I was at the building and I went often enough to Casement Park, surely to God I did, for the football and some grand games I saw, but I wouldn't live there. Thon's a tough town!"

"It's not so bad," I said loyally, while all the time looking beyond Paddy and past Geordie to where Narrow Water flashed past us and the hills of County Louth dipped their toes in Carlingford Bay.

"No, give me the Mournes," Paddy persisted. "Were yous ever in the Mournes?" He emphasised "in".

"Nawh," we told him. Geordie began to enthuse about our week journeying around the county.

"Sure yous have a great time of it," Paddy agreed. "I'll come with yous the next time. Work? Yous wouldn't know what work was. But boys, I'm telling yous this. Don't be leaving this day without going into the Mournes. There's a road yous could take, wouldn't be out of your way, so it wouldn't. After yous drop me off, go on towards Annalong on this road, and a wee bit outside the village on the Newcastle side there's a side road at Glassdrummond that'll take you up to Silent Valley. It's a straight road from here right through to Glass-drummond, boys. Yous can't miss it."

"That sounds good to me," Geordie agreed.

"Well, that's the best I can do for yous, boys. Come back some day and I'll take yous on better roads right into the heart of the mountains, but it'll be dark soon and snowing as well and my Kate'll kill me, so the Silent Valley'll have t' do yous. You'll be able to see where yous Belfast ones gets your good County Down water from to water your whiskey with and to wash your necks."

"Is Slieve Donard the highest of the Mournes?" I asked, trying to find my faithful guide book below Paddy's seat.

"Donard? The highest? It'll only take you a couple of hours

to climb up there; but, boys, you could see the whole world from Slieve Donard. That's where Saint Donard had his cell, up on the summit. You'll see the Isle of Man out to the east and up along our own coast all of Strangford Lough and up to the hills of Belfast and the smoke rising above them, and beyond that on a clear day Lough Neagh and as far as Slieve Gallion on the Derry and Tyrone border. And southwards beyond Newry you'll see Slieve Gullion, where Cúchulainn rambled, and Slieve Foy east of there, behind Carlingford town, and farther south again you'll see the Hill of Howth and beyond that again if the day is good the Sugar Loaf and the Wicklow Mountains'll just be on the horizon."

"That's some view," Geordie said in disbelief.

Paddy hardly heard as he looked pensively ahead at the open road.

"There's only one thing you can't see from Donard, and many people can't see it anyway although it's the talk of the whole place, and even if it jumped up and bit you it's not to be seen from up there among all the sights. Do yous know what I'm getting at, boys? It's the cause of all our cursed troubles, and if you were twice as high as Donard you couldn't see it. Do yous know what it is?"

We both waited expectantly, I with a little trepidation, for him to enlighten us.

"The bloody border," he announced eventually. "You can't see that awful bloody imaginary line that they pretend can divide the air and the mountain ranges and the rivers, and all it really divides is the people. You can see everything from Donard, but isn't it funny you can't see that bloody border?"

I could see Geordie's hands tighten slightly on the steering-wheel. He continued smiling all the same.

"And there's something else," Paddy continued. "Listen to all the names: Slieve Donard, or Bearnagh or Meelbeg or Meelmore – all in our own language. For all their efforts they've never killed that either. Even most of the wee Orange holes: what are they called? Irish names. From Ballymena to Ahoghill to the Shankill, Aughrim, Derry and the Boyne. The next time yous boys get talking to some of them Belfast

Orangemen you should tell them that."

"I'm a Belfast Orangeman," Geordie told him before I could say a word. I nearly died, but Paddy laughed uproariously. I said nothing. I could see that Geordie was starting to take the needle. We passed through Kilkeel with only Paddy's chortling breaking the silence.

"You're the quare *craic*," he laughed. "I've really enjoyed this wee trip. Yous are two decent men. *Tá mise go han buíoch daoibh, a cháirde*. I'm very grateful to you indeed."

"*Tá fáilte romhat*," I said, glad in a way that we were near his journey's end.

"Oh, *maith an fear*," he replied. "*Tabhair dom do lámh*."

We shook hands.

"What d'fuck's yous two on about?" Geordie interrupted angrily.

"He's only thanking us and I'm telling him he's welcome," I explained quickly. "Shake hands with him!"

Geordie did so grudgingly as the old man directed him to stop by the side of the road.

"Happy Christmas," he proclaimed as he lifted his box.

"Happy Christmas," we told him. He stretched across me and shook hands with Geordie again.

"*Go n'éirigh an bóthar libh*," he said. "May the road rise before you."

"And you," I shouted, pulling closed the van door as Geordie drove off quickly and Paddy and his box vanished into the shadows.

"Why don't yous talk bloody English," Geordie snarled savagely at me as he slammed through the gears and catapulted the van forward.

"He just wished you a safe journey," I said lamely. "He had too much to drink and he was only an old man. It is Christmas after all."

"That's right, you stick up for him. He wasn't slow about getting his wee digs in, Christmas or no Christmas. I need a real drink after all that oul' balls."

He pulled the van roughly into the verge again. I got out too as he clambered outside and climbed into the back. Angrily he selected a carton of whiskey from among its fellows and handed me a yellow bucket which was wedged in among the boxes.

"Here, hold this," he ordered gruffly. As I did so he held the whiskey box at arm's length above his head and then, to my surprise, dropped it on the road. We heard glass smashing and splintering as the carton crumpled at one corner. Geordie pulled the bucket from me and sat the corner of the whiskey box into it.

"Breakages," he grinned at my uneasiness. "You can't avoid them. By the time we get to Paddy's Silent bloody Valley there'll be a nice wee drink for us to toast him and the border *and* that bloody foreign language of yours. Take that in the front with you."

I did as he directed. Already the whiskey was beginning to drip into the bucket.

"That's an old trick," Geordie explained as we continued our journey. He was still in bad humour and maybe even a little embarrassed about the whiskey, which continued to dribble into the bucket between my feet on the floor. "The cardboard acts as a filter and stops any glass from getting through. Anyway, it's Christmas and Paddy isn't the only one who can enjoy himself," he concluded as we took the side road at Glassdrummond and commenced the climb up to the Silent Valley.

The view that awaited us was indeed breathtaking, as we came suddenly upon the deep mountain valley with its massive dam and huge expanse of water surrounded by rugged mountains and skirted by a picturesque stretch of road.

"Well, Paddy was right about this bit anyway," Geordie conceded as he parked the van and we got out for a better view. "It's a pity we didn't take a camera with us," he said. "It's gorgeous here. Give's the bucket and two of them glasses."

He filled the two glasses and handed me one.

"Don't mind me, our kid. I'm not at myself. Here's to a good Christmas."

That was the first time I drank whiskey. I didn't want to offend Geordie again by refusing but I might as well have for I

put my foot in it anyway the next minute. He was gazing re-
flectively up the valley, quaffing his drink with relish while I
sipped timorously on mine.

"Do you not think you're drinking too much to be driving?"
I asked.

He exploded.

"Look son, I've stuck you for a few weeks now, and I never
told you once how to conduct your affairs; not once. You've
gabbled on at me all week about every bloody thing under the
sun and today to make matters worst you and that oul' degen-
erate that I was stupid enough to give a lift to, you and him
tried to coerce me and talked about me in your stupid language, and now you're complaining about my drinking. When
you started as my helper I didn't think I'd have to take the
pledge *and* join the fuckin' rebels as well. Give my head peace,
would you, wee lad; for the love and honour of God, give's a
bloody break!"

His angry voice skimmed across the water and bounced
back at us off the side of the mountains. I could feel the blood
rushing to my own head as the whiskey and Geordie's words
registered in my brain.

"Who the hell do you think you are, eh?" I shouted at him,
and my voice clashed with the echo of his as they collided
across the still waters.

"Who do I think I am? Who do you think you are is more
like it," he snapped back, "with all your bright ideas about
history and language and all that crap. You and that oul' eejit
Paddy are pups from the same Fenian litter, but you remember
one thing, young fella-me-lad, yous may have the music and
songs and history and even the bloody mountains, but we've
got everything else; you remember that!"

His outburst caught me by surprise.

"All that is yours as well, Geordie. We don't keep it from
you. It's you that rejects it all. It doesn't reject you. It's not
ours to give or take. You were born here same as me."

"I don't need you to tell me what's mine. I know what's
mine. I know where I was born. You can keep all your emotional crap. Like I said, we've got all the rest."

"Who's we, Geordie? Eh? Who's we? The bloody English Queen or Lord bloody Terence O'Neill, or Chi-Chi, the dodo that's in charge now? Is that who we is? You've got all the rest! Is that right, Geordie? That's shit and you know it."

I grabbed him by the arm and spun him round to face me. For a minute I thought he was going to hit me. I was ready for him. But he said nothing as we stood glaring at each other.

"You've got fuck all, Geordie," I told him. "Fuck all except a two-bedroomed house in Urney Street and an identity crisis."

He turned away from me and hurled his glass into the darkening distance.

"This'll nivver be Silent Valley again, not after we're finished with it," he laughed heavily. "I'm an Orangeman, Joe. That's what I am. It's what my Da was. I don't agree with everything here. My Da wouldn't even talk to a Papist, nivver mind drink or work with one. When I was listening to Paddy I could see why. That's what all this civil rights rubbish is about as well. Well, I don't mind people having their civil rights. That's fair enough. But you know and I know if it wasn't that it would be something else. I'm easy come, easy go. There'd be no trouble if everybody else was the same."

I had quietened down also by now.

"But people need their rights," I said.

"Amn't I only after saying that!" he challenged me.

"Well, what are you going to do about it?" I retorted.

"Me?" he laughed. "Now I know your head's cut! I'm going to do exactly nothing about it! There are a few things that make me different from you. We've a lot in common, I grant you that, but we're different also, and one of the differences is that after Christmas I'll have a job and you won't, and I intend to keep it. And more importantly, I intend to stay alive to do it."

"Well, that's straight enough and there's no answer to that," I mused, sipping the last of my whiskey.

Geordie laughed at me.

"Typical Fenian," he commented. "I notice you didn't throw away your drink."

"What we have we hold." I took another wee sip and gave him the last of it.

"By the way, seeing we're talking to each other instead of at each other, there's no way that our ones, and that includes me, will ever let Dublin rule us."

The sun was setting and there was a few wee flurries of snow in the air.

"Why not?" I asked.

"'Cos that's the way it is."

"What we have we hold?" I repeated. "Only for real."

"If you like."

"But you've nothing in common with the English. We don't need them here to rule us. We can do a better job ourselves. They don't care about the unionists. You go there and they treat you like a Paddy just like me. What do you do with all your loyalty then? You're Irish. Why not claim that and we'll all govern Dublin."

"I'm British!"

"So am I," I exclaimed. "Under duress 'cos I was born in this state. We're both British subjects but we're Irishmen. Who do you support in the rugby? Ireland I bet! Or international soccer? The same! All your instincts and roots and ..." I waved my arms around at the dusky mountains in frustration "... surroundings are Irish. This is fucking Ireland. It's County Down, not Sussex or Suffolk or Yorkshire. It's us and we're it!" I shouted.

"Now you're getting excited again. You shouldn't drink whiskey," Geordie teased me. "It's time we were going. C'mon; I surrender."

On the way down to Newcastle I drank the whiskey that was left in the bucket. We had only one call to make, so when I asked him to, Geordie dropped me at the beach. I stood watching as the van drove off and thought that perhaps he wouldn't return for me. It was dark by now. As I walked along the strand the snow started in earnest. Slieve Donard was but a hulking shadow behind me. I couldn't see it. Here I was in Newcastle, on the beach. On my own, in the dark. Drunk. On Christmas Eve. Waiting for a bloody Orangeman to come back for me so that I could go home.

The snow was lying momentarily on the sand, and the water rushing in to meet it looked strange in the moonlight as it and the sand and the snow merged. I was suddenly exhilarated by my involvement with all these elements and as I crunched the sand and snow beneath my feet and the flakes swirled around me my earlier frustrations disappeared. Then I chuckled aloud at the irony of it all.

The headlights of the van caught me in their glare. My Orangeman had returned.

"You're soaked, you bloody eejit," he complained when I climbed into the van again.

He, too, was in better form. As we drove home it was as if we had never had a row. We had a sing-song – mostly carols with some Beatles' numbers – and the both of us stayed well clear of any contentious verses. On the way through the Belfast suburbs Geordie sang what we called "our song".

"O Mary, this London's a wonderful sight
There's people here working by day and by night:
They don't grow potatoes or barley or wheat,
But there's gangs of them digging for gold in the street.
At least when I asked them that's what I was told,
So I took a hand at this digging for gold,
For all that I found there I might as well be
Where the Mountains of Mourne sweep down to the sea."

We went in for a last drink after we'd clocked out at the store, but by this time my head was thumping and I just wanted to go home.

As we walked back to the van Geordie shook my hand warmly.

"Thanks, kid. I've learned a lot this last week or so, and not just about County Down. You're dead on, son," he smiled, "for a Fenian. Good luck to you anyway, oul' hand, in all that you do, but just remember, our kid, I love this place as much as you do."

"I know," I said. "I learned that much at least."

He dropped me off at Divis Street and drove off waving, on across the Falls towards the Shankill. I walked up to the Falls.

That was the last I saw of Geordie Mayne. I hope he has survived the last twenty years and that he'll survive the next twenty as well. I hope we'll meet again in better times. He wasn't such a bad fella, for an Orangeman.

(1992)

The Street and other stories

A Republican in the
Civil Rights Campaign

THE ARK WASN'T a big public house. Situated at the corner of Broadbent Street on Belfast's Old Lodge Road, it consisted of a public bar, which was partitioned from the more discreet back room and snug. That was it. A backdrop of shelved whiskey bottles fronted by a no-nonsense wooden counter which separated myself and the only other barman from the clientele. He and I were Catholics. The customers were mostly Protestant, mainly male, and totally working class.

Porter was the staple and non-sectarian drink. Firkins of it were delivered weekly from Guinness's yard on the Grosvenor Road, manhandled into place behind the counter and dispensed with much care into pint glasses. No Double X or draft beers. Wee Willie Darks, bottles of Red Heart or Carling Black Label were minority brews. Either a wee Mundies or the cheaper Drawbridge wine offered a more popular *deoch* (drink). A bottle and a half 'un were strictly Friday or Saturday night treats. Sales of spirits were minimal. An occasional gin for the women to augment their more economical small sherries or port. No vodkas. No liqueurs. And no Pope.

All the customers lived beside the Ark or in neighbouring streets. These streets lay between the Old Lodge Road and the Shankill Road on one side and the Crumlin Road on the other.

It was a loyalist area. The shipyard was the main source of employment and many of the Ark's male customers worked there. Or at least, as they put it themselves, they clocked in there most mornings. More lucrative jobs were the preserve of better-off areas. Some of the customers were unemployed. They spent their time commuting between their homes, the bookie's shop and the Ark. A few of them kept pigeons, some bred greyhounds. Rinty Monaghan, the former boxing champion, was the only celebrity to frequent the area.

The Twelfth of July provided an annual relief from the customary calmness. St Patrick's night in the Ark provided more entertainment. "When Irish Eyes Are Smiling" and "The Green Glens of Antrim" vied with "The Boys of the County Armagh" and "Danny Boy" – minus the third verse of course. On one occasion I was moved to render a verse of "The Sash" in Irish. A Somme veteran followed me with a rendition of "Kevin Barry". At the end of the night, as we cleared away glasses and empty bottles, everyone else stood for a collective voicing of "God Save the Queen". The Twelfth was a holiday. Not for bartenders of course, but for almost everyone else. Most of the Ark's clientele didn't go to the Field (where the annual Orange demonstration was held). Many of the men weren't in the Orange Order and none of the women were: they weren't allowed. We all watched the big parade of course and they crowded around the bonfires on the Eleventh night. They enjoyed themselves. There was no real harm in them. It was 1965. They felt under no threat and they presented no threat. That would come in its own time. They and we have only their leaders to thank for that.

In those pre-civil rights days I journeyed daily along the Falls Road, across the Shankill, and up the Old Lodge. Frequently I collected tripe, to be boiled with onions for a darts match buffet, from a Shankill Road butcher – no associate of his more notorious namesakes in later years (the "Shankill Butchers" were a loyalist murder gang) – and occasionally I took to the waters in Peter's Hill public baths at the bottom of the Shankill Road. On warm summer nights, including one Eleventh (of July) night, I walked to Ballymurphy along the Shankill and the

West Circular Road, through miles of loyalist territory, stopping for a fish supper in the Eagle Supper Saloon on the way. Nobody bothered me. Maybe I didn't look like a Catholic. Or maybe nobody cared. Polarisation was peaceful. My only aggravation had occurred much earlier when a short-lived schoolboy boxing career came to an end in a Shankill Road club when a Malvern Street sparring partner took me and his pugilistic skills more seriously than I did. That was in 1958. I was ten.

When I worked in the Ark I was already involved in republican politics. When the planners started the destruction of the Falls Road with the demolition of the Loney area – a district of densely packed tiny houses at the bottom of the Falls – and the building of the new slum of Divis Flats, I and other republicans joined local people in protest. When the same vandalism started in the Old Lodge Road I stood with the locals at the door of the Ark and watched as the bulldozers destroyed and displaced a community. No one protested. Everyone was sad. Some of the women showed a little anger, but none of the local men listened to them: They were only women after all. And no one listened to me; I was only a wee Catholic barman.

Outside the Old Lodge Road, however, the snail's pace of progressive politics was slowly taking on a new momentum. In May 1965 a hesitant exchange of ideas between republicans, communists and unaffiliated trade unionists led to a conference on civil liberties hosted by the Belfast Trades Council. As well as the above individuals it was attended by the Northern Ireland Labour Party (NILP) and the Campaign for Social Justice. I was on the perimeter of such developments. Like the customers in the Ark, I was only subconsciously affected by them. Although the NILP temporarily thwarted the fragile unity which was emerging among the elements who attended the conference, the republicans, encouraged perhaps by these developments, were slowly coming out of the closet to challenge the Stormont government's Special Powers Act and the banning of Sinn Féin. Easter 1966 was marked by a large republican commemoration in West Belfast, while a month earlier someone had blown up Nelson's Pillar in Dublin. And Ian

Paisley initiated a new quarter century of long hot summers by leading a highly provocative and sectarian march into the nationalist Markets area of Belfast.

For my sins, in a hilarious Keystone Cops diversion, I was arrested for selling the republican paper, the *United Irishman*, as part of a Sinn Féin plan to flout a Stormont government ban on it. But meanwhile, more serious incidents, including the murders of two Catholics and a seventy-year-old Protestant woman by the revived Ulster Volunteer Force led to the banning of the UVF by the Stormont government in 1966. Unionist boss Terence O'Neill had met Dublin Premier Sean Lemass the previous year, demonstrating that at least a section of unionism was being reluctantly dragged into the twentieth century on the eve of the new EEC era.

By now I was working in another pub, the Duke of York in the centre of Belfast. I left the Ark following a wage dispute. I had asked for the union rate for working a public holiday – the Twelfth. Instead I got the sack; my own personal lock-out. I was sorry to leave my friends on the Old Lodge Road, and they, diminished in numbers by the on-going levelling of their homes, were sorry to see me go. Though I never thought of it then, I probably got sacked at a good time. Peaceful polarisation was fraying at the edges. Ironically it was my Catholic employer and not the Protestant customers who evicted me.

I was spending my long lunch breaks from the Duke of York churning out leaflets in Sinn Féin headquarters in Cyprus Street on a geriatric duplicating machine and learning the ground rules of political agitation. The Wolfe Tone Society, a republican-oriented discussion group, had re-invigorated the initiative which had led to the 1965 civil liberties conference. Another conference was held in Belfast in January 1967. It decided to start the Northern Ireland Civil Rights Association (NICRA). At the same time, and while involved in the preparation of this hesitant groundwork for the civil rights campaign, the republicans had embarked on their own initiative to transform the banned Sinn Féin party into an open, legal organisation. Republican Clubs were formed for this purpose. They were banned as well.

In defiance of the ban, an open meeting of Republican Clubs was held in a room above a café in Belfast's Chapel Lane. We were pleasantly disappointed not to be arrested. A month later a meeting in the city's International Hotel elected an executive for the Northern Ireland Civil Rights Association and agreed on a constitution. We republicans were there in strength. We were acting on instructions not to pack the executive; it was sufficient to have an influence. We were also instructed to vote for Communist Party nominees. The meeting was uneventful with only the presence of a unionist, Robin Cole, providing diversion for the younger republicans. Most of us had never seen a unionist before, but he didn't look any different from anyone else. It was all a bit boring and I, for one, had no clear view of what it would come to mean.

For all that, it was an historic meeting. Over twenty years later at a conference in Coalisland to launch a '68 Committee, veteran republican Kevin Agnew gave me a hand-written list of those elected to that first executive. They were Dr Con McCloskey of the Campaign for Social Justice, Professor T.A. O'Brien, Noel Harris and Ken Banks of the draughtsman's union DATA, Professor Michael Dolley, Fred Heatley, Jack Bennet, Derek Peters of the Communist Party, Kevin Agnew, J. Quinn of the Liberal Party, Betty Sinclair of the Trades Council and Communist Party, Robin Cole, Joe Sherry of Gerry Fitt's Republican Labour Party and Paddy Devlin of the NILP. A backward glance over this first NICRA leadership shows how the republican voting strategy ensured a nicely rounded leadership for the parent Civil Rights Association. Business concluded, everyone, voters and voted, went home. Few of us, including me, or, I guess, the newly elected executive, realised we had set in train the beginning of the end of Six County politics as unionism and the rest of us knew it. After years of sterling and patient preparatory work by a small number of committed progressives, a new era had yawned itself awake in the International Hotel at the back of Belfast's City Hall.

A few months later and close to this spot, the RUC blocked a march by Queen's University students. They were protesting at the Stormont ban on Queen's University Republican Club.

Myself and a republican friend were walking by. Our curiosity aroused by this new spectacle, my friend went to investigate at close quarters. The students staged a sit-down. My friend was among those arrested. Subsequently, the Queen's students brought a new force into the slowly fermenting political agitation. Later they would form Peoples Democracy, which would add its own pinch of highly articulate and active ingredients to the civil rights melting pot.

That pot simmered gently until 1968. In the meantime, the remaining months of 1967 were more or less uneventful, that is if you discount the time that "Throw-the-Brick" Morgan threw a brick at the British Queen and her husband as their royal car was escorted down Belfast's Great Victoria Street. As "All You Need is Love" kept the Beatles at number one in the charts, Ian Paisley threw snowballs at Jack Lynch when he visited Terence O'Neill at Stormont. The day after that event an opinion poll showed that a majority in the Six Counties thought it unnecessary to legislate against discrimination. The civil rights struggle was set to be an uphill one.

The ingredients in the NICRA stew were diverse. They included civil libertarians, who were genuinely affronted by the lack of civil rights in the British state. Their interest was in removing these injustices. Others had a more radical and long-sighted view. They saw the civil rights platform providing a forum for political unity among progressive elements. Some of these saw the successful achievement of the civil rights aims creating a situation where such unity would, in a new democratic set-up, spread to the divided Catholic and Protestant working class, transforming sectarian differences into class unity. And some saw the civil rights struggle as a means of confronting an apartheid state, exposing its contradictions and building popular opposition to them and to the state itself. More because of the nature of the state and the crass stupidity of the London and Stormont governments than through any long-headed political planning or control by any of the above tendencies, that last scenario quickly became the almost inevitable conclusion to what was a modest campaign for reasonable, basic and just demands.

NICRA in its early days never had a unified strategy for confronting the state with these demands. It was modelled on the British National Council for Civil Liberties and began its existence by almost anonymously collating complaints of civil rights breaches. The leadership was cautious, perhaps rightly so, but the initiative never lay with it anyway. The initiative was on the streets and any campaign which involves street politics needs its leadership on the streets also; otherwise it ceases to lead. NICRA, whose perceived role was to lobby for legislative changes, tried to avoid street politics in the beginning. Then when these developed, almost despite NICRA, and on occasions quite definitely in spite of NICRA, a street leadership, which was already involved in separate campaigns in different parts of the Six Counties, filled the leadership vacuum in these areas.

This development was aided not only by the existence of separate agitations in Derry, Tyrone and Belfast, which had their own local leaderships championing localised campaigns against unfair housing allocation and other injustices, but by the spread of local civil rights committees which were largely autonomous. It was helped too by the reaction of unionist bullyboys, including the RUC, whose antics moved the whole situation on. As it turned out after 5 October 1968, a strange alliance of soon-to-be-SDLP leaders, some of the old guard NICRA leadership, the republican leadership and kindred spirits represented the gradualist tendency, while other republicans, the very energetic Peoples Democracy, and the vast majority of civil rights supporters formed a more combative tendency seeking to expose the contradictions of the Six County state.

The differences were mirrored within republican ranks. While the Dublin leadership had a clear enough view of the gradualist strategy, their Northern representatives, especially in Belfast, had a hazier view. This was partly a result of the Northern leadership's non-involvement in actual street activity, which permitted a degree of initiative to be wrested from them by rank and file activists who were taking a more realistic attitude than that laid down by the Dublin leadership. It also arose partly as a result of the fluidity of internal republican politics, which had still at that time to gell into the Goulding/MacGiolla leadership line – Cathal Goulding, a senior republican leader, and Tomás MacGiolla, president of Sinn Féin, were leading advocates of the gradualist, reformist politics which culminated in what is now the Workers' Party. The Belfast leadership, which was to toe the Goulding/ MacGiolla line in 1969, was in those less dogmatic times advocating or supporting pragmatic and at times, as we have seen, contradictory positions.

Thus there were two separate, if occasionally overlapping, agendas being followed by the republicans. One group was intent on exposing the irreformable nature of the Six County state; the other was following a gradualist approach to reforming the state. These elements were at least agreed on the merits of the civil rights campaign. Others, however, were not too sure. The absence of a united Ireland demand, a distrust of "politics" and a fear of reforms – the view that "If the civil rights demands are conceded, people won't want a united Ireland" – manifested itself in much grumbling and sidelines dissent.

More positively, the politicisation of the ailing republican struggle encouraged republican involvement with other forces in hitherto neglected issues, the fruits of which started to appear in the form of well-publicised demonstrations against housing malpractice in Derry and in the Caledon squat in County Tyrone, when republicans helped a local family to occupy a council house which had been allocated to a single young woman who worked for a local unionist candidate. Nationalist MP Austin Currie (later SDLP) got a lot of publicity for himself when he joined the squat fairly briefly, accompanied by TV cameras, but the groundwork had been done for weeks by the republicans. (Six years later Currie, as a Minister in the 1974 power-sharing administration, would impose punitive collection charges on people he had encouraged to go on rent and rates strike.) The confrontationist, though passive, nature of these activities, which spread also to Belfast, suited the mood of grassroots republican activists and was highly popular among discontented nationalists. Such activities, added to increasing republican impatience to move ahead on "their own" issues – the ban on Sinn Féin and on open political activity by republicans – also were at odds with the more cautious approach of the NICRA leadership.

The first NICRA protest rallies were held in Newry and Armagh in the spring of 1968 after the banning of an Easter Rising commemoration parade. The first civil rights march took place in August 1968 from Coalisland to Dungannon. Almost eighteen months after NICRA was formed, a hesitant beginning to the mass civil rights activity slowly developed. The 5 October march in Derry was to accelerate the process.

The local activists who organized this Derry march sought sponsorship from NICRA and from prominent people in the local community, including John Hume, then a local teacher who was prominent in the Credit Union movement and the campaign for a university for Derry. He refused his support. NICRA reluctantly and belatedly endorsed the march, which was going to go ahead anyway, and Stormont banned it. So it was that, courtesy of television coverage, the world saw the real face of British and unionist rule in the Six Counties. The RUC smashed into the relatively small demonstration, exposing the brutal nature of unionist domination and the ruthless denial of basic democratic rights. They split many skulls in the process. Nevertheless, a few weeks later 15,000 people demonstrated in Derry against RUC brutality and NICRA's demands received further widespread publicity. Universal franchise in local elections, an end to gerrymandered boundaries, the repeal of the Special Powers Act, an end to job and housing discrimination, and disbandment of the B Specials fronted the civil rights agenda.

These demands also became a focus for the emerging differences between the republican leadership and some rank and file activists. The leadership position had by now become clearer. The civil rights struggle was not only seen by them as a serious attempt to democratise the state, but to facilitate this process the national question, the issue of partition, was to be set to one side in order to allay unionist fears, and the movement was to be demilitarised. This strategy had one serious defect: it underestimated the reactionary and irreformable nature of the state itself and the reluctance of the London government and its Stormont management to introduce reforms. This reality was slowly dawning on many of us who came to believe that the major effect of the civil rights struggle, aside from winning some reforms or partial reforms, would be to show clearly the reactionary and colonial nature of the state and the responsibility of the British government for this situation.

We were also enjoying the breakdown of republican isolation, the political exchanges and interchanges, the pooling of resources and experiences arising from the informal alliances which were being developed in the "thick of battle" between the different elements of the civil rights movement. The traditional internalisation of republican activities and their restriction to a chosen few now seemed a thing of the past and, while the leadership plotted its gradualist approach, we felt, rightly or wrongly, that we were more in touch with reality. For example, Belfast republicans at Duke Street in Derry on 5 October were instructed to push visiting notables into the front line. A sensible instruction, but one which accepted that while attempting to democratise the state there was a need for dramatic confrontations in order to expose what was wrong with it. And these confrontations flatly contradicted the leadership's strategy of avoiding "provocation". They also moved the entire situation on and crystallised tensions within NICRA itself. These became most obvious following Terence O'Neill's "Ulster stands at the crossroads" television broadcast a few weeks after he had announced a five-point reform programme in November 1968.

Civil rights demonstrations had been opposed by loyalist counter-demonstrations, usually led by Ian Paisley; RUC brutality was an occupational hazard for civil rights activists and some B Specials had been fully mobilised by Stormont. In his "crossroads" broadcast O'Neill called for an end to civil disorder and agitation, and support for his reform package. He warned that Westminster might intervene if there was no improvement in the situation. NICRA responded by calling for a period of "truce", without marches or demonstrations.

The NICRA announcement led to much discussion among grassroots activists. Peoples Democracy took the lead when they announced that they would march from Belfast to Derry, beginning on New Year's Day 1969. Initial republican disagreement with this initiative saw a number of us being ordered not to take part. Days later this leadership position was submerged by the boots, bricks and batons of off-duty B Specials and their associates, as the RUC led the marchers into the ambush at Burntollet bridge. The Burntollet march showed that the reforms promised by O'Neill and the public relations exercise which followed his announcement were meaningless. It showed that nothing had changed. The British state had certainly not made reforms voluntarily. It would never of its own accord have even begun to move towards doing away with some of the things upon which the very existence of the state depended. Once there was any movement towards removing these, the foundations of the state became insecure. As the old order of things began to crumble, and as the British moved in to prop up their client state, the shortcomings and futility of a gradualist approach became increasingly obvious. Full civil rights and the existence of a partitionist and gerrymandered apartheid state were incompatible.

The struggle for civil rights was developing into a struggle for national rights. Northern republicans, including those in positions of leadership, were forced to reconsider the Goulding leadership's approach. Thus later in January 1969 it was republican stewards who took the initiative, discarded their armbands, and turned with gusto on the RUC at a banned march in Newry. The situation had developed rapidly. The civil rights demands were demands for rights which were taken for granted in Britain and western Europe. They were simple, modest and moderate, yet they evoked a ferocious response from the state and its supporters. The civil rights movement looked for the democratisation of the Six County state, but the state made it abundantly clear that it would not and could not implement democratic reforms. The civil rights movement had not demanded the abolition of the state, nor a united Ireland.

The civil rights struggle had not raised the constitutional question, but the reaction of the state and the active British intervention in support of the state brought the constitutional question to the fore, and the existence of the Six County state into question.

Parallel to this, the republican strategy of organising politically to achieve democracy within the state, which had involved a turning away from the physical force tradition, had run headlong into the reality of the irreformable sectarian state. It was a reality which the republican leadership was totally unprepared for and as the crisis within the state deepened, differences within republican ranks were exacerbated by events and by the return of some lapsed members who had disagreed with the general direction of the movement and who had been absent during the politicisation period. Under these pressures the loosely united tendencies which made up the republican movement came sharply into conflict. This would have occurred anyway, in time, because of the underlying strategic and ideological strains, but the civil rights struggle and the backlash from the August 1969 pogroms in Belfast dictated the timing and to a large degree the sharpness of the divisions. Latent personality conflicts were given a new vigour by the emotive events of 14-15 August 1969 – the attacks on the Catholic areas of the Falls Road, Clonard and Ardoyne – which saw the biggest forced movement of population in any part of western Europe since the Second World War, as Catholics fled from a state backlash which saw entire streets burned out and left eight people dead (six Catholics and two Protestants). The ramifications of those events affected all of Ireland.

The Goulding/MacGiolla leadership had got it wrong. Their failure to provide adequate defence, allied to the mishandling of an almost unprecedented opportunity to move the entire situation on, was bad enough. But when circumstances dictated and cried out for a leadership capable of unifying, or encouraging the maximum unity of progressives, anti-imperialists, socialists, republicans and nationalists, the republican leadership dithered and the republican movement divided. As the institutions of the Northern state tottered, both republican factions rushed belatedly to procure weapons. The political ground was left untilled, creating a vacuum which was later to be filled by a generally unchallenged SDLP. That the entire movement turned at this time to armed resistance was not entirely due to any ingrained militarism, but had everything to do with the stark reality of the situation.

That reality continues to this day. The British state in the north-east of Ireland is a failed political entity and since 1969 it has been kept in existence by a life-support unit of British occupation forces. The logic behind the Goulding/MacGiolla error on the national question has also continued through to this day in the pseudo-socialist posturings and at times two-nationist and partitionist approach of the Workers' Party. The republican movement also suffers from a legacy today, especially in the Twenty-six Counties, which is directly attributable to the distrust of "politics" which intensified in reaction to the Goulding/MacGiolla era. Only now is an increasingly politicised Sinn Féin attempting to recoup lost ground.

Now that we have reached the 20th anniversary of the civil rights struggle, the denials of democratic rights continue. They were rediscovered in the wake of the 1980-81 Armagh and H Blocks hunger strikes by the Irish establishment, who played no part in the original civil rights struggle and ignored the Northern crisis until it was forced upon them. These denials of democratic rights – "the causes of alienation" – were to be erased, we were assured, by the 1985 Hillsborough Treaty, or Anglo-Irish Agreement. But mentioning these issues in cosy chats at the intergovernmental meetings established under the Hillsborough Treaty has had no effect on the British. The inequities remain and there is ample proof in the recent past of British willingness to intensify them. There is a need today as there was in the sixties for a campaign for democratic rights in the Six Counties. The right to vote for which we marched and were batoned, and for which people died, has been eroded by British legislation. We were to learn that unless we cast our votes in accordance with the wishes of the British government, that government had little regard for the results of the ballot box. Thus after Bobby Sands was elected to Westminster in

April 1981, while on hunger strike, the British government introduced legislation to ban prisoner candidates, and when Sinn Féin won electoral support, the British declared that they would not meet or accept representations from Sinn Féin's elected representatives. When this disenfranchising of Sinn Féin voters was seen to have little effect on Sinn Féin's support in subsequent elections, restrictive and undemocratic obstacles were introduced for voters in the form of compulsory identity requirements (e.g. a driving licence or a passport). As this also had little effect and as the Sinn Féin vote remains remarkably solid, at the time of writing the British government is preparing a compulsory electoral pledge for candidates designed to try to prevent Sinn Féin from contesting elections.

British injustice continues in other areas also. Discrimination in employment and employment opportunity continues. Coercive legislation of the most brutal kind remains. The UDR has replaced the B Specials – a change only of name and uniform – and the RUC remains as sectarian as before, just becoming more numerous, more murderous and better equipped since 1969. They are ably aided today by a British army occupation force. This is what keeps the Six County state intact; without them it would not survive.

The present "unity by consent" formula is a fudge – a catch-22 – which shifts the terms of the debate about partition away from Britain's intransigence, and puts the responsibility for the British connection on the unionists. But of course it is not loyalty or love for the unionists which keeps the British government in Ireland. Even my friends in the Ark Bar knew that. British policy is a failed policy, that much is clear. What is needed is for the British government to change its current policy to one of ending partition and the union in the context of Irish reunification. That means withdrawing from Ireland and handing over sovereignty to an all-Ireland government.

The unionists have no right of veto over the unification of Ireland and the ending of the British connection. That is a matter of principle. But all sensible people agree that the consent of Northern Protestants is desirable on the constitutional, financial and political arrangements needed to replace partition. Northern Protestants have fears about their civil and religious liberties, and these liberties must rightly be guaranteed and protected. We who are denied our civil rights do not seek to deny these rights to others. What is needed is a regime of equality shaped by the diverse elements which make up our nation. The British government can play an influential role in persuading members of the unionist tradition that their best interests lie with the rest of the Irish people in building a new all-Ireland society. They can start that process by ending the unionist veto. While it remains, the unionists have no real incentive to examine any other option.

The important, crucial and most fundamental step is of course that the British government change its current policy. It will do this more speedily if it can no longer count on support from Dublin and the SDLP, and if it is faced with pressure from Dublin, supported by the international goodwill which Ireland enjoys and which we can enlist to support the Irish cause. Alongside such a strategy, which should include an international and diplomatic offensive by the Dublin government, there is an urgent need to win improvements on the ground on the issue of democratic rights. This calls for firm pressure on Britain and a campaign of international lobbying and publicity coupled with national political activity. By such means will Britain be forced to end the use of plastic bullets, strip searching, Crown forces' brutality, ill-treatment of prisoners, and torture in interrogation centres, and to change its attitude towards the repatriation of prisoners, the release of the SOSPs (prisoners serving indefinite sentences at "the Secretary of State's Pleasure"), discrimination in employment and high nationalist unemployment, the Prevention of Terrorism Act, reviews of life sentences, and cultural rights.

Of course, Dublin would be better able to pursue such objectives if it was free from criticism itself on similar issues. An array of repressive legislation, mostly based on British laws and including the obnoxious Offences Against the State Act, should be repealed. Similarly the non-jury Special Criminal Court should be abolished. Protestations by Dublin about unjust British special powers are little more than the pot calling the kettle black – a cynical exercise in the politics of illusion, re-fined and institutionalised by Hillsborough. If Dublin is gen-uinely concerned about, for example, the rights of prisoners in British jails, then it should end indeterminate sentences for life prisoners in Portlaoise Prison. These prisoners should be given release dates, and Don O'Leary, serving four years in Portlaoise for possession of a poster, should be released. Censorship laws, notably Section 31 of the Broadcasting Act, should be scrapped. Extradition should end. Some of the Irish taxpayers' money now used to maintain partition should be used to fund a European Court of Human Rights appeal by the Birmingham Six or to set up an international tribunal on their case and those of the Guildford Four and the Maguire family. The British government needs to be taught to respect the rights of Irish citizens. The education of the British government in this regard must start with our standing up for our rights and insist-ing that our public representatives do likewise.

The Irish establishment has failed not only to secure the most basic rights of citizens in the Six Counties but also to guarantee the rights of citizens in their own jurisdiction. Forced emigration and unemployment, cut-backs in housing, health and education, archaic social legislation and the sell-out of Irish culture are also part of the legacy of partition. The struggle for democracy must include the disparate victims of partition in both parts of Ireland and a national struggle must be forged which fuses social, economic and cultural discontent within a campaign for national self-determination.

Such a policy will ensure a permanent peace in the North and an end to sectarianism and division there. It will also ad-vance the economic, spiritual and social welfare of this nation and initiate the healing process which we all deserve and desire. Twenty years after the start of the civil rights struggle, is that too much to ask?

(1988)

Twenty Years On (ed. Michael Farrell)

FROM REFORM TO REVOLUTION

An té nach bhfuil láidir ní foláir dhó bheith glic.
(If you are not strong you had best be cunning.)

A s part of the "United Kingdom of Great Britain and Northern Ireland," the Six County state was part of "British democracy," enjoying some of the fruits of progressive British social legislation, and it was an administrative sub-section of one of the most prominent states in developed, modern, capitalist Europe. Such was the appearance and, to an extent, the reality. Yet a profound contradiction existed: this was an apartheid state in which a very substantial minority of the citizens were disenfranchised and denied social, economic, political and civil equality. It was a state fashioned by sectarian power and privilege, a state which practised wholesale suppression and discrimination.

Confronted by the civil rights movement, the contradiction exploded in the face of the British government and the state rapidly began to come apart at the seams. A generation of people stood up, cried "enough" and found the means to build a popular and implacable resistance to inequality and oppression. Previous generations had attempted to develop resistance, had opposed the state and its powers of suppression; republican activists had devoted lifetimes to the struggle and some had lost their lives in the fight. But their struggle had been isolated; carried out by small numbers of dedicated individuals, it had never been based on a broad sector of the population determined not only that change should come about but that it could and must come about. Catholics in the Six Counties had been as substantially opposed to the state before but, abandoned under the terms of the Partition Act, few had believed that they could achieve any significant change in the situation.

Some date the watershed to 5 October 1968, others to January 1969; the precise date is unimportant. What was exposed was that in the late twentieth century in the developed, modern European world, an utterly outdated, undemocratic regime was engaged in the violent suppression of those who were seeking the elementary demands of western democracy.

Whatever outward trappings of statehood the Six Counties have ever possessed, they have always been completely subservient to the British government at Westminster. The position is summed up in Article 75 of the Government of Ireland Act (1920):

Notwithstanding the establishment of the Parliament of Northern Ireland, or anything contained in this Act, the supreme authority of the Parliament of the United Kingdom shall remain unaffected and undiminished over all persons, matters and things in Northern Ireland and every part thereof.

It is a position which is expressed with admirable clarity and which has often been restated.

In recent years, the British government has attempted to suggest to international public opinion that Northern Ireland is attached to the United Kingdom by nothing more durable or binding than the will of the majority of its inhabitants. Nothing could be further from the truth: all relevant Acts exclude any right to secession, and the Northern Ireland Constitution Act (1973) states that: "It is hereby declared that Northern Ireland remains part of Her Majesty's Dominions of the United Kingdom."

The British attitude to the Northern state was prefigured in the approach of leading British politicians prior to its establishment. In July 1912, Bonar Law, leader of the Conservative Party, declared, "I can imagine no lengths of resistance to which Ulster will go in which I will not be ready to support them." Lloyd George, in May 1916, wrote to Edward Carson, "We must make sure that Ulster does not, whether she wills it or not, merge with the rest of Ireland."

In instituting the statelet and in imposing partition, the British government also instituted the full apparatus of sectarianism. The armed wing of Protestant unionism was institutionalised in the form of the "A", "B" and "C" Specials, which were armed, uniformed, organised and paid for by the British government. In the process of consolidating the British state in the Six Counties, 475 Irish people were killed and 1,766 injured in two years. In Belfast, 11,000 of the city's Catholics were put out of their jobs and 23,000 were driven from their homes; republicans were executed by RUC murder gangs and internment was widely used.

In the 1960s, people of my generation, even those who, like me, came from republican backgrounds, were aware only in the vaguest terms of how the state had been established. When Ian Paisley began his anti-Catholic crusade, when Catholic areas were attacked by the RUC and Peter Ward was killed, we heard some of the old people say that this kind of thing had happened before. But we were young and like most young people I suppose we believed that the lessons of the past were of little enough relevance to the immediacy of the present. We understood very little about the workings and dynamics of the state and of unionism. Nevertheless, it was clear even to us that the Six Counties was a puppet state, subservient to the British government, that nothing went on without the underlying and express approval of the British.

The Stormont parliament was in reality a menial regime and was debarred from legislating in relation to:

The Crown, peace and war, the armed forces, treaties with foreign states, treason, naturalisation, trade with any place outside Northern Ireland, radio, air navigation, lighthouses, coinage, weights and measures, copyrights and patents.

All the appurtenances, in other words, of statehood were denied to the Stormont "government" and were retained by Westminster. It was also denied control of the Post Office, savings banks and about ninety percent of its own taxation. What powers it did possess – over justice, policing, land purchase, agriculture and housing – could be withdrawn at any time.

The role of the Stormont government was to maintain the status quo, to carry out on the ground the logic of the partition that had ensured a permanent majority for the unionists by ceding three of Ulster's nine counties to the Dublin government. One-party rule was established and was guaranteed almost immediately by a system of ward-rigging and voting qualifications; proportional representation was abolished, business votes were established and franchise was limited at local government level to ratepayers and their wives. Unionists were placed in control of the entire political system. As part of the control of votes, Catholics were denied equal access to housing, and as part of the control of population – and thus of votes – Catholics were denied equal access to employment.

When the British government introduced universal suffrage, abolishing the restricted franchise for local government in 1945, the Stormont government secured the exclusion of the Six Counties from the provisions of the legislation. They also went beyond that by introducing, in 1946, their own Representation of the People Bill which restricted the franchise even more by taking the vote away from lodgers who were not ratepayers and retained company voting whereby up to six votes were allocated to the directors of limited companies. The thinking behind this legislation was eloquently expressed by Major L.E. Curran, the government Chief Whip: "The best way to prevent the overthrow of the government by people who had no stake in the country and had not the welfare of the people of Ulster at heart was to disenfranchise them."

To keep the lid on a blatantly oppressive system, coercive legislation was introduced, with the full approval, of course, of the British government. Under the Civil Authorities (Special Powers) Act, the Civil Authority (the Minister for Home Affairs) and the RUC were empowered to:

1.   Arrest without warrant.

2.   Imprison without charge or trial and deny recourse to a court of law or to Habeas Corpus.

3.   Enter and search homes without warrant and with force, any time of the day or night.

4.   Declare a curfew and prohibit meetings, assemblies, fairs, markets and processions.

5.   Permit flogging as punishment.

6.   Deny claim to trial by jury.

7.   Arrest persons it is desired to examine as witness, forcibly detain them and compel them to answer questions, under penalties, even if answers may incriminate them. Such a person is guilty of an offence if he refuses to be sworn or answer a question; this applies even when no offence is known, provided a police officer has reason to believe that one "is about to be committed".

8.   Do any act involving interference with the rights of private property.

9.   Prevent access of relatives or legal advisors to a person imprisoned without trial.

10. Prohibit the holding of an inquest after a prisoner's death.

11. Arrest a person "who by word of mouth" spreads false reports or makes false statements.

12. Prohibit the circulation of any newspaper.

13. Prohibit the possession of any film or gramophone record.

14. Forbid the erection of any monument or other memorial.

15. Enter the premises of any bank, examine accounts, and order the transfer of money, property, vouchers or documents to the Civil Authority. If the bank fails to comply an offence is committed.

16. Arrest a person who does anything "calculated to be prejudicial to the preservation of peace or maintenance of order in Northern Ireland and not specifically provided for in the regulations."

The Civil Authority was the Stormont Minister of Home Affairs, and he was empowered to delegate the powers granted him under the Act to any RUC man he wished, and he was also authorised to make new regulations and new laws without consulting parliament. The Special Powers Act, as it became known, was renewed every year from its inception in 1922 until 1928 when it was renewed every five years; it eventually became permanent in 1933 and was superseded in 1973 by the Northern Ireland (Emergency Provisions) Act. Such powers, fully sanctioned by the British government, were no mere passive presence in the background; they were the active means by which the existence of the state was maintained and all opposition was suppressed. Organisations, meetings and newspapers were banned. Curfews were imposed, whole (Catholic) areas were searched, and internment without trial was used in 1920-21, 1922-24, 1938-45, 1956-61, 1969 and 1971-75.

It is hardly surprising to learn that Mr Vorster, who was then South African Minister for Justice, remarked in 1963 that he "would be willing to exchange all the legislation of that sort [Coercion Acts] for one clause of the Northern Ireland Special Powers Act".

People such as myself knew little about the precise provisions of the law; we simply absorbed a general awareness that if they wanted to get you they could, that power in all situations rested with them – with the state, the RUC, the law courts. We were not of a class that understood terms such as habeas corpus and, while we were aware that the Campaign for Social Justice and others were complaining about the state of affairs, we had no real understanding of how the unionist system worked.

Blatant discrimination in access to jobs and housing allocation was something one took for granted, almost like part of the landscape. In 1969, out of 109 people employed in the technical and professional grades of the civil service, only thirteen were Catholics; of the 319 employed in the higher administrative grades, only twenty-three were Catholics. Of the 115 people nominated by the government to serve on nine public boards, only sixteen were Catholics. Yet I registered the fact that the conditions I knew in the Falls were similar to those I saw in the Shankill Road and the Old Lodge Road, both Protestant areas; the conditions in Catholic Ballymurphy were similar to those in Protestant Moyard. The fact was that conditions in the Six Counties for working class people were pitiable, irrespective of whether they were Protestant or Catholic.

As I absorbed all of this I came to understand the centrality of partition in the whole dreadful scheme. I also realised that without a proper understanding of the reason and consequences of partition there could be no understanding of the problem, and thus no solution. Partition was, and remains, the main means by which equality is denied us and the principal method by which self-determination is withheld from us. Partition aborted a national independence struggle in the 1920s and secured Britain a toehold in a part of Ireland from which she could influence all of Ireland; it divided the Irish people into two states, and within one state it established a unionist monopoly which divided us once more.

The break-up of monolithic unionism in the late 1950s began as a result of moves initiated by unionism in its own self-interest. When the linen and ship-building industries were in their heydays, which coincided largely with the two World Wars, there had been an industrial base in the north-east of Ulster which was integrated into British and British Empire markets. This provided the economic foundation of the narrow concept of unionist self-interest which was expressed in the notion of Stormont as "a Protestant parliament for a Protestant people". The Unionist Party was then the property of the landed gentry, people who probably would have felt more at home in the British House of Lords and who were in many instances related to the British aristocracy.

When Terence O'Neill took over as Prime Minister from Lord Brookeborough in March 1963, the basis for the old narrow self-interest had already been succeeded by a new dynamic. The linen and ship-building industries were in steep decline and O'Neill, a former Minister of Finance, perceived the need to attract multinational capital. The evidently anti-quated social relations which characterised the Six County state did not appeal to the British, European and US compa-nies he sought to attract in the build-up to EEC membership and in the wake of the decline of the British Empire, and so he tried to modernise the style of government and to project an image of the state which was more in tune with the twenti-eth century.

The process required at least an appearance of some kind of partnership, both in relation to the other state on the island, the Twenty-six Counties, and in relation to the minority which had been so systematically excluded from having an equal role in the society of the Six Counties. The most obvious grievances of the nationalist population and the crudest facets of unionism gave the Dublin government a problem. The Prime Minister of the Twenty-six Counties, Sean Lemass, could not afford to be seen to deal with people who were bla-tantly mistreating a sizeable section of the population. And this led to a new era of unionism characterised by certain lib-eral noises which were expressed not just by Terence O'Neill but also by publications such as the *Belfast Telegraph*, which had previously expressed a traditional Protestant ascendancy perspective.

All political ideology is based on either the self-interest of those who support it or on what they perceive to be their self-interest. The self-interest of unionism was to keep the "papists" down. This playing of the Orange card, this ex-ploitation of the perceived self-interest of working-class unionists, was an essential element in keeping unionism intact and united; and despite social contradictions between ele-ments of its support it still remained a monolith, firmly set on the foundation of supremacist ideology.

When O'Neill tried to alter the appearance of the state, he ran into major difficulties. There were two reasons for this: firstly, those who saw their self-interest as being sectarian, narrow and anti-papist rose up against any such liberalisation, even when its value was explained to them in the most schoolmasterly language. It was at that point that one found Ian Paisley throwing snowballs outside Stormont at Sean Lemass's cavalcade. The second reason for O'Neill's difficulties, which was totally coincidental in relation to this development in unionism, was the rise of the civil rights movement.

O'Neill has largely escaped criticism and has in a quite unrealistic manner been portrayed as a liberal who, if only he had been given a chance, would have achieved social progress. A rather parochial answer to that view is provided by what a man said to me one day several years ago in the Falls Road. "I don't mind a bigot," he said, "because a bigot doesn't know any better. I don't mind a bigot, but I can't stand an educated bigot." Terence O'Neill was an educated bigot. He was just sophisticated enough to know that the self-interest of unionism could no longer be sustained by the crude methods of the past, but the Orange monster which unionism and the British colonial ethos had created could not take the chance. At the same time, the demand for ordinary civil rights could not be dealt with, as it had been previously, by straightforward coercion.

An important factor in the difficulties which unionism faced with the civil rights movement was television. For example, in the early sixties Brian Faulkner had been engaged in aggressive provocations in the Longstone Road, but they were not covered by television. The RUC action on 5 October 1968 was not the first action of its kind by any means, but it was the first time that such brutality had been enacted in front of television cameras. Years later, the killing of John Downes was by no means unique: other people had been killed by plastic bullets; thousands of rounds had been fired; numerous people had been injured. The killing of John Downes was different because it was seen by the media. The fact was that in the electronic age, unionism and later the British could not cover up all that was happening.

O'Neill's attempt to modernise the appearance of the state, combined with the rise of the civil rights movement, began the break-up of the unionist monolith as the cover-all philosophy which had been able to unite all kinds of different strands and

114

strata. When it had suffered small cracks in the past – when the NILP had been able to win Protestant votes, for example – it had cemented itself again with the glue of sectarianism. It could do this easily when it did not have to make any gestures of goodwill towards its non-citizens, the Catholics. These days were now gone, and the divisions within unionism widened as a result.

O'Neill attacked the Burntollet march as "a foolhardy and irresponsible undertaking" and civil rights marchers as "mere hooligans". He ignored the violence inflicted upon peaceful demonstrators by the sticks and stones of loyalists, ignored the fact that about one hundred of the ambushers were members of the B Specials, and ignored the assault by drunken RUC men on the Bogside in Derry. Instead, he warned that he would mobilise the B Specials. Yet, despite O'Neill's vitriol against the civil rights marchers, he found himself under attack from the extreme right. In an attempt to bolster his po-sition, he called an election for 24 February 1969, hoping to emerge with an increased number of his supporters in Stormont. It was an election which saw the Nationalist Party lose ground to civil rights candidates, but, more importantly in terms of unionism, the election exacerbated the tensions within the Unionist Party between pro- and anti-O'Neill fac-tions and heralded the emergence of the fledgling Paisleyite party. The fundamentalist branch of unionism had begun to achieve new prominence.

The Unionist Party had always enjoyed the support of the disparate elements in the Protestant community because it had been able to ward off any threat to Protestant privilege. For centuries the Protestants had been told that they were the chosen people and that the Catholics were scum. "I wouldn't have one about the place," said Prime Minister Brookeborough. Religious demagogues pumped out their mes-sage of hatred against "the purple whore" and the "Fenians breeding like rats". The reactionary nature of unionism grows from the fact that they have to defend the indefensible. When one cannot defend one's position in an honest and rational way, one naturally adopts a kind of laager mentality and forgets about trying to convert world opinion. In this sense the unionists have the same problem as the old white regime in South Africa used to have.

Terence O'Neill (later the great white hope of Dublin middle-class opinion as represented by *The Irish Times*) expressed his own difficulties in terms which achieved a typical combination of condescension and prejudice:

It is frightfully hard to explain to Protestants that if you give Roman Catholics a good job and a good house they will live like Protestants, because they will see their neighbours with cars and television sets.

They will refuse to have eighteen children, but if a Roman Catholic is jobless and lives in the most ghastly hovel, he will rear eighteen children on National Assistance...

If you treat Roman Catholics with due consideration and kindness they will live like Protestants, in spite of the authoritative nature of their Church.

Little wonder that O'Neill failed to convince anyone, not least his fellow unionists. Not only did they successfully depose him but, in classic *coup d'état* style, they blasted electricity installations and the Silent Valley reservoir in the process. The IRA, which was blamed for these operations, during this time had to content itself with petrol bombing a number of Belfast post offices in retaliation for the beating to death of Samuel Devenny by the RUC in Derry.

The unionists appeared to have everything, including bigger bombs. Nevertheless I, for one, did not have a clear understanding then of what unionism was and certainly did not identify any of the ordinary Protestants I met daily as having anything to do with the open sectarianism and coercion of the state.

In rural areas it was different. There the folk memory of the perceived superiority of political Protestantism over Catholics remains very strong to this day. People can show you the land that was taken from their family three or four hundred years ago, and they will name the families that took it. In fact, this is not unique to the Six Counties; one finds it all over Ireland. The indigenous population were dispossessed of their land by

116

planters, and from time to time these planters had to fight tooth and nail to retain that land by means of various forms of coercion, including the Penal Laws. These laws effectively created an apartheid system, with the Catholics placed in basically the same situation as the blacks in South Africa. In terms of the land, the oldest male child of a family could only inherit land if he converted to Protestantism; otherwise the land passed to all the male heirs. This quickly reduced the size and viability of Catholic-owned farms.

In modern times, this apartheid system was supported at every turn by the assurances of senior British political figures or the British government itself. The institutionalised form which their assurances took was the loyalist veto. Unionists refused, and refuse still, to deal with their Catholic neighbours as equals because they didn't need to. Unlike their black counterparts in South Africa, however, the Irish Catholic labour force, both rural and urban, wasn't necessary for the wellbeing of the state. Deserted by Dublin, displaced persons in their own country, they had no political or economic muscle with which to gain equality. And the refusal of the unionists, though I didn't understand it then, was, in the circumstances, understandable from their point of view. They had been told by the British government that their privileged position as an ascendancy would remain for as long as the union with Britain remained, and that would be for as long as they desired it. As if to underline this, in April 1969, 500 extra British troops were flown in from England to guard installations against further IRA attacks. The attacks, of course, had been the work of the UVF.

In the beginning I was puzzled by all this, and by the state's reaction to even the most passive form of dissent. Why should we be forbidden to sell our newspaper, to wear an Easter lily commemorating the Easter rebellion of 1916, to fly a tricolour flag? Why couldn't jobs be provided and what was so rebellious about asking this? What was so treasonable about demanding a decent home? Where was the subversion in the demand for equal voting rights?

I did not have a very clear understanding of the Northern

Ireland state, of what it was. Our housing agitation was as much aimed against the old nationalist politicians and their failure; they seemed to be involved in a very sterile, do-a-favour-for-a-constituent type of politics. Our approach was that the people have a right to a house, so let's get them a house. Being young and enthusiastic we didn't see why we should have to wait, when you could go into the Housing Trust and do a sit-in and get results. It wasn't clear to me in the beginning that the housing problem had anything to do with the state as such, or even with voting.

At that time there was cross-community communication, which I don't want to exaggerate, but it was there. I knew a lot of Protestants, I worked in a Protestant area; there were differences, but they seemed only to come to the surface around the Twelfth. But, even then, I watched Twelfth of July parades and bonfires and I enjoyed them. The nasty side of sectarianism hadn't manifested itself yet.

It was only as I started to meet reactions that I started to ask why: why did small things lead to over-reaction? Over the Sherlock squat a number of us got something like fifty-seven summonses; at that time we laughed about it, but in retrospect it was a gross over-reaction. The RUC activity of landrovers patrolling the Loney area of West Belfast was a similar over-reaction. When I started to go to debates and listen to people who obviously had well-documented proof of discrimination, I began to go through a process of politicisation, and that, combined with my experience of the reaction of the RUC, pushed me to clarify my views of the situation. I began to re-alise that Catholics were being denied houses because that meant that they could be denied votes. I discovered that gerry-mandering in Derry was a conscious practice carried out to maintain one-party control. In a very parochial sense, I began to realise that this kind of sectarianism wasn't just a blind hatred of Catholics but was something which was being used tactically for unionist political advantage.

I was, as mentioned before, about eighteen months in Sinn Féin before I realised what I was in. Then, as I started to ex-amine the situation, I began to see that we were not dealing with just a unionist hatred of "papists" but that it was actually in the state's interest to stop, for example, the sale of republican papers, to stop the ideas of republicanism being promoted.

When William Craig reacted immediately by banning the Republican Clubs, I realised that the unionist government was opposed to the organisation of political opinion which was radically different from theirs. Through that process I began to get an understanding of the state. The British government claimed ultimate responsibility over the Six Counties area. It was thus responsible for the situation, but it had deluded public opinion at home and abroad into believing that responsibility rested with the Stormont regime. This regime was refusing to introduce the minimum reforms demanded by the civil rights agitation, and the British government was unwilling to force such reforms upon its puppet government. The republican leadership's strategy of progressive democratisation could not succeed in the face of such intransigence. But neither could the British continue to disguise their role. Increasingly they were being forced, by the contradictions inherent within their statelet, into taking a more dominant role. Many of us saw this as a useful development, with the potential for ridding us of the barrier administration at Stormont and placing the responsibility clearly where it belonged – with the colonial power in London.

In 1963 I hadn't even been sure what the border was. Going to the Donegal Gaeltacht, I looked out to see where the border was and what it looked like. I didn't know in 1960 or 1961 what the IRA was. I remember myself and a friend in school trying to work it out and deciding it was the Irish Rebel Army. There was a certain bravado in singing a rebel song, in shouting something at the RUC. There was the famous case of a fellow known as "Throw-the-Brick". He was working on a building site and when the British Queen came to Belfast on a visit he threw a brick at her. Everybody wanted to meet him, and when he came out of prison you'd be delighted if you saw him on the street because he was famous, but you didn't really understand what it was all about. It was enough to know that it wasn't our Queen he'd thrown the brick at. The only face of unionist power that I really encountered was the RUC; in rural areas, harassment by the B Specials was a constant fact of life, but in Belfast they were not a particularly significant feature.

Most working-class Catholics were overwhelmingly fatalistic and apathetic. One older man, a veteran of the IRA's 1930s campaign, was unaffected by my youthful zeal and probably spoke for most of his generation when one day he told me wearily: "Never bother yourself. It'll be all the same in a thousand years." People weren't politicised, most were finding it hard to make ends meet and there was a high level of emigration. But the feeling of isolation, of alienation from the state, was not confined to the Catholic working class, who were mostly resigned to their fate. The professional class were also affected.

A new generation of young Catholics with expectations of being able to rise socially, having fulfilled the educational requirements, found it difficult to accept the status quo which denied them their place in the sun. The student radicals, the most prominent of whom was Bernadette Devlin, were articulate and defiant; they weren't going to be chased back into the ghettos and they were well able to state their case on television. This new element combined with others to act as a catalyst for the mobilisation of the non-unionist population.

The state at any time could have undermined the civil rights agitation by moving swiftly on what were normal democratic demands; and perhaps in the global sense, if wider issues had occurred earlier, the natural consequence of EEC membership would have been to modernise the state. But movement came too late. In fact, whatever civil rights reforms were granted were only granted after the holocaust, after the whole thing was up in the air.

By 1969, well before the pogroms, I sensed that we were playing with something extraordinarily dangerous. I had numerous arguments with Liam McMillan because I didn't think that the Belfast or Dublin leaderships understood what was happening. They appeared unable to give proper direction in the face of the small riot situations which were beginning to develop in Ardoyne and Unity Flats. Elsewhere throughout the Six Counties, tensions were also rising. The RUC, the B Specials and loyalist counter-demonstrators were clashing frequently with Catholic civilians. In July, renewed attacks by the RUC in the Bogside area of Derry lasted three days, and in Dungiven they batoned a Catholic man to death.

Our agitation around Divis Flats was becoming a series of ever more frequent skirmishes with the RUC, whose ferocity was a revelation. The particularly frightening aspect of it was that we, the small group of republican activists, had been identified by this stage as leading the local agitations, so that – and I've had this experience many times since – we found ourselves, as we ran like hell, looking over our shoulders at the baton chargers passing other protestors and obviously heading for the republicans, heading for us.

I felt, in the eye of the storm, that we were moving rapidly towards catastrophe, and I was absolutely frustrated that the people who were in the leadership of the republican movement did not appear to understand what was happening. Maybe they did. Maybe I was too young and too dogmatic.

I remember on one occasion at Hastings Street barracks, where there was frequent rioting, there was a baton charge and people turned to face it and the RUC fled back into the barracks. We then proceeded to the barracks door and, armed with a telegraph pole, about fifty of us started to use the pole as a battering ram against the door and then, through a series of shouts, another fellow and myself were accepted in as a delegation. There was a feeling of recklessness, that we had them, and we relished that feeling. I saw the same thing later, in 1971 in Ballymurphy, where young people went into the barracks there and drove out the British army landrovers.

Being nineteen or twenty years old and not having any responsibilities; being fit enough to go and spend three, four or five nights in succession sitting in a squat, going to Unity Flats, to Hooker Street, and in between times off for a weekend in Dublin or to a fleadh, an Irish music or dance festival. There was a sense of freedom, a youthful, naive and mistaken feeling that the revolution was happening all around us and that the world was beginning to respond. By July we were actively involved in trying to get people in Ardoyne and Unity Flats organised to defend themselves against further RUC and loyalist attacks during the Orange parades. In the meantime, the republican leadership was in no way prepared for any sort of military defence, never mind an offensive. It was, instead, engaged in semantics.

By August the balloon was up. There were days of heavy rioting in Ardoyne and in Unity Flats. Patrick Corry, a Catholic, was beaten to death in an RUC barracks. The first Catholic families were being intimidated out of the Crumlin Road area by loyalist gangs. In Derry, a Bogside Defence Association had been established by republicans in preparation for expected loyalist and RUC attacks during the annual loyalist parade on 12 August.

On 8 August, Prime Minister Chichester-Clark, his Home Affairs Minister and James Callaghan the British Prime Minister met in London to discuss the situation. British troops were put on stand-by in Derry and Belfast in support of the unionist regime. The highly provocative loyalist march was going ahead and the "croppies" were expected to lie down once again. But they didn't. Instead, the battle of the Bogside began.

RUC armoured cars attacked the Bogside barricades and, for the first time, CS gas was used. Defenders hurled stones, bricks, broken paving slabs and petrol bombs, and the tricolour flew from a tower block alongside the flag of James Connolly's Irish Citizen Army, the Starry Plough. The siege continued day and night, but even with a force of 700 at their command, with armoured cars, batons and CS gas, the RUC could not subdue the Bogside.

On the second day, at an emotional meeting of NICRA in Belfast, we heard a tape-recorded plea from the Bogside for help. A proposal to draw the RUC out of Derry, or at least to prevent reinforcements being sent in, was enthusiastically endorsed. Rallies were to be organised throughout the Six Counties. On behalf of the West Belfast Housing Action Committee, I informed the meeting that we would hold a

122

protest march and meeting on the Falls Road. A NICRA delegation was later to go to Stormont to plead for the withdrawal of the RUC from the Bogside. We left the meeting to make petrol bombs. The NICRA request was refused and the Six Counties erupted.

At 5 p.m. on 14 August 1969, British troops entered Derry and took up positions. The RUC and B Specials were pulled back and the troops remained outside the Bogside. In Belfast, barricades had been erected on the Falls Road. Loyalist mobs, in many instances led by B Specials, attacked and burned Catholic houses. The RUC, with Shorland armoured cars and Browning heavy machine-guns, fired into Divis Flats, and in Ardoyne they opened up with sub-machine-guns. Seven people were killed in loyalist and RUC attacks, including John Gallagher, who was shot dead in Armagh by the B Specials. The IRA had virtually no guns with which to resist the attacks, but a small number of weapons was mustered and played a role in driving the loyalists and Specials out of the Falls Road.

Arms were rushed up from the Twenty-six Counties and barricades were strengthened to meet the continuing loyalist attacks. British troops took up positions on the Falls Road; they did not intervene to take down barricades, but neither did they intervene when loyalists burned down the whole of Catholic Bombay Street and a young Fianna boy, Gerard McCauley, was killed trying to defend the street. As the RUC and loyalists attacked Ardoyne, another Catholic street, Brookfield Street, was burned down. In all, 1,820 families left their homes in Belfast, 1,505 of them Catholics, during July, August and September.

The situation had developed rapidly. The demands of the civil rights movement had been demands for rights which were taken for granted in western Europe, and they were demands for rights which existed in the rest of the so-called United Kingdom. In retrospect they were, in themselves, unremarkable, simple and moderate demands. Yet they had evoked a ferocious response from the state and its supporters, and the consequence of that response had left the authority and stability of the state in tatters. When I had first become involved in political action I had asked myself what was so rebellious about asking for jobs, what was so treasonable about demanding a decent home, so subversive about seeking equal voting rights. I had received my answer, as had we all.

The civil rights movement had been looking for democratisation of the state, but the state had made abundantly clear the fact that it would not and could not implement democratic reforms. The movement had placed its demands on the state; it had not demanded the abolition of the state, nor a United Ireland. Now, however, with the reaction of the state and the intervention of the British army, the constitutional question had come to the fore and the whole existence of the Six County state stood in question.

The republican strategy of organising politically to achieve democracy within the state, which had involved a turning away from the physical force tradition and a dumping of arms, had run headlong into the reality of the irreformable sectarian state. That the republican movement now turned to armed resistance had nothing to do with any ingrained militarism, but had everything to do with the stark realities of the situation.

The republican movement of the 1960s had proved incapable of responding adequately to events as they evolved in the Six Counties. The spontaneous popular uprising of August 1969 – uncoordinated, locally organised, lacking any general plan – and the subsequent effects in the Twenty-six Counties found the movement ill-prepared and unable to cope with the needs and potential of that period.

Failure and inadequacy did not relate solely to the question of defence for beleaguered nationalist areas. Indeed, lack of guns was not a primary problem as it was made up quite rapidly. The primary problem was lack of politics, a shortcoming which was to remain even after guns had become plentiful.

This lack of politics, affecting all tendencies in the then disunited republican movement, arose from an inability to understand what was happening on the ground, its causes, effects and possible consequences. Many of those who

124

warned, quite correctly, of the need for armed defence contingencies, many of those who were strident in their condemnation of the republican leadership's failure to provide such necessities, did not understand the political requirements of that time. But the leadership was clearly lacking in political understanding and this led to their failure to prepare properly on all fronts, not least on the question of defence.

Understandably in the circumstances, their failure was seen simply in terms of military preparedness, and this view, allied to a suspicion amongst the older republicans of the politicisation process in which the movement was engaged, led to the split in 1970, a major set-back for the republican cause. It also ensured that the reinvigorated republican struggle which emerged then was an inadequate one, because the only republican organisation which arose from the ashes was a military one: it had little or no proper educational process, no formal politicisation courses, and there was scant regard paid by the leadership to such needs.

Everyone connected with the movement at that time was, of course, responsible for such shortcomings, and perhaps the situation could not have been otherwise. As in the case of any radical movement, republicans have had to grapple not only with the movement's historical shortcomings but with the whole question of finding a strategy for moving towards the independent republic. This is an on-going task requiring continuous analysis, co-education, good internal and external communications, re-assessments, flexibility and, most of all, agreement on the final objective. At some stage in the late sixties, the republican leadership lost sight of most, if not all, of these requirements, and the lessons of that period are as important today as ever. Any leadership which ignores these lessons will, like the Goulding leadership, do so at a terrible cost to itself and the people it seeks to serve.

(1986)

The Politics of Irish Freedom

SHANE

OUR SHANE COST £10. In 1968 £10 was a tidy bit of money. I bought him off Billy Bradley in Springhill. Billy bred Alsatians; he called them German Shepherds. Shane was the only sable-coloured pup in a large litter of black-and-tans in Billy's coal-shed.

He was a big pup, heavy-boned and thick-coated. I paid for him in two instalments. To tell the truth, I have a vague recollection that our Paddy may have paid £5. At least I remember us having an argument, half-joking, half-serious, about who owned what half of the dog, so I suppose that means our Paddy must have been a half-owner. I must ask him about that the next time I see him.

A few weeks after I got Shane, Billy give me his papers. I was pleased about that at first but later I must confess I got a wee bit sceptical. That was after Barney McLavery scoffed when I showed him the papers one day. Barney had remarked on how fine-looking a pup Shane was. Barney bred greyhounds.

"He's champion stock," I said proudly, "pedigree breeding. I've the papers."

"Aye," said Barney, "I wouldn't pay much heed to papers. Doggymen always have papers about the place. But he's a nice pup all the same."

After that I put the papers away.

We always had a dog in the house. In fact, when I got our Shane we already had a red-haired collie-type mongrel called

126

Mickey I got for nothing from a man in Moyard. Before Mickey we had Rory. I remember when Rory disappeared that I cried for a week. Rory and me and my friends used to roam the Black and Divis mountains every summer. He was a great dog. So was Mickey, and he and Shane made a nice pair. I suppose it's a good thing rearing a young dog with an older dog. The older dog puts manners on the pup.

Then when he was about nine months old Shane got sick. I took him down to the free vet in May Street. Shane had distemper. The vet gave him an injection and told me if he didn't improve that I'd have to get him put down. I was shattered. I took him home on the bus and my da let me keep him in the back hall. He was very, very sick. I gave him penicillin tablets, force-fed him honey to bring the phlegm up, and washed the mucus from his nose.

"Make him eat," Billy Bradley advised me. "Keep his strength up."

I sat up all night for a week spoon-feeding Shane with scrambled eggs, milk, rusks and water. When he got better I was really proud of myself. Even now, thinking back on it, I'm still proud of myself. And of Shane too, of course. He was banjaxed; anybody would be. But after a few weeks you'd never think he'd had anything wrong with him. Except when he was tired, like after a long walk: then you'd see his back legs a bit weak. Other than that he was all right.

He and I used to go everywhere together until, as things became more hectic, I started spending less time at home. Even then, though, I would still see him regularly and we would walk together maybe three or four times a week. I've always thought there is nothing as relaxing as strolling with a dog. Shane was a really fine-looking animal, and biddable as well. Big as he was, he was quite docile. Mickey was a different kettle of fish. I suppose he had to be. In Ballymurphy small dogs live very combative lives, especially small small ones like Mickey.

When the British Army arrived on the scene my visits home became more infrequent. At times I may only have been a few streets or even only a few houses away, but 1970 and '71 weren't actually great dog-walking years, so Shane and I cut down on our excursions. I still saw him, of course. Our Liam or our Seán would walk him down to wherever I was and we would have an hour or so together. The problem was that when it was time to part Shane used to go wild. He would rear up on his hind legs, crying and shouting and barking and yelping. It got so that our Liam or our Seán could hardly hold him as he jerked away from them, pulling and straining on his lead and bawling out to me. In a way it used to please me, I suppose. Once I got a week off and we spent our time wandering through the fields of Aughyneill down south, far away from British Army patrols, but he fretted for days on returning to Belfast when we went our separate ways again.

In 1971 the Brits killed Mickey. They killed a lot of dogs in Ballymurphy. The dogs gave an early warning that the Brits were in the area. The dogs used to give them gyp and with our house being raided so often Mickey would go crazy whenever he caught sight or scent of a British soldier. After they killed him our Dominic cried for a week.

Then in 1973 Shane vanished. The Brits took him, of course. Somebody saw him up in the Henry Taggart British Army base but there was nothing we could do. My Ma phoned the barracks and complained but of course it was pointless. We had always been afraid that the Brits would get him – they are always keen to get any half-decent dog. They had tried to take Shane before, but my Da caught them and got him back. This time, though, we didn't get him back. I was in Long Kesh by then, interned in Cage Six.

We used to get very frequent British Army raids in the cage; at times they even raided us twice in one night. Usually they raided at about half-four in the morning. They would sneak into the huts, slipping into place at the foot of our beds and then, as the one in charge snapped on the lights, they all beat hell out of the beds with their batons.

"This is a British Army search!" one of them would scream at us. "When told to do so, you will take your knife, fork and spoon and go to the canteen."

We would be escorted one at a time through a gauntlet of British troops to spend the morning in an empty hut.

Sometimes we would be put on the wire, legs and arms and fingers splayed wide and holding the body weight. It was hard going, especially at half-four in the morning. After the first hour you forgot what end of you was up.

One morning we got a Brit raid which was no big deal. They took it easy enough and none of us wanted any trouble. When the raid was over we were taken back from the canteen to our hut, one at a time as was the routine, through two lines of British soldiers. Sometimes some of the Brits would slabber at us or use their batons and occasionally they would "seize" their war-dogs, setting them on us. This particular morning nothing untoward happened and the worst we were hit with were the usual and predictable insults.

Just as I turned the corner of our hut I saw Shane. He was about fifty yards from me, close to the gate of the cage, and accompanied by a small, stocky British Army dog-handler.

I had about ten yards to walk. Our Shane was clearly in my view. I shouted out to him but he didn't move. Then I whistled, the way I always whistled for him: one long, three short, then one long whistle, all in the one breath.

He tensed immediately, ears cocked, head alert, his body on point. Jesus, he was a smashing-looking dog!

"You! Fuck up!" the Brit nearest me said.

I whistled again and slowed my pace. Our Shane saw me just as I reached the end of the hut. He jerked towards me and the Brit dog-handler, just like our Liam and Seán before him, could hardly hold him. Shane was rearing up on his hind legs, crying and shouting, barking and yelling. I thought he was going to break free as he lunged forward, jerking away from his handler, pulling and straining on his lead and howling out to me.

Then a Brit shoved me around the corner and into our hut. I could still hear Shane crying. The lads behind me told me that he had to be taken out of our cage, still pulling and straining against his handler. And still crying.

(1992)

The Street and other stories

A LIFE BEFORE DEATH?

THE WHITEROCK ROAD was pitch black and the occasional young couple, hurrying home, clung their way past McCrory Park.

A few stragglers leaned together outside Jim's Cafe. An overcrowded black taxi laboured up the hill. Few people noticed the two figures walking down towards the Falls Road. One was a thickset man in black overcoat, white open-necked shirt and white drill trousers. He wore a cap pushed back on his head, and walked with one hand in his pocket. He didn't seem to be in any hurry. His companion, a younger man dressed in jeans and an anorak, had to shorten his natural stride to match the older man's. They walked in silence alongside the cemetery wall until they reached the Falls Road. They turned right at the bottom of the Whiterock and strolled slowly up the road. The young man cleared his throat. His companion glanced at him.

"Come on, we'll cut down here."

The younger man nodded. They hurried down Milltown Row and went more cautiously then, the older man in front bent forward with one hand still in his pocket. Down and over the football pitch, across the Bog Meadows and up towards the graveyard.

The moon peeked out at them from behind clouds. Cars on the motorway below sped by unknowing and uncaring. The man with the cap was out of breath by the time they reached the hedge at Milltown Cemetery. The cemetery waited on them, rows and rows of serried tombstones reflecting the cold moonlight. It was desperately quiet. Even the sounds from the motorway and the road seemed cut off, subdued. They forced their way through the hedge and on to the tarmac pathway. Nothing stirred. They waited a few tense seconds and then moved off, silently, a little apart, the young man in the rear, the man with the cap in front. It was twenty past eleven.

The young man's heart thumped heavily against his ribs. He was glad he wasn't alone, though he wished the older man hadn't worn the white trousers. They wouldn't be long now anyway. Ahead of them lay their destination. As the moon came from behind a cloud he could see the pathway stretching before him. His companion cut across a grassy bank and the young man, relaxing a little by now, continued on alone for the last few yards.

He thought of the morning when they had last been there, the funeral winding its way down from the Whiterock, the people crossing themselves as it passed, the guard of honour awkward but solemn around the hearse. He thought of the people who had crowded around the graveside. Men and women long used to hardship but still shocked at the suddenness of death. Young people and old people. Friends of the family, neighbours and comrades of the deceased. United in their grief. And in their anger too, he reflected.

He sighed softly, almost inaudibly, to himself as he came alongside his companion again. The older man whispered to him. Wreaths lay on the grave which had been dug that morning and the fresh clay glistened where the diggers had shaped it into a ridge. The two men glanced at each other and then, silently, they stood abreast of the grave.

They prayed their silent prayers and the moon, spying from above, hid behind a cloud. The men stood to attention. A night wind crept down from the Black Mountain and rustled through the wreaths. The older man barked an order. They both raised revolvers towards the sky and three volleys of shots crashed over the grave.

The young man was tense, a little pale. The man with the

cap breathed freely. He pocketed his weapon. The young man shoved his into the waistband of his jeans. They moved off quickly. The moon slid from behind the clouds, the wind shook itself and swept across the landscape. All was quiet once more. The two men, moving across the fields, reached the Falls Road. They walked slowly; they didn't seem to be in any hurry. Few people noticed them as they walked up the Whiterock Road. It was five past twelve. Jim's Cafe was closed. An occasional young couple, hurrying home, clung their way past McCrory Park. A car coming out of Whiterock Drive stopped to let the two men cross its path. As they did so the cemetery wall was caught in the car's headlights.

The white graffitied "IS THERE A LIFE BEFORE DEATH?" flashed as the vehicle swung on to the main road and headed off towards Ballymurphy.

The two men paused and looked at each other. Then they, too, continued on their journey.

(1992)

The Street and other stories

THE REBEL

MARGARET BECAME A rebel when she was fifty-three years old. She remembers exactly when it happened. It was 2 July 1970 at about half-past two in the afternoon. Up until then Margaret had been no more rebellious than anybody else. She was a cheerful, witty little woman with a family of five boys and four girls. Margaret's husband, a tall, stern-looking man, didn't get too involved with rearing the children. That's not to say that he neglected his paternal duties; on the contrary, he was a dutiful father. But he was a father of the old school, Victorian to a degree in his attitudes, working hard always to keep his family fed, and strict in the administration of discipline.

He had been a rebel once, in his younger days. Only Margaret knew if he retained any of that instinct or whether his paternal responsibilities had smothered it. It can be hard to be a rebel with so many mouths to feed and so many bodies to clothe. That was Margaret's preoccupation also and ironically that's what led indirectly to her becoming a rebel.

Margaret's son Tommy was arrested on the night of 1 July and brought to Townhall Street RUC station for an overnight stay before a court appearance on a charge of riotous behaviour the following day.

Margaret received this news with some shock when Sean Healy, one of Tommy's friends, arrived breathless and excited at her front door with the tidings. She didn't know

133

what way to turn, and when her husband came in later she was relieved that he knew precisely what had to be done.

"Give me my dinner, Mother, please. First things first," he told her a little testily when she greeted him with the dramatic news.

Later, as he settled himself in his chair by the fire, he delivered his judgement.

"That young Healy lad isn't too reliable. I think you or one of the girls should go down to Mrs Sharpe's and phone the barracks. That way we'll know where we stand. And if it's true, well then a night in the cells will do our Tommy no harm, Mother, so don't be worrying. There's nothing we can do about it tonight except phone." He paused for a moment. "You'll have to go to the courts in the morning if he is arrested and," he reflected a moment, "we'll probably need a solicitor. Bloody fool, our Tommy. Go on, Mother, go down and find out what's what, like a good woman."

Margaret said nothing. She was glad to get out of the house. Teresa went with her to Mrs Sharpe's.

"M'da's a geg," Teresa sniffed indignantly as they hurried along the street. "He sits there like Lord Muck giving his orders. You're too soft, Ma."

"Oh, don't mind your father. That's just his way. He's as worried about our Tommy as we are. He just finds it hard to show his feelings. Here we are now. You phone for me, Teresa. I'll go in the back with Mrs Sharpe. Okay, love?"

Later that night while the rest of the family were asleep, Margaret lay in bed beside the still form of her husband and sobbed a little into her pillow.

The following morning, with children and father dispatched to work and school, she and Mrs Sharpe made their way to the Petty Sessions. Neither of them had ever been in court before and they were unprepared for the babble of noise, the heavily armed RUC men and women, the multitudes of people and the crowded confusion in the large foyer of the court building. They stood timorously until Mrs Sharpe noticed a section of the crowd milling around a notice-board.

"Wait here, dear, till I see what that is," she said.

Margaret watched anxiously as Mrs Sharpe disappeared into the notice-board scrum. She re-emerged victorious seconds later.

"Your Tommy's in Court Number Three. Here it is here," she pointed to one of the doors leading off from the foyer. They pushed their way between the heavy swinging doors and into the cool quietness of Court Number Three. There they sat silently for two and a half hours.

Then the court rose for lunch. There was no sign of Tommy. Margaret was beside herself with anxiety by this point. She and Mrs Sharp edged their way out of the wooden pew from which they had watched an apparently endless procession of accused appear before the bench. A young man who seemed to have been representing most of them approached Mrs Sharpe.

"Are you Tommy Hatley's mother?" he asked.

"No; that's her there, son."

"Mrs Hatley," he shook hands with them both, "my name's Oliver McLowry. I'm representing your son."

"Is he all right, Mr McLowry? What happened to him? When will he be up?"

Mr McLowry took Margaret gently by the arm and led her and Mrs Sharpe out of the court and into the now almost deserted foyer.

"Don't be worrying," he told them, "Tommy is in good form. He'll be up about two o'clock this afternoon. I'll see if I can get him bail."

By now the trio – Mr McLowry in his dark suit between the two middle-aged women in their brighter summer coats – were picking their way down the court steps and into Townhall Street.

"I've to rush back to the office for an appointment, ladies. You'll get a tea or coffee over there in that pub. We'll see how Tommy gets on this afternoon and," he handed Margaret his card, "here's my office number. Phone me tomorrow and my secretary will make an appointment for us to get together to discuss the case. Don't be concerned if Tommy doesn't get bail today. There were a lot of arrests last night and the DPP is opposing bail. Your Tommy has no previous record so he might just be one of the lucky ones."

He smiled again. Margaret scarcely heard what he had been saying.

"When can I see our Tommy?" she asked.

"If he doesn't get bail you'll get a visit after he's up. He's all right, dear. Try not to worry. I must run now."

He shook hands with them both again and hurried off towards Chichester Street. Margaret and Mrs Sharpe wandered down towards the pub at the corner. They didn't go in: neither of them had been in a pub before. Instead they walked around to the back of the City Hall and had tea and sandwiches in the International Hotel. They barely had their bus fares left when they came out again.

"I'll fix you up, Mrs Sharpe, later on," Margaret promised. "It's not fair on you spending all that money for such tiny wee sandwiches and not even a crust on them. I'll fix you up as soon as we get home."

"Oh no you won't. You needn't bother your barney fixing me up for nothing. That's what neighbours are for. And anyway, sure didn't I only pay for what I ate myself. Wait till I tell our ones about me and you swanking it in the International."

Margaret chuckled. "Our Tommy'll pay, so he will. It's the least he can do for putting us to all this trouble. He's lucky we let him off so lightly. Let's go back round now and make sure to get our seats."

Tommy was up at two o'clock. He looked pale and dishevelled as he stood alone and vulnerable in the dock. He smiled at his mother when Mr McLowry pleaded his case and he waved at Mrs Sharpe as the magistrate responded, and then he was led away again.

"What happened?" Margaret asked in disbelief.

"He got remanded for a week," Mrs Sharpe told her.

"What? A week? What about his bail?" She looked helplessly towards Mr McLowry, but already he was engrossed in the affairs of another client.

"C'mon," Mrs Sharpe comforted Margaret, "let's get out of here." She allowed herself to be led from the courtroom.

"We should go home now. The children will be home from school and you're worn out. We can phone Mr McLowry's office from my house later on," Mrs Sharpe advised.

"I'm seeing our Tommy, Mrs Sharpe, so I am, before I go anywhere." They were standing in the foyer. "Mr McLowry said I could see our Tommy after he was up, so that's what I'm going to do. You go on home and I'll call in on you when I get back. There's no point the two of us waiting here."

"Are you sure?"

"Of course I'm sure, so I am. Your children'll be in. Just do one more wee thing for me. Nip in and tell our Teresa to put on the potatoes if I'm not back in time. And tell her there's money behind the clock if she needs it; tell her to go easy on it, too," she added. "And thank you, Mrs Sharpe. You're one in a million."

"No problem," Mrs Sharpe replied. "Tell your Tommy I was asking after him. Tell him I'll bake him an apple cake with a file in it. Cheerio, Margaret. I'm sorry I have to rush off and leave you here."

"Catch yourself on. G'wan out of this with you. I'm going to ask your man the score about seeing our Tommy," Margaret nodded towards a big RUC man standing near by.

"Good luck," said Mrs Sharpe. "And don't forget to tell Tommy I was asking for him."

"That door down there, missus," the RUC man told Margaret. "The sergeant in there'll have information about prisoners."

Margaret thanked him and made her way to the door marked Enquiries at the end of the foyer. She knocked on it a few times and when there was no reply she pushed it nervously to find herself in front of a counter in a small room. A bald-headed RUC man looked at her with indifference.

"I want to see my son, Tommy Hatley," Margaret informed him. "I was told to come here to see the sergeant."

"Well I'm the sergeant, but whoever told you that doesn't know what he's talking about, missus," he replied coldly.

"My son's a prisoner here. He was just up in Court Three. He's on remand. Mr McLowry's his solicitor."

Margaret fought down the panic rising in her stomach. The sergeant turned away from her.

"There's no visits with prisoners here, missus."

"I want to see my son, mister," Margaret's voice rose and to her own surprise and the sergeant's annoyance she rapped the counter indignantly with her clenched fist.

"Missus, dear, I've told you: there's no visits for prisoners here."

"I have a right to see my son," Margaret's eyes welled up with tears.

"Missus," the sergeant smiled at her, "you have no fucking rights. Now," the smile switched off, "get out of my office before I arrest you as well."

"I'm not going anywhere," Margaret replied.

"Is that right?" The sergeant's smile returned again.

The sound of the door opening behind Margaret interrupted their verbal duel. It was the RUC man who had sent her to the office. He looked from Margaret to the sergeant.

"All right, Sarge?" he asked. "Your son's up in the Crum", missus," he told Margaret. "C'mon." He shepherded her out of the office.

"Don't mind him," he told her kindly, looking at his watch. "You'll be too late for a visit today but you should get one first thing in the morning."

"He said I've no rights," Margaret told him.

"Well, be that as it may, there's no use us arguing about it," he smiled at her.

"Thanks," Margaret replied. "Thanks for your help."

"No problem, missus."

"By the way," she asked as she walked away from him, "what's the right time?"

"Just after half-two, missus."

That's how Margaret was able to remember more or less exactly when she became a rebel. Or maybe, as she would have put it herself, that was when she started to become a rebel. She doesn't remember a lot about the rest of that day. The house was in bedlam when she got home and although Teresa had done her best the younger ones were complaining and playing up. It was only after her husband got in from work and had his dinner and she told him all her news that she remembered she hadn't had dinner herself. She didn't tell him about the tea and sandwiches in the International Hotel. She was still feeling guilty about that when she went down to Mrs Sharpe's after the children were safely in bed.

"Margaret, you're wired up," Mrs Sharpe chided her. "What men don't know'll do them no harm."

The thought was a new one for Margaret. It was also an enjoyable one; it was like when she was a child playing a trick on grown-ups. She chuckled at Mrs Sharpe's wisdom.

"Maybe you're right, Mrs Sharpe."

She went to Belfast Prison at Crumlin Road to see Tommy the following morning. He never got bail. Instead, a month later he received the mandatory six-months sentence for riotous behaviour. Margaret's routine changed with this new development; now she had to make time for prison visits. She also missed Tommy's wages. She didn't tell her husband that, but he must have known because he gave her a little extra each week.

"For Tommy's parcel," he said, "and maybe he'll want the odd book."

He wanted lots of books. Margaret took to going to Smithfield market each week after her visit to pick through the secondhand bookshops for the novels and political tomes on Tommy's list. She got into the habit also of having tea and a scone in the ITL cafe before heading for home again. That was a new luxury for her as well. She got friendly with one of the booksellers, a woman of her own age called Mary. When Margaret eventually confided to her that the books were for her son in prison, Mary insisted she would send him some as well. She took payment for Margaret's selection only when Margaret threatened not to return if she didn't.

"Here," she laughed, "take this one for yourself."

"Ach, I never get time to read," Margaret protested.

"Make time. Be kind to yourself," Mary said in mock sternness. "You'll get no thanks otherwise."

That's how Margaret started reading, in the ITL cafe over

her weekly cup of tea and scone.

That night Teresa and her sisters heard their father's voice raised in exasperation in the bedroom next to them.

"Woman, dear, are you never going to let me get to sleep? I don't know what's come over you!"

They listened intently for a reply. It didn't come for a full minute.

"I just want you to promise not to call me "mother" again. I'm not your mother. I'm your wife."

"Yes, dear."

"Promise."

"I promise, Margaret, I promise. Anything for peace and quiet.".

Teresa smiled to herself. She knew her mother was smiling also. "Good for you, Ma," she whispered.

"What's wrong?" her younger sister asked.

"Nothing," said Teresa proudly. "Our Ma's just become a women's libber."

Margaret didn't think of herself like that. She had two grown-up children married and living away from home; the rest, the youngest of whom was ten, were all living together in a tiny house, they and their father all making demands on her and her time. But she took Mary's advice and Mrs Sharpe's, and started to make time for herself.

Tommy got out of jail after his six months but was interned a year later in the big swoops. The British Army took his father as well but he was released after a few days. Margaret was up to her neck looking after refugees, taking part in protests: she didn't get to bed for three nights.

When she awoke after fourteen hours solid sleep her husband brought her dinner to her on a tray.

"You never did that before," she smiled in pleased surprise. "Even when I was sick, even when I had our babies. The neighbours or our ones did it."

"I'm not the only one who's doing things they never did before," he replied awkwardly. "There's been a queue of people here for you. There's a list of messages. And there's a meeting in St Paul's, Mrs Sharpe says."

"What was on the news?" Margaret propped herself up on the pillows and settled the tray on her lap.

"The whole place has gone mad," he replied morosely. "More shooting last night: two killed; more arrests, bombs in the town, people hurt. Will I go on?"

She looked at him quietly. "No, you're okay."

"Where did you get the food?" he asked her, watching as she devoured the sausages and potatoes he'd prepared.

"That's for me to know," she teased him, "and for you to find out. You oul' fellas are all the same; yous need to know everything. Well, for nearly thirty years you've been feeding us and for the last three days I've been feeding us, and I feel good about it."

He looked at her in amazement.

"Ach, love, I'm only joking," she laughed. "You never could take a slagging. I got the food down in St Paul's. We set up a co-ordinating committee in the school to look after the refugees and to distribute food, especially baby-food and the like. That's what happens when you get arrested, you see. I go mad for the want of you."

She put down her tray and lunged towards him in mock attack. He retreated to the door in embarrassment.

"The whole place has gone mad," he said again. "It's time you were up, woman."

She chuckled at his discomfiture. "I wonder how he gave me all those children," she thought cheerfully.

"My oul' fella never worked," Mrs Sharpe said to Margaret. "You're lucky. Yours is never idle. I used to say my man put on his working clothes when he was going to bed."

They were sitting together after the meeting.

"It's funny about men," Margaret said. "They are all bound up in wee images of themselves. You know: they're the providers, they take the decisions. They decide everything."

"Or they think they do," Mrs Sharpe said.

"I know, I know," Margaret agreed, "and as long as we let them think that it's fine and dandy. But as soon as we start to let them see that we can take decisions too and make choices, then their worlds become shaky and their images get tarnished. They, even the best of them, like to keep us in our places."

"Blame their mothers."

"Nawh, that's too simple."

"But it's true."

"I don't know. Young ones nowadays have a better notion of things. I'm no different from my mother, but our ones are different from me."

"You're no different from your mother?" Mrs Sharpe looked at her. "Who're you kidding? Could you see your mother round here doin' what we're doing?"

"No," Margaret replied. "But then she never got the chance: a year ago I couldn't even see myself doing what we're doing."

She got slowly to her feet. "And now I suppose we better get back to our oul' lads. Mine's only started to get used to being married to me. And," she looked at Mrs Sharpe with a smile in her eyes, "he ain't seen nothing yet."

They laughed together as they locked up the school for the night. Outside, people were gathered at barricades and street corners. They all greeted Margaret and Mrs Sharpe as they passed. At Mrs Sharpe's the two women parted and Margaret walked slowly up the street. She was tired, middle-aged and cheerful as she made her way home to liberate her husband.

(1992)

The Street and other stories

CAGE ELEVEN

I'M IN BED at the moment, covered in breadcrumbs and skimpy grey British Army blankets, my knees tucked up under my chin and a blue plastic mug of blue plastic tea in my hand. The eejit in the next bed is doing his staunch republican bit. "McSwiney taught us how to die," he is saying to his locker, and him only two weeks without a visit. The visits get cancelled regularly here. I think we are only entitled to one visit a month; the other three are "privileges" to be withheld as the prison Governor decrees. After the first visitless week or so men take to their beds. It's not a pretty sight. Your Man has retired for the night already, pink pyjamas neatly creased and rosary beads in hand. And it's only seven o'clock.

During such phases the huts here are like some surrealistic limbo; made of corrugated tin sheets, they are unpainted Nissen huts. Leaky, draughty, cold, they are locked up at nine o'clock every night and unlocked at 7.30 every morning. We're inside them, of course: us and our lines of bunk beds, lockers, our electric boiler, a kettle, a row of tables, a television set and a radio.

Somebody has just decided to brush the floor. Big floors in here, and thirty men lying, sitting, squatting, sprawled and splattered all over it. Nowadays there's thirty to a hut; it used to be worse. There are four or five huts to a cage, depending on the size of the cage; two-and-a-half huts or three-and-a-half for living in; an empty hut for a canteen of sorts, and the

143

other half-hut for "recreation", with a washroom and a "study" hut thrown in. Wired off with a couple of watch-towers planted around, and that's us.

Oh, and the drying hut. I can't forget that. The drying hut is where we hang our wet clothes. When we don't hang them on the wire. The drying hut is also the only place in here where you can be on your own. If nobody else is in it, that is.

All the gates open inwards. They probably do the same out-side but you notice it more in here – that's called doing "bird". And everyone walks in an anti-clockwise direction. I don't know why. Internees do it, Loyalists do it as well. "Will you do a lap?" or "Fancy a boul?" or "Ar mhaith leat dul ag siúl?" and away you go around and around. And always against the clock. Maybe some instinct is at work. That's the funny thing about this place: a simple thing becomes a matter of life and death. I suppose it has always been like that. If you walk the other way you get the back ripped out of you.

Jail is unnatural. Even the men in this hut are wired up. Imagine thirty men of different ages, the oldest sixty-three, the youngest eighteen, all locked up together for years and years. I don't know how they stay in such good form. A well-informed comrade told me years ago that if he was building a sty for his pigs he could only keep twenty-odd pigs in a hut like this.

"Apart from the size," said he, "there isn't enough insulation and the walls must be breeze block or brick." Nowadays when he feels outraged at something or other he is heard to mutter: "This place isn't fit for pigs," but sure that's another story.

The floor is clean now and some of the boys are waiting for the late news. Sometimes we miss it and then there's a shout-ing match. Marooned as we are on the desert island of Long Kesh, television has become our electronic window on the world. The news programmes are of paramount importance. So is *Top of the Pops*; it has a consistently large audience while the audience for the news programmes go up and down de-pending on what's happening outside. News comes from other sources as well. From visits, from rumours. You would be surprised at the rumours which go the rounds here. *Scéal* is the word used to describe the widest possible generalised interpretation of the word "news". It includes real news as well as gossip, scandal, loose talk, rumour, speculation and prediction.

Much of it is manufactured by my friends Egbert, Cedric and Your Man. They do it almost by instinct now, and the thing about it is that by the time it does the rounds here its source gets totally lost in the telling and retelling, the digesting and dissecting. What starts as an apparently innocent, throwaway remark from any of the aforementioned comrades soon becomes attributed to a BBC news-flash, an absolutely impeccable source on the IRA Army Council or a senior civil servant in the British Northern Ireland Office. And of course everyone adds their own wee bit; in fact, that's our main pastime. We manufacture it most of the time in our cage and sometimes shout it across to other cages, or we talk at the wire when we are out of the cage for visits, football or other excursions. We also throw "pigeons" to each other. A pigeon is a well-tied snout (tobacco) tin containing a *scéal* note and a few pebbles for weight. We hurl our pigeons from cage to cage and thus have a line of communication which the screws can't penetrate. If you're a good thrower, that is.

The prison grub is awful. It comes to us from the "kitchens" in big containers on a lorry. At the cage gates the containers are transferred to a trolley; then whichever POWs are "on the grub" trundle the trolley across the yard and load the containers on to a "hot-plate" in the empty hut which poses as a canteen. If the food is particularly gruesome it will be refused by the Camp or the Cage Staff. If not, anyone who is "on the grub" serves it to whoever has the courage, constitution or Oliver Twist appetite to digest it.

In the internment cages we rarely ate the prison grub, but then we were permitted to receive a fairly wide selection of cooked food which was sent in from outside by our families or friends. Here in the sentenced end the food parcels are more restricted and less frequent and so, alas, we have to eat the prison grub. At least some of the time. Apart from Seanna, that is, who eats it all the time. Sometimes we find more appropriate uses for certain alleged items of nutrition, and the cakes, which remain hard even with dollops of custard on them, came in handy on one occasion. During a British Army riot here we managed to keep them out of the cage for long enough by loosing volleys of gateaux at their ill-prepared ranks.

We usually dine together in food clicks – it took me years to establish that click is spelt clique. Some of our more ideologically correct comrades call them co-ops, and for a while the word commune was favoured by a few free spirits, but click is actually a more accurate description. A food click shares out its members' food parcels, usually on a rota basis, and divides the duties of cooking, plastic dish washing, tea making and so on in a similar fashion. Periodically someone drops out or is ejected from a food click. Occasionally others, for less quarrelsome reasons, go solo – known here as creating a "thirty-two county independent click" – but mostly collective eating predominates.

Cooking usually means reheating on the hot-plate, or on one of the ceiling heaters from the shower hut, removed and suitably adapted for the purpose, or even on a wee fire lit outside in a corner of the cage.

We drink loads of tea here. The Cage Eleven intelligentsia drink coffee. The water for both beverages is boiled in a communal boiler, which each hut has. Being "on the boiler" means being Gunga Dinn the water carrier for a day. When I was in solitary once, I was able to make tea from a second-hand tea bag with water heated by placing a water-filled brown paper bag on the pipes. It took eighteen hours and was only tepid but it was still tea. I think. Without milk. Or sugar.

In between praising the food and manufacturing *scéal*, receiving *scéal*, discussing *scéal* and passing on *scéal*, we read a wee bit, back-stab each other a wee bit, talk a great deal and engage in a little sedition, which is mainly a matter of getting to understand the political situation which has us in here in Long Kesh. This process is occasionally revealing, sometimes amusing and always, next to *scéal*, the most time-consuming activity of most sane POWs. Other, less sane, POWs make handicrafts, but that's a habit I've avoided so I can't really comment on it. A lapsed handicrafter told me once of his belief that the making of harps, Celtic crosses, purses, handbags and even soft toys was addictive. Painting hankies with coloured marker pens was, he believed, less serious – merely a phase all POWs go through.

We also go through phases of depression – the big D. On the outside marriages break up, parents die, children get sick; all normal worries intruding into our impotent abnormality. Some comrades have nervous breakdowns. Some do heavy whack. Comrades also die in here through lack of medical facilities and in one case a British Army bullet, and people are dying outside all the time as the war goes on. It all has its effects in this bastard of a place. That's one thing POWs have in common: we all hate Long Kesh. But we try not to let it get us down.

Some POWs sing or play musical instruments which is one of the reasons why others try to escape. Would-be escapees cause the prison administration a great deal of anxiety, but the prison administration doesn't like being anxious. So to relieve the prison regime's anxiety we are forced to endure British military raids when, at an unearthly hour in the morning and entirely without notice, a British Colonel Blimp makes a commando-style raid into our huts and orders us to "put your hands on your blankets, look at the ceiling, then when told to do so you will get dressed and take your knife, fork and spoon to the canteen". Just to show he's serious he is accompanied by a few regiments of combat troops. Why we're told to bring our knives, forks and spoons I'll never know. We never get fed. Sometimes they tell us we can take our "treasures" with us; I've never been able to understand that either. Sometimes they spreadeagle us on the wire and sometimes they beat us. They always make a mess of the place.

As you can see from all this, the prison administration takes its anxiety very seriously, which is more than can be said for most of the rest of us. They tried to give us prison numbers, taking away our names and calling us prisoner 747611 or prisoner 726932. But we refused to use our numbers and now the screws have given up using them too. After all, we're only here because of bad luck, stupidity, miscarriages of justice, being in the wrong place at the wrong time. And, of course, because our respective parents conceived us in or near that part of north-east Ireland which is under British occupation, at a time when we were assured of reaching imprisonable age just when some citizens of this state decided they had had enough of it. And once we were here in Long Kesh, like Topsy we just growed and growed.

Sometimes we give ourselves a hard time. As Your Man says in his wounded way, "Are the men behind the wire behind the men behind the wire?" But mostly we save up our resentments for the prison administration. We mess up head counts, make hurling sticks out of prison timber, protest regularly, organise our own structures, read books they don't understand, ignore their instructions, try to escape, succeed in escaping. Generally we just do our own thing. We enjoy political status in Cage Eleven . We would do all of the above anyway even if we didn't have political status. In fact we would probably do worse, but for now we co-exist in our strange little barbed-wire world, enduring a unique experience under and because of the unique political apartheid which exists in this little British colony in the top right-hand corner of Ireland.

Your Man says we'll all be out by April 24 next year. I don't know about you but I wouldn't believe a word of it. How would he know anyway? He's a bit of a hallion. Maybe his brother told him. His brother's best friend is married into a family which has a son who is engaged to a woman whose father works for a man who is very thick with some old chap who works as a civil servant at the British Home Office in London. And he would know, wouldn't he?

April 24. Let me see. That's a Monday. Funny now, that being a Monday. Your Man wouldn't be quick enough to figure out that for himself. You see, Monday's a good release day. Now if it had been a Sunday, well then you could say for certain Your Man was lying. But it's not so easy now, is it? I wonder if Egbert or Cedric know anything about this. Egbert knows Your Man's brother pretty well. I think I'll go and suss him out.

"Ah. Egbert. Just the man I'm looking for. Did you hear about the letter from the British Home Office? About releases in April? You did? What do you mean there's a copy of it on the wall in the Governor's office? Egbert, c'mon. Give us a bit of *scéal*."

Only one hour, four minutes and one thousand and six hundred and twenty-four days to go.

(1990)

Cage Eleven

SCREWS

I HOBBLED TO the doctor's during the week. Luckily I had been able to time the spraining of my ankle to coincide with the weekday hours in which the prison regime allocates a doctor for the thousand or so prisoners here. I was feeling pretty pleased with myself because if you are going to sprain your ankle (or anything else for that matter) in Long Kesh there's nothing like getting the time right. Timing is everything. If you make a mess of that you could die waiting for the doctor to come. On the other hand, if you're perfectly healthy it's pretty good *craic* going to see the doctor here. For one thing, it gets you out of the cage.

First stop is the cage gate. It opens into a wee wire tunnel. That's where the screws rub you down. Out of the tunnel (the regime calls it an air-lock) then out, via the other cage gate. A brisk hobble takes us to the wicker gate in the wall which now surrounds our cages. All movement of prisoners is recorded at each gate. Passage through all gates is accompanied by your screw shouting "one on" or "one off" depending on whether you're leaving or arriving. The screw on gate duty then makes his mark in a little ledger, denoting your departure from or arrival into the area controlled by his gate. All very elementary. Three gates within yards of each other with screws at each one. Big screws, wee screws, strong screws, weak screws. Screws of all shapes and sizes: smart, clean, regimental screws; washed-out, bogging, scruffy screws. Security screws, visit screws, sports screws, friendly screws and nasty screws. Screws performing all kinds of functions, every role programmed to suit their capabilities. Every role programmed to subvert our attitudes.

Beyond the wall now and on to the road which runs alongside the visiting boxes. Lots of muck about the place. Building workers escorted by screws, sentry-boxes inhabited by screws; screws in vans, screws at gates, screws to-ing and fro-ing – all programmed, all functioning well. When I feel fit enough to go to the doctor's I have my own special screw to keep me company. He is a remarkable piece of humankind – a right pockel. I pause, he pauses; I hobble fast, he hobbles fast; I stop, he stops. I smirk at him, he smiles shyly back; I glare at him, he looks away; I address him as "my good man", he grins stupidly; I ignore him, he observes me sleekitly. I go to the doctor's, he goes to the doctor's.

I think he really hates me. Deep inside his blue uniform, I reckon he really, really harbours a burning hatred for me. Like, I'm not sure of that, of course, but the majority of screws here behave, most of the time, as if they hate the prisoners.

Just me and him then. Almost at the doctor's. Brit watchtowers within range, more building workers, the whole place being assembled on grip-work and overtime. Out of the ashes of Long Kesh arose the Maze Prison. Only one more box and one more gate to go. Only one more screw to pass: this one is programmed to open and close gates and to write down names. A breakthrough in time and motion. Usually they train two screws for complicated performances like that. One to open gates, one to do the names. This looks like an experiment, something like the one-man buses when they came out at first. Inside another cage now, my screw following closely. I'm glad we both made it. I tell him this and ask him, in my most regal tone, to open the door. He scurries forward, fumbles, gets embarrassed, succeeds. I ignore him and we step inside, me into a partitioned "waiting room", he into a corner.

No one else about. I examine the graffiti: "P.J. Can we ask for a retrial?", "Wee Arthur, 15 years! Wait for me Sadie I love you", "6 into 32 won't go", "This place is hereby renamed Lourdes – if you get cured here it'll be a miracle", "Bump", "Jim O'Toole, 12 years", "Mickey" ... a whole wall of them. An interesting but unprintable one on the window-sill. Another one about that much-maligned old Italian republican, Red Socks himself. The place is pigging. I sit down. My screw looks away again. A young lad comes in: a skinhead haircut, tattoos across his knuckles. He's a YP – a young prisoner. There is a swelling below his left eye, a bruise on his forehead. He sits down, ill at ease; I grin at him, ignoring the screws, and offer him a cigarette. He takes two drags while the screw has his back turned and then hands it back to me. The poor kid is frightened to death. He still hasn't spoken a word.

"Do you want some snout?" I ask. I give him another drag and wait for his answer, feeling protective, disdainful of the screws.

Suddenly he leans across to me: "Can you get a complaint made about a screw?"

"Aye, I'll get our OC to see the Governor."

"It's about .... He beat me up. He beats all of us up." His words rush at me in a frenzied whisper. He hesitates, then, ".......... is a bastard. He beats us up all the time. He's the worst screw of the lot."

The screws at the door must know what he's telling me. They must know what's happening. They pretend they don't. They ignore us. The YP gets cockier and pockets the cigarettes I give him. He is about fifteen or sixteen, pale-faced bar the bruising. I ask him for his name. He gives me his surname. He looks uncomfortable again as I leave. I hear the screws say something. I go into the doctor's.

More screws – three of them in white coats. Clean screws called medics. We examine my leg together. I wince, they wince; I explain how it happened, they nod their heads sympathetically. The doctor prescribes something or other. The screw with the pen calls me mister. I wonder how they will deal with the YP. I consider telling the doctor about him, just to get rid of my frustrations, just to get shouting a bit. Then I look at them all and I feel lost for a second. They know there is something wrong: they're programmed for that eventuality. They move away and I go out. Past the YP. He pretends he doesn't see me. Past the screws, who look sheepish. My own personal screw tags along behind me and we hobble back. Back past the gates, across the road. When my screw slips in the muck I mutter "idiot" at him.

I notice heavy cable beside the wicker gate: they must be going to make it automatic. I pass more screws. We head for the cage, but I hobble past our cage towards the next one. My screw follows uncomplainingly. I talk with our Camp OC at the wire, giving him a rundown on the YP's complaint. Afterwards my screw and I part company at our cage gate. I ignore him. He says goodbye. He uses my first name. I come through the gates, in by the tunnel. Through the next gate and across the yard. He heads off towards the gate in the wall.

Inside the hut I drink my tea. Outside the huts the screws continue their patrols. Outside our cages they hunch against the wind. At their gates they jangle keys. In sentry-boxes they huddle against the cold. Don't ask me why they do it. I'm not programmed like they are so I couldn't give you an answer. It took the British Army, the RUC, a British judge and a few Special Branch men to get me in here. Screws serve their sentences voluntarily.

Well, they do so for a lucrative wage plus overtime. I don't really hate them. I'm not so much against anything or anybody, it's just that I'm for a lot of things. None of them include screws.

But then nobody here likes screws. No one likes thinking of Paddy Teer dead in the prison "hospital". Teddy Campbell dying his last few years here to be released to a premature grave. Jim Moyna breathing his last agonising breath as he fought to keep living against all the wire, all the screws and all the gates between his cage and the doctor's. Frankie Dodds dying at the gate of the cage – just outside the wire tunnel.

My personal screw whined when I called him an idiot. He is programmed to do that. If he had me on my own in solitary I couldn't say that or if I did he wouldn't whine – not while he had assistance. That's the way screws are programmed.

And now here in Long Kesh the screws are being programmed to take political status off us. But they know and we
know it won't be an easy job. The H-Blocks will be their
Waterloo. The ones like .... who beats up YPs don't understand. But then they never do. That's why they're screws.
They're not all like that, of course; some of them are decent
enough; but most of them aren't.

They are out there now, outside this hut, hunched against
the wind, huddled against the cold. They are out there, outside this window watching in, jangling their keys. They are
out there now, they and the British Army, keeping us in here.
For the time being anyway.

(1990)

Cage Eleven

CRATUR

H E WAS FROM somewhere near the border and he got his name from his habit of addressing everyone as "cratur". He rarely volunteered conversation but, on request, would say, "Sin sin, cratur", (That's that, cratur) or perhaps, "Okay, cratur". He was a man of amicable disposition but, because of his aloofness, Cratur didn't make many firm friends. Everyone treated him with respect and some with caution; others didn't treat with him at all.

On one occasion, having offered to clean out the drying hut, he did not content himself with merely cleaning and tidying. Instead he gathered every last item of clothing that had been deposited there since the introduction of internment in August 1971 and expelled them from the hut. And he didn't just deposit them outside the hut but carried them out to the gate fence and flung them over. Some snagged on the German razor wire where they flapped colourfully in the breeze; others lay in a large pile in no man's land, all now inaccessible to their owners. The Cage OC, besieged by POWs complaining about their losses of favourite shirts, pullovers, Y-fronts and even socks, demanded an explanation.

"Why did you do that?" he growled at Cratur.

"Ach, sin sin, cratur," came the reply. Agus sin mar a bhí sé. (And that's how it was.)

Uneventful days passed – uneventful, that is, by Lazy K standards. Of course, the odd complaint about this and that did

155

the rounds, but only when the Great Sunday Paper Scandal came to light did things get serious again. In the study hut the Cage Staff deliberated their next move.

"As I see it," said the very short-sighted Cage Adjutant, "We have not got one Sunday paper today; the screws are holding them. They are probably sitting reading them now. OC, I propose that we take militant action, OC." Now you know why he was Adjutant.

"OC," he crawled, "I propose we stop the visits."

"We don't get visits on Sundays," interjected the Cage Intelligence Officer whose duty it was to have information like this. "And, furthermore, the screws have told me that the papers did come in today."

"And who, may I ask, received them?" asked the Adjutant, knowing full well that he could ask what he wanted.

"Cratur got them," replied the IO, proudly victorious in the verbal battle.

And as it was said, so it was also revealed – *Sunday Newses* and *Sunday Worlds, Sunday Presses* and *Sunday Independents* could plainly be seen sticking out from under Cratur's mattress, while supplements and reviews peeked coyly from beneath his pillow.

"What are you doing with those?" screamed the OC.

"Ach, sin sin, cratur," came the smiling reply from atop the mountain of newsprint. Agus sin mar a bhí sé.

And then the Brits came in. Half past five one cold morning. "This is a military raid! Put your hands on your heads. Look at the ceiling!" barked the uniformed English accent. "You will get dressed! One at a time! And stand at the wire! Do not move until you are told!" And so, sleep-befuddled Brit lunatics in uniforms threatened, ordered and cajoled even more sleep-befuddled Irish lunatics in underpants out into the cold night.

"I'm not standing at the wire," said Cratur to a forty-five-year-old private.

"Oh yes you are, you Irish ..."

"Nawh, I'm not," said Cratur. "I've got a bad heart and I'll faint in this cold."

"Get that man against the wire!" screamed a tall, thin, Sandhurst accent.

"Right, Sir," said a corporal as he fell beneath the full sixteen stone, ten pounds of fainting Cratur.

"Okay," said the medic, "put him back to bed."

We all took turns cleaning out the huts. It was called being on the floor.

"You're on the floor in the morning."

"Right, cratur," said our friend.

"Lights out now lads."

The hut slipped into sleep, beds creaking as men moved restlessly in the night. The wind wailed its way through the wire, screws patrolled their mercenary beats. All was as usual. Then a mop bucket clanked and the sound of running water washed away the silence. Splash. And a gallon of water cascaded up the hut. Splash. Splash. And splash again.

Roused out of his bed, the Hut OC swam towards Cratur. "What the hell are you doing, you half-baked eejit!" he choked.

"I'm washing out the hut, cratur," came the reply, and the OC went down under a tidal wave which swept through the hut. "Ach, sin sin," said Cratur as he waded back to bed.

Months and months later and still things got no better. Cratur "sin sinned" his way over, under, by, through and on top of cage regulations. Never did he break a rule: always he carried it out to the letter. A careless order to "put the bins out of the cage", was met with bins being flung over wires and gates. "Brushing out the hut" meant mangled bodies caught unawares amid milk cartons and bed-fluff. Brit Military Police were soaked with holy water on one raid, prisoners were almost killed on another. And yet everyone liked Cratur. He was the exception and his notoriety was secretly welcomed by his comrades.

"You would think they'd let him out, wouldn't you?" we said to one another. "He's dead sound, only they shouldn't keep him here." But they did. Not that Cratur cared. He grinned and scared screws.

"You can't do that," declared a stern-faced, pimple-ravished Governor.

"Ach, I can, cratur." And he did and grinned as he did so.

"You're the Devil," said Cratur one morning to a young man of impeccable background. "You with your black beard and dark face. You're the Devil," he snorted as he hurried from the hut.

"What will I do?" pleaded the accused.

"Ach," said the OC, "It will be okay. Cratur never did anybody any harm. You'll be okay."

But he wasn't. That night he awoke to find a tall, bulky figure in priest's vestments at the foot of his bed. "Begone Satan!" intoned the priest's vestments in a country brogue, "Begone! Begone!"

"Mommy!" cried the condemned and helpless victim. "Help. For God's sake, somebody help!"

And the priest's vestments sighed. "Sin sin," they sighed and slid away, leaving the exhausted and exorcised child to change his soiled bedsheets.

And then, one morning *scéal* had it that Cratur was being moved to Muckamore Mental Home or some place like that. Everyone was sorry and sad to see him go. Comrades, exorcised and bedevilled alike, came to bid him farewell.

"It's the best thing really, you know," they said to one another. "This place wasn't doing him any good at all. But still, I'm sorry to see him leaving."

"All the best," they yelled.

"Ach, sin sin, cratur," came the reply, and away Cratur went.

"I feel cat about that," said a usually hardened RTP (Rough Tough Provie). "I don't like him going into a home, it's a pity on the poor man. Sure, he wouldn't do anybody any harm."

And RTPs and screws for once agreed that it was a bad job and, having agreed, they went their separate ways.

And Cratur went his. "Sin sin," he said.

And "Sin sin, cratur," whispered the shadowy figure to himself as he slid noiselessly through the open window of the mental hospital later that night.

"Could I have a pint of stout please, and a wee one," he asked as he hoisted himself on to a bar-stool in Dundalk the following day. "Sin sin, cratur," he chuckled into the telephone, "I know I can't talk to the Camp Kommandant himself. Just give him a message, will you? Tell him it's long distance and just say 'Sin sin, cratur'. He'll know what you mean."

And a few customers smiled to themselves at the tall, bulky figure who stood that night, pint in hand, singing "The Men Behind The Wire". And he smiled back at them and winked. "Sin sin," he grinned. "Sin sin, cratur."

Agus sin mar a bhí sé.

(1990)

Cage Eleven

SLÁINTE

"**D**ID ANY OF you see Cedric?" Egbert asked.
"He's with Dosser," a voice shouted back down the hut.

Egbert left with one of his smug little smiles on his face.

The Dosser was our brewmaster, our distiller. He and a motley crew of apprentices gathered up the ingredients, prepared them and stored them in containers which were then carefully hidden. While the rest of us waited, the Dosser performed intricate little rites, tests and other perambulations until, satisfied that his potions had matured, he commenced to erect his still. Then, as he explained it himself, he proceeded to "purify the brew by extracting its essence through heat vaporising it, and then condensing it with cold and collecting the resulting liquid".

That's what he was doing the day Egbert was looking for Cedric. It didn't take Egbert long to find the Dosser; he tracked him down to his hidey-hole with a homing instinct an excise man would have envied.

"Is Cedric here?" he called.

"Nawh, he couldn't stand the pace. He left a while ago," Your Man, who was acting as assistant, replied good humouredly.

The Dosser said nothing. The making of *poitín* is an intricate process requiring great concentration and he was totally engrossed in his art. He was studying a list of figures, written

160

neatly in a little black notebook. Dosser was a perfectionist.

"Did youse let him drink?" Egbert enquired.

"Couldn't stop him," Your Man smiled. "He had a note from his mammy."

"Very funny," Egbert snapped. "It's well seen youse don't have to live with him."

He went off in high dudgeon. The Dosser finished his calculations.

"I think we'll be okay," he turned to Your Man and Igor, "It's three o'clock now; this run will be finished and the other one started before five. That will get us finished by eight. We'll have everything stashed away before lock-up."

"An bhfuil Cedric anseo?" (Is Cedric here?) Egbert shouted into the Gaeltacht hut.

"Nawh, ní fhaca mé é," (Nawh, I didn't see him) someone shouted back. "Nach bhfuil sé leatsa?" (Isn't he with you?)

"If he was with me I'd hardly be lookin' for him, would I?" Egbert snarled.

"Ná bí ag caint as Béarla," (Don't be talking English) the Gaeltacht Hut OC commanded.

"Go raibh bloody maith agat," (Thanks very bloody much). Egbert left.

The making of *poitín* requires a certain finesse and a degree of expertise. Especially in Long Kesh. Of the *poitín* makers I have known, the Dosser was probably the best organised, at least among the sentenced men. The internees had their own champions, and most of them swore by the Commander. Nevertheless, the honour of being the best makers of *poitín* would have to go to men from North Antrim, Tyrone, South Armagh or South Derry, some of whom can recall when every Irish village had its own distillery. That, they will tell you, was before 1661, when a tax was introduced. Nobody in South Derry, North Antrim, South Armagh or Tyrone paid it, nor would they drink the new "parliamentary whiskey". *Poitín* was their man. Here in Long Kesh their business is conducted on a small, selective scale – for gourmets. The Dosser and the Commander, like John Power and Arthur Guinness, cater for a wider clientele.

It is said that the Commander placed a monthly levy on all the occupants of his cage. Two pounds of sugar or six pounds of fruit were expected; with about 140 internees in his charge, that made for a goodly amount of raw material. The Commander came up with the yeast and he and his trusty men then laboured manfully to produce and consume gallons of alcohol with the regularity of a conveyer belt. Bushmills would have been threatened by such industry had the Commander taken up brewing as a legitimate concern. Dickie Glen, however, claimed that the Commander cut corners. In times of fruit shortage or blight, potatoes were bribed from the camp kitchen to become an experimental and highly potent potato wine, which the Commander described as a cheeky little vintage.

The Commander held that you can make alcohol from nearly anything as long as you have sugar and yeast; the rest is just for taste, it's the alcohol which is important. He had an almost permanent slur in his speech and an increasingly punch-drunk, John Wayne walk. The Dosser took a different view: for him the taste was almost as important as alcohol content. Apples and oranges were his preferred and most constant base though, in rare circumstances, he had been known to use jail jam. He nearly always had some kind of concoction fermenting away somewhere. Most Long Kesh distillers, like the Commander, calculated when the next raid was likely. They hurriedly squashed together their ingredients, fermented them for about eight days, ran them through a worm and got drunk. But the Dosser was different: his hiding places or dumps were carefully constructed and some of his brew survived for six months, simmering gently in the innards of our cage until the potent smell demanded that it be moved on to the next part of the process. The Dosser left nothing to chance. All his deposits were graded according to age, content, quantity and temperature of the dump. All relevant information was recorded – in code, of course.

During the first part of the fermentation process the Dosser checked and rechecked his cellars, notebook and pen in hand and the ever faithful Igor, his number one apprentice, by his side. When the Dosser was satisfied that everything had reached its optimum maturity he assembled his still and the distilling commenced. Then and only then were the chosen and carefully selected batches brought forward.

The first run was the most potent and normally it had to be diluted. If it was a big run or if he was feeling particularly generous, Dosser presented a sample to his helpers. Cedric had received such a sample the day he went into hiding from Egbert. At least, Egbert says he went into hiding: Cedric says he never went anywhere, he just became invisible. In fact he fell into a drunken slumber behind the shower hut and it took almost two hours for Egbert's searching, sober eyes to locate him. When Cedric would wake an hour later, he would be a changed person.

Meanwhile, Dosser had assembled forty-two pints of clear-spirited moonshine. He also supplied a sort of scrumpy – nine gallons in this batch – for those who liked a pint with their wee ones. It was approaching eight o'clock when the last of the *poitín* was drained from the wash. Dosser was well satisfied.

"Let's get cleared up, men," he suggested. "A wee walk before lock-up would be just the ticket before we get down to some serious drinking."

Back in the hut Big Duice thought he should try to console Egbert about Cedric's unprecedented absence.

"Maybe Cedric got a transfer to another cage," he suggested delicately.

Egbert never even bothered to answer him but just smiled his crooked little smile.

Cedric was lying in the yard, his face painted bright green, with two yellow strokes where his eyebrows had used to be. His eyebrows and half of his moustache had been shaved off. Egbert had done his work well: having used only the best leather dyes, it would be three weeks before Cedric's visage would return to its normal rosy pallor. But Cedric was oblivious to all this. He was stocious; he felt great. He managed to get a finger-hold in the tarmac and inched his way towards the wire. He sang Leonard Cohen ditties tunefully to the ground.

He elbowed himself slowly over on his back. "Songs for a suicide," he chided the stars. "Let's sing something more in keeping with our mood. 'Moonlight and roses bring wonderful memories of you,'" he crooned.

It was fifteen minutes to lock-up. Dosser's still was now once again part of the plumbing in the shower hut. His customers had received their supplies – all except Cedric and Egbert; Your Man brought their bevy to Egbert's bunk.

"Here you are, old friend," he told Egbert, "that's free, gratis and for nothing for you and your mucker."

"He's still not in," Egbert replied. "I hope he hasn't got himself into trouble." He barely smothered a grin.

Cedric had reached the cage wire. A British soldier, complete with a large Alsatian dog, faced him on the other side of the wire.

"Alsatians once again, Alsations once again," Cedric sang to them both, to the air of "A Nation Once Again".

"I see you're taking your mother for a walk," he said pleasantly to the Brit.

"Fuck off! Away from that wire, you Paddy lunatic fucker," the Brit snarled, unnerved at the green-faced apparition which crouched before him.

"G'wan back to your own country, you foul-mouthed English glyp," Cedric retorted.

He pulled himself up slowly, fingers clutching the wire until he was in a vertical position. The Brit faced him uneasily. The war-dog growled manacingly. Then, finally erect, Cedric addressed them. His strong, proud Ulster voice boomed across the wire and even the dog was silenced as Cedric proclaimed:

"We are the indomitable Irishry. You are mere tools of the colonisers. You cannot defeat us. You do not understand us. Time has triumphed," he orated, "the wind has scattered all. Empires are lost. Even England will bite the dust. Or in other words," he continued,

"Ireland was Ireland, when England was a pup,
Ireland will be Ireland, when England's buggered up."

The Brit drew his baton and struck the wire at Cedric's face while the dog lunged forward snarling and snapping.

"Ach, catch yourself on," Cedric chortled.

"You can stick your wooden baton up your hole," he chanted.

"You can stick your wooden baton up your hole.

You can shove your wooden baton, shove your wooden
     baton,

You can shove your wooden baton up your hole," he laughed.

The Brit kicked the wire and smashed at it with his baton. Cedric stood back.

"A wee bit of order," he cried. "Bígí ciúin. One singer, one song. A wee bit of order for the singer. I'll start youse off with this wee one, and then youse can join in the chorus. OK?

"Show me the man who does not love the land where he
     was born,

Who does not look on it with pride no matter how forlorn.

I only know that I love mine and I hope one day to see

Oppression driven from our shores and Ireland one day
     free.

"This is the chorus," he intoned. "Join in if you like.

"Let friends all turn against me, let folks say what they will,

My heart is in my country and I love old Ireland still.

"Arís – all together now. Let friends all turn ..."

The Dosser burst into the hut. "There's trouble at the wire!" he exclaimed. "It's that stumer Cedric! He's winding up a Brit. If we don't get him away before the screws arrive in for lock-up he's going to get our drink caught," he informed Egbert.

"That's all you're worried about, isn't it? No thought for anyone else. No thought for poor Cedric. If the OC sees him he'll be on punishment for a year," Egbert lamented as he leapt from his bunk.

At the wire Cedric had Egbert in his thoughts. "OK," he challenged the soldier. "The next raid just ask for Egbert. That's me. That's my hut," he gestured and then, seeing Egbert speeding towards him across the yard, "Just ask for me," he concluded, "'cos I want to knock your bollocks in. You and me: a fair dig. Up the Murph!"

"Whoa," Egbert cut in. "Hold your horses, comrade," he told Cedric. "Can you not leave him alone," he chided the enraged Brit. "Pick on someone your own size next time, OK?

"C'mon, mucker," he led Cedric away from the wire. "Do you fancy a wee drink? Who did that to your face?" he queried. "Let's go in now before lock-up. We don't want any trouble, do we?"

They laughed together, each delighting in his own mischief-making, unaware of the other's.

"Trouble? Trouble?" Cedric stopped and braced himself. "You don't know the half of it, Egbert," he chuckled, his green visage wrinkling in a smile.

"I know you don't," Egbert agreed.

"Trouble?" Cedric queried. "I'll give them trouble.

"If you hate the British army, clap your hands," he sang.

"If you hate the British army, clap your hands.

If you love the IRA, if you love the IRA,

If you hate the Lazy K, clap your hands."

Egbert opened the door of the hut and dunted Cedric, still singing, inside. Your Man handed them both a drink.

"The night is young," he announced with a flourish towards the waiting pints of pure. "I like your make-up," he told Cedric, who stared back at him, green and uncomprehending.

"Let's have a toast," Egbert suggested.

They raised their jam jars in salute to each other.

"Sláinte," said Your Man to Cedric.

"Up the RA," Cedric declared, his green face beaming at us all.

"Up the RA!" we all replied in unison.

Then, raising our drinks to him and to Egbert and to Your Man in a happy chorus, we grinned and toasted one another.

"Sláinte!" we proclaimed.

(1990)

Cage Eleven

REMEMBERING A HEDGEHOG

T HERE WAS A big house in Huskey's Field. In days long
past it was probably the local manse, but everyone in
Ballymurphy just called it Huskey's. From the
Springfield Road a long, tree-lined avenue provided entrance,
while another more humble path cut from the side of the
house towards the river which flowed down from Rock Dam.
Perhaps long ago the owners of the dam and the flax-works
connected with it lived in the big house. Maybe Huskey knew
their history, but no one bothered asking him. When the big
house became a school he became its caretaker and when it
became an occasional clinic he earned a uniform, and a reputation which he probably didn't deserve.

Huskey's field, you see, was well stocked with chestnut trees
and no amount of "Trespassers Will Be Prosecuted" notices
could keep us from raiding them during the cheeser season.
Nor, indeed, could we be prevented from playing Ralioh,
lighting fires, or knocking wood for the 15th of August.
Below Huskey's the brickyard held its own fascination, while
the Pithead, stretching from behind Beechmount, was a place
over which a gang from Westrock (Tintown) held an uneasy
reign. Rival gangs from the Rock and the Murph provided
consistent, if unorthodox opposition to Tintown's supremacy,
while Durango, an RUC speed-cop, messed everyone about
equally as he chased combatants, often mounted on stolen
gypsy ponies, if and when they strayed out of the area.

On Mondays, Wednesdays and Fridays queues formed at Huskey's for rations of cod-liver oil, orange juice and milk tokens. They came from Ballymurphy, across the wee bridge at Divismore Park and up through the cheeser trees. Local protests led to the building of a new clinic on the Springfield Road, beside the entrance to the long avenue, and after that workmen arrived to cut down the chestnut trees. Pipes were laid alongside the river and rumours of a new RUC barracks being built in Huskey's swept the area. They didn't build an RUC barracks, though; they built Springhill, and as a small group of warehouses crept from opposite Whiterock Orange Hall to envelope the Pithead, and as Curry's Timber Yard climbed up over the Brickie, the new estate emerged from the grip-work and brown muck of Huskey's. Grey, barrack-like houses replaced the cheeser trees and a memory of the tree-lined avenue was retained in name, if not in deed, by Springhill Avenue, the only street of any length among the rabbit's warren of entries and alleyways.

In 1971, while thinking all these thoughts, I walked through the Whiterock towards Ballymurphy. It was about one o'clock in the morning. The Paras were garrisoned in the area but we usually got plenty of warning from the local people as to their whereabouts, so I strolled along letting my thoughts wander with me. Coming along Westrock Drive I noticed a small bundle huddled close to the kerb on the road beside me. You probably won't believe this, but there I was a few seconds later, kneeling on the road face to face with ... a hedgehog. I got pretty excited, never having met a real live hedgehog before, so I pulled off my anorack and with much caution lest I was bitten or, even worse, speared by one of its spines, I edged it into my clothy container and headed for some safe refuge. Bridget's was the nearest and most obvious place, so I cut across the gardens, close to where the cheeser trees had once stood and Huskey's – for all they had done to it – didn't seem so far away.

To my dismay, however, no one in Bridget's shared my excitement. They had tolerated me long enough so they weren't surprised to see me arriving as I did, in the middle of their session, shirt-sleeved and with a destitute hedgehog wrapped up in my jacket. But they were not amused, and Bridget gave off about fleas as I deposited my prickly friend on her sofa; only Dorothy, the daughter of the house, was at all interested in my story. Bridget's was one of those houses – an aluminium bungalow, in fact – in which neighbours gathered for a late-night bingo session and a bit of *craic*. I had disrupted all this and I suffered as a result.

"What are you going to do with that?" asked a girl, who, incidentally, I later married.

"I'm going to set it free," I declared.

"If the Paras catch you it'll look good in the papers," Bridget threw in: "'Charged with possession of a hedgehog'." The neighbours laughed, I took a redener and the hedgehog rolled itself up even tighter.

"Well, I'm going to have to do something with it," I said lamely.

"You're not leaving it here," Bridget warned, "a dirty oul' thing like that. Throw it over Corrigan Park wall. That's probably where it came from."

"The Brits use Corrigan at night," Dorothy said. "Look, it's stretching itself out!" she exclaimed.

And so it was. A small, wet, pig-like snout and two bright, intelligent eyes had emerged from the bundle of prickles on the sofa as the hedgehog adjusted to the heat in Bridget's front room.

"He's making himself comfortable," someone declared.

"Are we going to get on with our game?" another more crabbit neighbour moaned. "Take him out of that and let's get on with our bingo."

"C'mon into the back," Dorothy suggested to me. "Here, you carry it." So into the back we went.

"Flip me," I complained, "I'm always in trouble. What am I going to do?"

"Take it to Riddel's Field. I'll watch out for the Brits for you and it will only take us a minute anyway. We could skite up and down before me Ma knows we're away," Dorothy whispered excitedly. "C'mon, if we don't leave it somewhere safe the dogs'll ate lumps out of it. No use sitting there with a big long face on you. I'll switch off the lights and we can sneak out." And so we sneaked out.

Back we went along the way I had walked earlier, across the bungalows and into the 'Rock, where we visited Mrs Crowe's for a few minutes, and then off again with Dorothy willing the Brits away from us and me nervous in the now deserted streets with their dark, sleeping houses. On till we got to the Giant's Foot. A minute later I was up and over the gap in the wall and the hedgehog was dumped amid the undergrowth along the outskirts of the field. I returned a little breathless to Dorothy and together we hurried back towards her mother's. The excitement was over and our journey home seemed longer and sillier with every shadow we passed. "If I get caught I'll kill you, wee girl," I hissed.

"You'll be all right," she laughed. "You're always gurning about something. You wouldn't have wanted your stupid hedgehog killed, would you? Sure, here we are, home again. I told you it would be easy. They probably didn't even miss us."

And they didn't. We told them but they thought we were stupid, and they were right of course. Getting caught for the sake of a hedgehog would have been as thick as champ. At least I thought so. Dorothy didn't. She reckoned it was sound. "After all," she exclaimed, "you couldn't let the poor wee thing die, now could you?"

A few short months later Dorothy herself was dead. She and Maura, her older sister, heard of a Brit raid in the Falls while they were at a party. They rushed off in a friend's car to warn the people there. A Brit patrol opened fire on the car and killed the two sisters. It was early in the morning, a morning just like the one we spent bringing the hedgehog to safety. And Dorothy, who had grown up near Huskey's Field, became the first volunteer soldier of Cumann na mBan to be killed by British troops. Bridget Maguire lost her two daughters, and myself and the girl I later married lost a friend.

Anytime I think of Huskey's Field, of Westrock, the Murph, Springhill, the Giant's Foot, or of hedgehogs, I think of Dorothy. She was nineteen. She will be five years dead next month. You wouldn't think it was as long ago as that. Isn't it strange how Long Kesh sharpens memories like these?

(1990)

Cage Eleven

Dorothy Maguire and Maura Meehan were shot dead by the British Army on 23 October 1971.

MOLES

THE DERRY WANS were talking about Derry. About the Bog, the Creggan and Shantallow. Your Man beside me smirked and burst into a chorus of "Danny Boy" as he slid down off the roof where we had been taking our ease and more than our share of sunshine.

I pull myself to my feet and gaze around at Long Kesh. Cage upon cage stretch away in every direction. Black tarred roofs and grey metallic ones; black roofs where new cages have replaced those burnt out and grey ones where work has yet to begin. Away to my right the motorway shimmers in the bright sunshine and behind it green fields climb backwards to meet the horizon. The odd farmhouse dots the landscape and a whitewashed church sits comfortably between us and the motorway. The British Army posts frown down on us, and nearer at hand screws' watch-towers roast in the heat. Cars and lorries whizz up and down the M1. Two new Brit posts monitor the open ground between the perimeter fence and the motorway itself. That's where Hugh Coney was shot. Out there, between us and them; between Long Kesh and freedom; between motorway and concentration camp.

Did you ever dig a tunnel? Down into a shaft. A make-shift trap-door overhead and then in. In, into clay and gravel and rocks and water, everywhere seeping water, and the pitch blackness and bad nerves making bad air taste worse.

"A good trap's the thing," say the experts. "You must have a good trap-door or you're lost."

We lost quite a few times but then we were only amateurs. Cage Five was the place for tunnels. They had them everywhere, but one by one they were discovered. Screws fell down them while patrolling the yard, tunnels collapsed and men were dragged back from clutching clay and clinging gravel. They used to call Cage Five "The Moles". Other cages had tunnels too, of course, where internees and sentenced men worked hard towards perimeter fences and freedom. But up in Cage Five, nearer the fences, boggers rarely stopped push, push, pushing, and soon below ground the cage must have been a maze of half-finished tunnels.

Hugh was shot coming out of a tunnel. You don't hear much about it now and it's not even a year yet. Just after the fire it was. There were tunnels in Cages Four, Two and Five, and only for the distance they would have been going in all the cages. But Cage Two's collapsed and then Cage Four's. They filled the shafts in again so the screws wouldn't find them. Hard work, after digging muck out, to have to put it back again, but nobody complained. It had to be done because loose talk being loose talk, everyone knew that Cage Five must still be going.

These were pretty good days. All around us Long Kesh lay razed to the ground. Everyone sprouting beards and everyone and everything bogging with dirt. Paddy the Lad, rummaging through twisted timbers and finding souvenirs for all who wanted them. Men sleeping in the open or, like the most of us, in makeshift huts and shelters. Sing-songs at night and concerts. Paddy B singing "Mule Train" and "The Music Man". I wet myself one night listening to him singing "The Music Man". And Big Dominic and Billy R conducting campfire style sing-alongs.

No visits, no parcels and few letters getting out, but up in Cage Five digging, digging, digging. I wasn't there myself, but the stories came back. Stories of flooding and collapsing, of no shoring and "bad air". Of "It's stopped, it's finished," and then: "It's started again! I wonder will they make it? We're bound to get a raid some day now, you know. It must be tight by this time." And it was, part of it under water and long twists in it to avoid obstacles, and the air must have been stinking.

We didn't know it was through until we heard the shooting. Out there it was, away to the right, between us and the M1. Between Long Kesh and freedom. We were just walking around our cage when the self-loading rifle spat out its message. We stopped for an instant. "It must be Cage Five. They've shot somebody. Head for Cage Four. Mess up the head count. Move!"

Then the long night. After the first charge which took us through the wire and over into Cage Four; after the stomach-wrenching CR gas; after the doubt, the uncertainty and the rumours; after all the digging and toiling. After everything.

"One man has been shot dead in Long Kesh." The half-seven news with its impersonal message, the message from outside brought into us on a transistor radio. "This is the end of this news bulletin."

Sin é. One dead. A Brit soldier dispensing justice from the muzzle of his SLR. Lying out between us and freedom, weapon cocked, safety off, waiting for us. One POW dead or dying. Long Kesh in the news again. Hugh Coney, IRA volunteer and internee, shot dead. Out there, away to my right.

Out there close to the motorway that he was trying to reach. Out there where the cars and lorries whizz up and down the M1, past the whitewashed church, past Long Kesh, past Cage Five, past reality.

I lie back on the roof and gaze skywards. That's the only way to get a long-distance look in Long Kesh. All the horizons here are artificial, barbed-wire ones. You can't see any distance at all, except skywards. So I gaze at the distant sky and think of other escape efforts.

The tunnel from Cage Seven was inching its way towards the perimeter fence. It headed, at a worm's pace, towards the area where the H-Blocks now stand; by Big Ned's reckoning it was eighty-foot long. In Cage Eight a shorter tunnel was started in the grass verge. It only had to cover thirty-odd feet but as it was being worked in the open, right under the screws' noses, progress was much slower. In Cage Twenty-two as well a shaft was sunk, and the men began to edge along underground in an effort to join with the others.

Digging tunnels isn't much *craic*. In fact it's scary, because even in summer it's difficult to stay above the water level. Dry digging is impossible and constant seepage makes sudden shifts in the ground inevitable. Even the shoring is unreliable and prone to collapse at the slightest touch. The water seeps in everywhere because Long Kesh is built on a bog.

The name itself comes from *Ceis Fhada* which translates from Gaelic as "the long ditch" or "basket". Even the new Brit term, the Maze, comes from the Irish *An Má* – the plain. Methinks it should have been called *An tUisce* – the water. At any rate, for all these reasons, I've always avoided going down tunnels. I was perfectly willing to bale out water, hide dirt, wash clothes, clean up, cut shoring, make tools or keep watch. I was even prepared to undertake the awesome job of digging through two feet of concrete floor with only the most basic of home-made chisels. Anything as long as I didn't actually have to go up the tunnel. And, anyway, I was no good at digging.

None of this made any difference, of course, because orders is orders. They say you can ask questions afterwards.

Afterwards?

So there I was, feeling foolish in a pair of shorts, letting on to be indifferent to the death that surely awaited me. Joking casually to Your Man. There was no way out of it.

Your Man went down first, disappearing slowly as the shaft swallowed him up. I followed reluctantly, feet first. Things got a bit tight when I was waist-deep in the floor. There wasn't enough room to get my arms through so I forced my body into position forty-four (yoga, of course) and then down I slid.

There were two inches of water at the base of the shaft, cold water which lapped in little waves around my ankles. The tunnel mouth was only two feet square and as I hunkered down I could see it narrowing as bags of returned dirt bellied their way out from the sides. Your Man's feet, toe-deep in silt, glared back at me as I resignedly began my journey.

We were soon hard at work. Slow, tortuous work. He scraped at the face with a makeshift shovel and I lay on his legs, holding him steady, doing my best to minimise movement. Wishing I were somewhere else. We were only down for twenty minutes. I think I could have stuck it longer, lying there petrified, but then suddenly Your Man let off one of his great, slow, strangled farts. I don't want to make it sound melodramatic, but in that cramped space, far below Long Kesh's tarmacked and concreted surface, I panicked. Well, I think that's why I panicked. In any case, it was as good, as original and as believable an excuse as any other, so we shuffled our way backwards towards the shaft and the abnormality overhead.

They never let me go down again. Nobody said anything, of course. They just put me to hiding dirt. I looked disappointed, suspected Your Man of back-stabbing, and offered a silent prayer of thanksgiving to St Jude.

In the meantime things continued above and below ground and by the end of the second week we were feeling pretty hopeful. Cage Seven had almost reached the perimeter, Eight had survived a heavy fall of rain, and we had scraped through two British Army raids. The Beard and Wee Owen were even planning a holiday in France; Cedric had sent all his clothes out, and Your Man talked of the propaganda that his return to the struggle would warrant. I thought quietly to myself of the safety of West Mayo and spoofed along with the rest.

On Saturday we were moved. No warning or advance notice from the prison regime. We tried to talk our way out of it, of course, but you know the score yourself. There's a hard way and an easy way; you move or the Brits move you. We moved. As a sort of consolation we left our gaping hole in the floor unmarked and unhidden with a note for the head of prison security poking out of its mouth. That at least would get somebody into trouble – the screws are supposed to stop us digging, you see.

Our second day back here saw the start of another tunnel. The one in Seven looked a sure thing and none of us wanted to be left behind. We didn't get as far this time, of course. The shaft was only finished when it was caught. Cage Eight's collapsed a few days later. It nearly killed the screw who disappeared into it.

And the one in Cage Seven? The water got it. It filled up to the ceiling one night along its complete hundred-feet length. It was bound to happen: winter is no time to dig. The heavy rainfall turns the ground into silt and apart from anything else it's a devil to hide.

Now, the summer's different. Your Man reckons that if we just keep below the hardcore we should be OK. He thinks we can manage to stay above water-level that way; if we hit clay we'd be flying. The thing to do is to keep at it. Like, we've nothing else to do anyway, have we?

(1990)

Cage Eleven

ONLY JOKING

"**B**IG DOMNIC O'FILIBUSTER was the best mixer I ever met," Your Man was adamant.

"Nawh," Cedric snorted scornfully. "He was only a wee boy compared to Dipper Dedalus."

"What are you arguing about?" asked Egbert.

"About who was the best at stirring things up, putting in the mix, before we all settled down to do our whack," I explained.

"Awh, that's easy. Domnic!" Egbert replied knowledgeably.

"Listen to him," Cedric almost screamed. "He'd rather be wrong than be quiet. He's only here a meal hour. How would you know who was the best mixer?" he accused Egbert.

"Well," Egbert replied quietly and with a finesse that both Domnic and Dipper would have envied, "it's easier to be objective if you're not involved. Yours is a subjective recollection, probably biased by your closeness to the situation. I'm uninvolved and therefore impartial and objective, and Domnic gets my vote."

"Domnic's not looking for your vote. You're not even in this conversation!"

"Hold on, Cedric," Your Man pleaded, "Egbert's got a point."

"My arse!" Cedric spluttered. "He's winding me up. He knows nothing about Big Domnic or Dipper."

"Is that so?" Egbert asked smugly. "Remember the time

178

Domnic asked the new screw to get him a bap and the *Irish News*?"

"Aye," Your Man's face lit up at the memory. "He went out to the gate about half-eight one morning, gave the new screw a ten-bob note and asked him to run down to the shop for ten Park Drive, a bap and the *Irish News*."

"I remember that," Cedric conceded warmly. "That was quare *craic*. Especially when the screw came back half an hour later and returned the ten-bob note."

"He said he couldn't find the shop," Egbert chortled.

"And 'member he asked the Gov'nor for a piano?" Cedric continued. "The negotiations went on for weeks. It was an English gov'nor and he hadn't much sense. Domnic really wound him up."

"Just proves my point," said Egbert.

"Wha'?"

"I'm just saying that you're proving my point," Egbert repeated softly.

"No way. I, I never said Domnic wasn't a good mixer. I only said he wasn't as good as Dipper."

"What about Big Mick?" Your Man asked.

"Now there was a man who was born with a wooden spoon," Cedric was glad of a reprieve. "He never stopped stirring. Remember he set up a mousetrap in Cage Six? He fixed electric wires to a steel tray, then plugged it in and set it just beside the hut toilet."

"Was he trying to catch the mice doing a piddle?"

"No, he was trying to catch us doing a piddle. No laughing matter when you're dying for a piss in the middle of the night, in the dark. 'If you splash, you flash,' Big Mick used to shout from his bunk."

"A really crazy man," Egbert volunteered. "He used to walk around the yard, stark naked, pretending he was walking a dog. He had a piece of cable, almost rigid it was, which he fashioned into a dog lead and he walked around with an invisible dog on the end of it. The new men never knew what to make of him. We used to set them up: 'Never mind Big Mick,' we'd say."

179

"What about the escapes?" I asked.

"Aye, they were great – Big Domnic's speciality," Egbert reminded us.

"There was more than Big Domnic set men up for escapes," Cedric retaliated. "Dipper was great at that. Most new men fell for it; we would ask them to create a diversion," he explained to me, "and of course there would be no escape at all. It was quare *craic*. Men fainting in front of screws; or keeping watch with their faces blackened, ready to sing out if they heard a noise. Of course, we always arranged that for them. Then as they raised the alarm by singing we'd switch on the lights. Ha, ha, ha, I can still see their wee black faces as the whole hut erupted laughing and they realised they were set up."

"Aye," Egbert agreed, excited at the memory, "and the water fights and putting bread on the roof of another hut so that the seagulls came down for breakfast and wakened everyone."

"That was banned quickly here," Your Man recalled. "It caused awful rows. Scores of seagulls pecking and fighting on the tin roof at dawn isn't very comradely."

"What about Domnic getting the new men to go to the gate with their towels, waiting for a bus to take them out for a swim," Egbert returned to his theme. "Dipper never did anything as good as that. They used to stand there in a queue!" he roared at the memory.

"And there was a young fella called Dusty used to make a lot of noise in bed every night. And then Domnic painted a big eye on Dusty's bed-sheets with the words *We're watching you* below it. Dusty was furious. He changed his sheets around, and on the other side there was a big ear with *And we're listening to you as well*! I thought he'd explode when he saw it," Egbert burst out. "Still, it soon quietened him down at night, I must say."

"I was talking about Dipper," Cedric started valiantly.

Egbert ignored him. "What about the confessions? I've great stories to tell about confessions. When new lads came in on remand we'd tell them the priest was in and if they wanted to go to confession he'd be in the study hut. Well, we told them that, with very serious parental faces on us, and of course it nearly always worked. Off they'd go to the study hut, but instead of a priest, inside ..."

"Would be Big Domnic," Cedric mimicked. "Everybody knows this yarn. He'd have a blanket up and half the men in the cage behind it and the other half hanging off the hut like blue-bottles around ..."

"Sshhh," Your Man interrupted. "Let Egbert tell it. It's his story."

"It's everybody's story!" Cedric protested.

"Well I started it so I'll finish it," retorted Egbert.

"It'll be the first thing you ever finished."

"Domnic," Egbert repeated slowly as he glared across at Cedric, "Domnic would be behind a blanket draped across the hut and he'd have a boxing glove on. You get the picture? He'd begin the confession just as any priest and he'd start to ease all the lad's sins out of him and then, when the lad admitted some particular offence, he'd shout: 'You did what?' and he'd whack out with the boxing glove! It was really something to see. An arm with the boxing glove on the end of it coming round the edge of the blanket. The young lad staring at it in disbelief, then wham!

"And you, ha, ha, you know, nobody ever looked behind the blanket. Even when they got whacked a few times. They just went on with their confession. Ha, ha, ha. One young lad ended up cowering in his seat in dread of the boxing glove as he made a clean breast of things."

"What kind of sins did they confess?" Your Man asked with interest.

"Oh nothing much. I mean, no mortal sins; all venial ones. Only telling lies, losing their tempers, masturbating – that was worth two punches. Ha, ha, ha. Oh, Big Domnic was a geg. I remember another time ..."

"I remember a time too," Cedric shouted, grimly determined to have his say. "I remember a time when some of us worked a double-mix around confessions. There was a guy in our cage when we were on remand and he'd do the confessions and he'd always wind the new wee lads up, asking them had they got a girl and did they ever drop the hand."

"That's bad talk," Egbert put in. "Trust you. You bust in here mouthing off about Dipper and then you start to bring sex into it. It's not on."

"Hang on, hang on," Cedric huffed with indignation. "Let me finish."

"Aye, let him finish," Your Man agreed.

"Well, one day we got a new lad and then we set up our friend." He paused; "We'll call him Bloggs. We set him up as nice as could be. Bloggs did the confession business as usual and we were in behind the blanket with him and the new lad was out in front.

"'Well, son,' said Bloggs, 'have you a girlfriend?'

"'I have, Father, and I'm afraid I'm in a bit of trouble.'

"Bloggs nearly burst. He had a job keeping back his laughter. 'He's in trouble,' he whispered to us behind the blanket and then barely containing himself he asked,

"'What kind of trouble, my son?'

"'She's pregnant, Father.'

"By now," Cedric continued, "Bloggs was nearly beside himself. He had half his pullover shoved in his mouth and every other second he'd nudge us. He was delighted.

"'Would you like me to visit the girl?' he asked.

"'Father, I'd be very obliged if you would. She lives in Andersonstown.'

"'That's where I live,' Bloggs whispered to us between mouthfulls of pullover as his face grew redder and redder and the tears started down his face with the effort not to laugh out loud.

"'Whereabouts in Andersonstown, my son?'

"'In Andersonstown Terrace, Father.'

"'Awh,' Bloggs wheezed at us from the floor, tears tripping him up and the giggles starting to burst through. 'That's my street. What a cracker!'

"'And what is the girl's name?' he asked eventually.

"'Bloggs, Father. You might know her Da.'

"Gee whizz," Egbert whistled in admiration as the rest of us burst into applause. "That's a great mix. What happened?"

"There was holy murder. Bloggs went through the blanket at the wee lad. He never, ever forgave him. And he had to get a special visit before he'd believe it was a mix."

"Like the time the Brits came in and challenged Ed to a fair dig," Egbert offered. "When he refrained they got very annoyed, calling him a welcher, and then they beat him up. Ed was shattered. He didn't mind being beat up, but his pride? He used to be proud when he was young. His pride was hurt at being called a welcher. Later we discovered it was Todler's fault. Unbeknownst to Ed he had pinned a notice on the bottom of Ed's bed, warning that Big Ed was a lean, mean, fighting machine. It suggested he ate Brits. Poor Ed wouldn't hurt a fly. The Brits weren't a bit pleased. Nor was poor Ed. Ed was very annoyed at Todler for that, so he was."

"That's like you taking the needle when the legs of your jeans were sewed up the morning there was a British Army raid," Cedric chuckled.

"I didn't take the needle," Egbert contradicted him. "I was just a wee bit upset. It wasn't fair, making an eejit of me in front of the Brits. Not a very republican thing to do.

"And it wasn't really having my jeans sewn up that annoyed me. When I tripped getting them on I twigged to what was wrong. It was when I got another pair out of my locker and they were sewed up as well and then the sleeves of my jacket too! I never did find out who did it. I got three days solitary for hitting a Brit who laughed at me. That wasn't funny."

We all laughed. "You were always too angry for anyone to admit it," Cedric told him. "Anyway, now that you seem to be over it, I'd be delighted to tell you."

The rest of us waited in anticipation as he paused at the door of the hut.

"Do you want to know, Egbert?" he teased.

"Cedric, I don't really care if I never know. There's mixing and mixing and that was out of order, but I wouldn't like to fall out with anyone now about it so don't tell me."

"OK, old friend," Cedric agreed as he slammed the door behind him. A second later the door re-opened and he poked his head in again. "Who did you say was the best mixer?"

"Domnic," Egbert replied without hesitation.

"You're right."

"What?"

"You're right!"

"I thought you said Dipper was the best."

"I did, but Dipper never sewed up all your clothes. That was a classic. That was Domnic."

The door slammed closed again.

"You know," said Egbert in disgust, as he looked around at our laughing faces, "there are smart-alecs all around Ireland and the British government chooses to put most of them in this cage and me with youse. Just remember," he snapped, "remember! He who laughs last, laughs last. I'll get my own back on the lot of youse!"

(1990)

Cage Eleven

DEAR JOHN

"WHAT!" I EXCLAIMED.

Your Man sighed sadly. He leaned back in his chair until it was tilted on two legs with its back resting against the wall of the study hut. He eased his legs out from under the table and balanced himself with his feet on the table-top. He stared at the ceiling, then, swallowing hard and averting his gaze from mine, he replied, "Sinead has left me. She's taking the kids to live in England."

"When did you find this out?"

"Today. On the visit. Well, I found out for definite today. She talked about it before; we both did. Remember last year? When I told you she wasn't coming up because she was sick? Well, she wasn't sick. She was just browned off with the searches and the British Army outside the camp, the screws on the visit, and all the messing about getting ready and the annoyance with the kids. And then before we'd know it the half-hour would be up and it was time to start waiting for the next half-hour – the following week."

Your Man's tone was despondently even. He continued to stare at the ceiling.

"To make matters worse we don't ... " he corrected himself, "we didn't live in a republican area. So she used to come up on her own in her brother's car. You know the way all our people come up on the bus, well most of them do, and they get a bit of *craic* and, you know, it all helps. Sinead always felt a bit of an outsider."

"You should have said. Sure there's plenty of our people to give a wee bit of support," I protested. "She could have – she could still go out with Colette and Anne-Marie and all that crowd. Why don't you arrange for ..."

"Nawh, mucker, it's too late," he interrupted me. "And don't be annoying yourself. I suggested all that. I even got my sisters to take her out. Nawh, it isn't that. Sinead just never got married for this. She got married to be married. It's not her fault. It's a wonder she stuck it so long – it's three years now. Our Sean's five and wee Mairead's nearly four. Not much of a life for any of them, is it?"

He swung his legs down off the table and hunched forward in his chair. He stared blankly at the study-hut door. I could see the tears welling up in his eyes.

"I'm going to miss the kids," he declared eventually, sucking in his cheeks and blowing out a long, deep breath. "That's why Sinead didn't go before this. She knew I loved the kids up on a visit."

"Maybe it's a phase she's going through. Once it's out of her system she'll be all right," I offered.

"Nawh," Your Man smiled wryly at me, "this is no phase. This is for keeps. Sinead's a realist. I've another nine years to do, you know. That's not much of a future. So we decided that we'd separate."

"You agreed!" I exclaimed.

"Aye," he replied. "What did you expect me to do? I was a beaten docket. I'd no choice. Like, I'll still see the kids during the summer. They're going to come back to stay with her Ma and our ones will bring them up to see me. They'll probably have wee English accents by then. Who'd have thought it would turn out like this? Poor Sinead; poor kids. Poor me," he gave a false little smile and then stood up.

"It's a hard oul' station." He smiled again, a wee, sorry smile.

"C'mon and let's go for a walk. It's no use the two of us going into a big D. I'll be all right, I'm glad I got talking to somebody about it. You're the first one I've talked to except for Sinead. Just shows you the type of relationships we have in here. By the way, don't say anything to Egbert or Cedric. I'll tell them the morra."

We pulled the door of the study hut shut behind us. It was a bright, starlit night. We paused, hesitating, unsure of ourselves.

"Are you sure she's going to go away?" I asked, more for something to say than anything else.

"Her plane left Aldergrove ten minutes ago," Your Man answered, with a touch of impatience creeping into his voice.

"I'm sorry," I said, "I didn't mean to annoy you asking stupid questions."

"It's OK. It's not your fault. It's nobody's fault. It's just the way the cookie crumbles, as my Da used to say. The only problem is ..."

He started to walk. I fell in alongside him.

"The only problem is, old comrade, that I love Sinead and Sinead still loves me."

He stopped in mid-stride and for the first time he looked me in the eyes. "You don't understand that, do you?"

I said nothing.

"Well, maybe you're right," he continued, "I don't understand it either. But that's what I believe and I'm going to keep believing it," he asserted determinedly, "until I'm able to come to terms with this mess. Then I'll probably be ready to believe something else. OK? But not before that. OK?"

"OK," I replied.

We walked in silence.

"You know why I need to believe that?" he asked after a short while. "You know why?" He continued without waiting for an answer. "Because in this place," he waved his hand expansively at the maze of wire and lights and watch-towers which surrounded us, "in this place you need to believe in something and right at this minute I don't have a lot to believe in. But I believe Sinead loves me."

He glared fiercely at me. Tears of anger and frustration and sorrow welled up again in his eyes.

"She just couldn't take it. And that's not her fault. OK?"

"OK, old friend," I said quietly.

"You know something else?" he asked.

"What?"

"I'm fucked." His voice finally broke. "OK?"

"OK," I replied.

I didn't look at him. I didn't need to. I knew he was crying. Not the body-wracking, sobbing convulsions of uncontrolled and disbelieving grief; no, Your Man's tears were the silent, proud and dignified longing for a lost love. He was almost regal in his sorrow.

He didn't look at me. He didn't need to. He knew I cried with him, sad little tears of solidarity and love. No one in Long Kesh saw us weeping that night as we journeyed slowly around the yard. Or if they did we didn't notice them. We were impervious to our surroundings.

We thought only, each in our different way, of Sinead and the two kids, flying high over the Irish Sea. Your Man never mentioned her to me again, not for about two years. And she never came back.

(1990)

Cage Eleven

UP THE REBELS

SEAMUS HAD BECOME institutionalised. He had been serving terms of twelve months, or six months, or three months in Belfast Prison for as long as he or anyone else could remember. It had gone on for so long now that he had forgotten how to cope with even the simplest realities of life outside. Three meals a day, a bed in a cell and the absence of decision-making on any issue, from going to the toilet to what to eat, had made Seamus into a passive, if likeable, human zombie.

Every time he finished one sentence, back he came again within a week or so, to do time for some equally trivial offence. His family, who were both well-to-do and well-respected, were embarrassed by his behaviour. Once they even sent him from the family home in Armagh to Belfast for examination by a psychiatrist. Seamus, for his part, was so disturbed by this experience that he stole the psychiatrist's car and promptly ended back in the relative safety of Belfast Prison again.

That's when I met him. I was on remand at the time he returned to his old job as orderly in A Wing. He used to "bump out" the wing three times a day, and when I was on my way from my cell on the bottom landing or sitting in it during lock-up I used to see or hear Seamus "bumping" his way up and down the well-polished floor. "Bumping" meant polishing the tiles which stretched a hundred yards from the "circle" up to the end of the wing, and Seamus had been doing it for so long that he now took a certain pride in the dull red glow which was produced by his endless to-ing and fro-ing. He used a bumper, which is like a brush but bigger, with a wooden box where the brush-head should be. The box was weighted down with bricks and its base covered with blankets. It was heavy and tedious work pushing and pulling this contraption over the tiles, all the time trying to coax a shine from them. Seamus didn't seem to mind. The screws didn't really bother him except when they wanted their tea made or some menial task performed. When they did require his services he complied with a slow yet unhesitating obedience. Sometimes one or two of the nastier ones would poke fun at him, but he was so much a part of the place that everyone usually took him for granted.

On Sundays, during mass in the prison chapel when the political and the ordinary prisoners came together, we would pass him cigarettes and at night when we were locked up and he was still bumping up and down the silent, deserted wing we would slip newspapers under our cell doors for him.

He was always extremely cautious about associating too openly with us. We were fairly rebellious, holding parades in the prison yard, segregating ourselves from loyalist prisoners and dealing with the prison administration only through our elected OC. We were continuously on punishment, being subjected to loss of privileges and petty restrictions.

As he bumped back and forth, Seamus was a silent, indifferent observer of the daily battles between us and the screws. Or so, at least, it appeared to us. Then one day a screw spilled a bucket of dirty water over Seamus's clean floor.

"If you don't keep this place cleaner than that," the screw guldered, "I'll have you moved to the base."

Seamus looked at him in dumb disbelief and then, with tears trickling slowly down his face, he went on his hands and knees at the screw's feet to mop up the water which was spreading like a grey blemish over his floor. The screw was a new one, and that incident was only the first of many. It got so bad subsequently that poor Seamus was even afraid to accept our cigarettes and we found the newspapers which we slipped into the hall for him still lying there when we slopped out the following morning.

There wasn't much we could do about it. We willed Seamus to resist and our OC went as far as to make a complaint about the screw, whom we all spontaneously ostracised. But we were beginning also to despise Seamus for showing no signs of fighting back, and in his own way he seemed to be blaming us for his troubles.

And then Seamus rebelled. I was coming from the toilet at the time. He stood only a few yards from me, bumper at hand, looking at a group of screws loitering outside the dining-hall.

"Fuck yous!" he screamed, his words echoing along the wing and up along the tiers of the high glass ceiling.

"Fuck yous!" he screamed again. "Yous think yous are somebody ordering me about. And you," he rounded on me with a vengeance. "Fuck you too and your cigarettes and your stupid bloody newspapers. I'm sick of yous all and your awful bloody floor."

At that the wing exploded into noise, with prisoners banging their cell doors, rattling the bars and generally making a hectic, frantic and frightening clamour.

"Tell them to bangle their floor, Seamus."

"C'mon, Seamus, let it all out."

The screws, caught unaware by the suddenness and the ferocity of the din, moved hesitantly out of the wing and into the circle. There, safe behind the heavilybarred gates, they looked up towards where Seamus and I stood, unescorted and alone, in the middle of the wing. The closed cell doors stared blankly at us, the floor stretched sullenly to meet the prison walls and the noise continued unabated from all sides. Down at the circle the screws had drawn their batons, and one of them was phoning for assistance.

"Shit," said Seamus to me, a slow, sheepish grin creeping across his face as he surveyed the scene and heard the shouts of encouragement ringing out from all quarters.

"Ah, c'mon," I said, glancing nervously at the circle where reinforcements had begun to arrive. "We better go down there and let them quare fellas know there's nothing wrong." I had to shout to be heard above the continuing noise. "If this keeps up they'll think it's a break-out and you and me'll be murdered."

Seamus ignored me and sat back on his bumper. He took a crumpled roll-up from behind his ear and lit it, slowly and defiantly exhaling the smoke towards the circle.

"I've only a week to do anyway," he muttered. "Sit down and take it easy. We'll go when I'm ready."

And so we did, he to the punishment block and me back to my cell.

He didn't appear back on the wing for a few days after that, but the screws told us that he was okay and for what that was worth we were content enough. A new orderly came to bump the wing and life returned to its monotonous normality. Then, on a Thursday, Seamus returned: we greeted him with a shouted, uproarious welcome. The screws didn't seem to mind. He was due for release anyway the following day and there was little they could do about it.

That night, after lock-up, a muffled knock brought me to the cell door. I peered through the narrow chink between the heavy door and the door-frame.

"Do you want a cup of tea?" Seamus hissed in at me. "Hurry up if you do."

I grabbed my mug, delighted at the thought of such an unexpected luxury, and hissed back at him: "How're you going to get the tea in here?"

"Shut up," he ordered. "Houl' your mug up to the chink."

I did as I was told and smiled to myself as the end of a folded newspaper appeared through the narrow gap.

"Widen out the end of the paper and houl' your mug below it."

As I did so a trickle of strong, hot tea poured down the funnel-like folds of the newspaper into my waiting mug.

"Enjoy that," said Seamus. "There's no bromide in it." He withdrew his tea-sodden paper.

"I've more for some of the other lads but I'll have to hurry up before the screws come back." He hesitated for a second:

"I'm sorry for giving off the other day. You know the score yourself: I was doing heavy whack. Anyway, I won't be back here again," he added with feeling, "so good luck."

"Good luck, Seamus," I whispered.

He moved from the door, then turned back again. Through the chink I could see his lips widen into a grin.

"Up the rebels," he smiled.

That was the last I saw of him. I was released myself a few months later and I forgot about Seamus. That is, until this morning, when his photograph stared out at me from the front page of the *Irish News*.

Twenty-nine-year-old Co. Armagh man shot dead after crashing through a British Army road-block in a stolen car.

At least he never did go back there again, I thought to myself. But you never know. Maybe he was on his way back when he was killed? Probably not though. Whatever institutionalised refuge Belfast Prison held for him had been lost during his last stay there. They'd never let him bump out A Wing floor again after his last outburst. We'd made sure of that.

No, he probably knew what he was doing when he crashed that road-block.

What was it he had said to me that night he gave me the tea? Up the rebels?

"Aye, Seamus, up the rebels."

(1992)

The Street and other stories

THE IRA/ÓGLAIGH NA HÉIREANN

*Irishmen and Irishwomen: In the name of God
and of the dead generations from which she
receives her old tradition of nationhood,
Ireland, through us, summons her children to
the flag and strikes for her freedom.*
1916 Proclamation

THE CLASSIC PERIOD of republican struggle, the period which is impressed upon one's mind as the definitive image of the IRA, is the Tan War, with its flying columns taking on the Black and Tans. At its height, it was a military campaign with a background of incipient forms of alternative government apparatus functioning through the republican courts in certain parts of the country. The flying columns moved about as fairly self-contained units; they were fed and accommodated in sympathetic households or sometimes they commandeered unionist houses and lived off the occupants.

In the 1930s and 1940s, the IRA enjoyed no such background in the country, and its military actions took place in England, in the Twenty-six Counties and only in one or two places in the Six Counties. The 1950s campaign was restricted to the border counties – there was literally no activity in Belfast – and a lot of the IRA people involved came from the Twenty-six Counties and presumably worked around the border counties or maintained small flying columns based in Fermanagh, Tyrone and South Armagh. By the end, this campaign, like those before it, consisted of just five or six active republicans skipping between five or six houses.

The current phase of armed struggle is different from any other, apart perhaps from a resemblance to the situation in the Black and Tan War in those areas that enjoyed some kind of governmental status. In the 1970s, the struggle developed into a broad political and armed campaign, but even the military aspect developed its own politics of physical force.

What particularly characterised this phase is that the IRA fought within the occupied area and existed cheek by jowl with the British forces, which had at their command a massive array of technological resources. The IRA is one of the few guerilla forces in the world which has operated in and from within the occupied area, and, despite the long duration of this phase of struggle, the IRA has continued to enjoy unsurpassed community support.

I wish that physical force had never been part of the political struggle in my lifetime in Ireland. But a statelet which was born in violence has maintained itself throughout its seventy years of existence by violence and has been supported in so doing by the British army and government. The conflict which has resulted in the deaths of over 3,300 people began, in 1966, with the UVF campaign of assassinations of Catholics; it continued in its early stages with attacks by loyalists and RUC on civil rights marchers and graduated to the joint loyalist/RUC attacks on Catholic streets in Derry and Belfast, and the first member of the RUC to be killed at this time was shot by loyalists on the Shankill Road. The IRA's armed struggle in this period originated as a defensive response to the combined attacks of the RUC, loyalists and the British army, and it has always been massively outgunned. There are in the Six Counties today something like 123,000 legally held guns, and these are not in the possession of the IRA. There are approximately 30,000 members of the British forces, between British soldiers, the UDR, the RUC and the RUC Reserve. They are armed with sophisticated weapons, with armoured cars, a massive battery of electronic surveillance equipment, with cameras trained on many streets of West Belfast and Derry, and they are backed by the law which, in Brigadier Frank Kitson's phrase, is "just another weapon in the government's arsenal ... little more than a propaganda cover for the disposal of unwanted members of the public".

From defensive origins the IRA campaign developed into an offensive against the state, and there is no denying the fact that innocent bystanders were killed and injured as a consequence of IRA actions. Death by violence is always a sickening tragedy and no talk of "the inevitable casualties of guerrilla warfare" can do anything to alter the fact. I deeply regret all the deaths and injuries which occur in the course of this struggle and, although I have never tried to justify civilian casualties or fatalities of IRA actions, I am challenged constantly by some journalists and television interviewers, imitating the attitudes of their political masters, with having placed myself and the whole republican movement outside the bounds of political debate by refusing to condemn the IRA, and the IRA is commented upon in an unreal way as if its motivation were the pursuit of violence for its own sake. It is commented upon in a way which ignores and diverts attention away from the circumstances which account both for its origins and for the continuation of its armed activity.

Óglaigh na hÉireann takes its historical and organisational origins from the forces which engaged in the Easter Rising of 1916, though one can trace its ancestry much further back if one wishes. But the circumstances which shaped the recent support for the IRA are, above all, the experience of the barricade days from 1969-72. Those days are of continuing importance not just in terms of the IRA but because they saw the development of tremendous community solidarity, more than a memory of which remains today.

In response to joint RUC and loyalist attacks, nationalist Derry was barricaded from August 1969 until July 1972; in

Belfast, for a much shorter period, there were barricades in up to twenty-six Catholic enclaves, with the major concentration in West Belfast. Massive shifts in population caused by the loyalist pogroms – the biggest forced movement of population in Europe since the Second World War – led people to open up their homes behind the barricades to refugees. Everyone had to develop self-reliance and mutual solidarity in order to cope with the situation. Working people took control of aspects of their own lives, organised their own districts, in a way which deeply antagonised and traumatised the Catholic middle class, and particularly the Catholic Church hierarchy. It was an experience of community oneness, of unselfishness at every hand. And, when more than barricades were required for defence from the armed forces of the RUC, loyalists and, soon, the British army, this generation of the IRA emerged.

The IRA was, in August 1969, disorganised, almost completely unarmed, and unable to play the role it had played in previous pogroms, in the 1920s and 1930s, of defending the areas under attack. In one or two instances, firearms were produced by individual republicans in attempts to hold off attacks, but the IRA was in no shape to offer any organised response. Yet, by March 1972, the IRA had not only created a defensive force of unprecedented effectiveness, they had also carried out a massive offensive which had succeeded in its aim of bringing down the Stormont government.

In the days, weeks and months after the August 1969 pogroms, republicans worked with frantic energy to raise money, to procure arms and to reorganise the IRA to meet the demands of a situation of armed siege. In a remarkably short time, a people's army took shape; closely knit with the nationalist community, it was made up of the sons and daughters of ordinary people, its members indistinguishable to any outside observer from the rest of the community. Whether people in the nationalist areas agreed or disagreed with the IRA and all its actions, they recognised it as their army, knew for the most part which of their neighbours were members, and referred to it simply as the "ra".

Streets, houses, people and even churches were under

197

attack, and IRA volunteers – most of whom were very young – put their lives on the line to protect them. At first, sticks and stones, petrol bombs and unsophisticated guns were used against the forces of the state, which were equipped with the most up-to-date weaponry. And, in the midst of days of rioting and skirmishes, the IRA was screening, training and attempting to instil discipline into large numbers of new recruits. Much had to be done under intense pressure and at breakneck speed; but, before long, the IRA had adopted clear structures for its operations and had acquired explosives and guns that stood a chance of generating an effective counter to the firepower being directed against the nationalist areas.

When the barricades were up there was a great sense of euphoria; this was perhaps naive, but it was nonetheless real. When the IRA campaign began, the civil rights campaign was still going on, albeit on a smaller scale than previously, and the honeymoon period immediately after the arrival of the British troops was over. For the first time in the Six Counties one had the combination of armed struggle and mass popular struggle. Most of the Catholics had withdrawn from the institutions of state and, when internment came, they all withdrew. The armed struggle began to be waged with great intensity and with major support and tolerance. There was also the feeling that things were happening in Dublin, as reflected in the Arms Trial crisis in Fianna Fáil, and that tended to give Northern Catholics succour.

When Prime Minister of the Six Counties Faulkner said things like "We have them on the run" and the IRA came back the next day with a devastating series of operations, the effect that had in lifting people's morale was enormous. The free run for republicans in the barricaded areas meant that the areas were almost entirely free of petty crime, and this had more to do with an identification with the struggle than with any policing methods of republicans.

The ambassadors for the British government on a daily basis were the British soldiers. They were "welcomed" initially because they were seen as relieving a siege, whether in the Falls Road or in Derry, but it was an uneasy welcome. They got tea in only a few households. People did not know whether to cheer or what to do. Even in the past when Catholics had joined the British army for lack of available jobs, their families had been inclined to feel a bit guilty about it. At the very least, there was a consciousness that these were British soldiers and that, in one sense or another, we were Irish. Another factor which came quickly into play was the racist attitude of many British army regiments. They antagonised whole communities by their behaviour and especially by their attitude to women-folk. So, while there were initially mixed feelings about the British army, once it became apparent what their role was, all ambiguity went out of the window. Within a very short space of time, people were shouting insults at the soldiers and people were suddenly talking about memories of the Black and Tans.

Bombay Street, and, two months later, Coates Street were burned down by loyalist gangs and the RUC after the British troops had arrived and after the larger scale burnings had already taken place. Whole streets of houses were burned out, people were killed and about a hundred injured during the two-day attack on this Catholic area in the Lower Falls. The fact that the British army did not intervene taught nationalists an important lesson.

The Falls Road curfew, in July 1970, made popular opposition to the British army absolute in Belfast. Three thousand British troops invaded the Falls Road and, from helicopters, voices over PA systems announced that the area was under curfew and that anyone on the streets was liable to be shot. Five civilians were killed, more were injured, and 300 were arrested. The invasion and curfew lasted for two days, during which 1,600 canisters of CS gas were fired. Troops smashed down the doors of houses, pulled up floors, wrecked people's homes. The siege was broken, at great risk to themselves, by hundreds of women who massed together and simply marched past all the "squaddies", who did not know how to cope with this direct expression of popular feeling. After that, recruitment to the IRA was massive. IRA organisation and capability increased so dramatically that, by June and July of 1971, they were able to carry out as many as 125 bombings in those two months – an average of more than two per day. The Stormont government and the British army were not succeeding in their attempts to crush the resistance.

The shooting dead, in Derry, of Seamus Cusack and Desmond Beattie marked a critical turning point. Prime Minister Faulkner had, in May, given the British army carte blanche to fire on anyone acting "suspiciously"; on 8 July 1971, they obliged, and two unarmed Catholics were killed. The struggle for civil rights had continued, despite the RUC beating people to death, despite loyalist attacks, despite the Battle of the Bogside, the upheavals of August, and the shootings of people in the Falls Road. But the shootings of Cusack and Beattie marked a change, and this change was cemented by the use of the British army forces as the implement of repression. Before that it had been primarily a battle between beleaguered nationalists and the Stormont administration for equal rights; then it became a battle between beleaguered nationalists and the British establishment.

The British government could have defused the situation, could have prevented it reaching the stage of open armed conflict. If they had understood and taken note of what the Campaign for Social Justice was saying in 1965, they could have moved then to introduce the norms of democracy at a time when republicanism was virtually dead. In such circumstances it would have been impossible for the IRA to survive. If in London the will had existed to make even limited changes, the long-sighted agitators would have pointed out how small the changes were and how unsatisfactory, but the British government would have succeeded in undercutting support for republicanism.

Instead of defusing the situation, the British government copper-fastened popular support for the IRA. In Ballymurphy in West Belfast, for example, there were six semi-active republicans and ten supporters in 1969; today Sinn Féin draws its biggest vote from that area. The crucial transformation came about when a British army regiment came into Ballymurphy and attempted to beat its people into submission. If they had come in with kid gloves they would still have been unwelcome, but they would not have generated the same phenomenon of implacable republican resistance.

Internment, introduced on 9 August 1971, had a major effect in making people conscious participants in the struggle. Those who were already politicised were not surprised by the introduction of internment, but there were many Catholics who did not believe that such a thing could happen, and to them internment came as a crucial indication that the road to reform was blocked off. Brutal confirmation came with the shooting dead of unarmed demonstrators in Derry on Bloody Sunday, 30 January 1972. Óglaigh na hÉireann was inundated with new recruits.

When Stormont fell in March 1972, it was a time of complete and utter jubilation. I remember talking to a middle-aged man in Ballymurphy in the midst of a colossal gun battle. (Although many people might not realise this, a lot of those big gun battles fought to defend an area from attack – in this case attack by the British army – had as many as two hundred people standing and watching what was happening.) This man, who had lived through the imposition of partition and the setting up of Stormont, kept saying, almost as if he were drunk, "Jesus, you'd never think you'd see the day!" He represented a feeling that, so quickly after the events of 1968-69, something that was hated, something that was symbolic of all that was wrong in the state, had been removed. And probably most people who were anti-unionist felt, quite rightly, that they had played a part in the removal of Stormont. The IRA was clearly seen as acting on their behalf.

The fall of Stormont was very decidedly a watershed. The feeling was that "we'll never go back to that again".

The impact of the fall of Stormont on the unionists, as well as the disarming and disbanding of the B Specials, must obviously have been catastrophic. Having said that, the actual impact may have been exaggerated by commentators. Just after the fall of Stormont, I found myself committed to the Maidstone prison ship, which was anchored in Belfast Lough in the hinterland of loyalist East Belfast, and we felt very vulnerable to attack by an Orange mob enraged at the abolition of their Protestant parliament. The Vanguard Party was in its heyday, with its parades and rallies featuring fascist salutes. Unionist leaders were making threatening noises, and, if there was going to be a real Orange backlash, that was the moment at which it should have occurred. But it didn't, and, in assessing the dangers of a future loyalist backlash, one must take this into account. They said they would not accept the fall of Stormont, but they did; they said they would fight to the last man, but they didn't.

What loyalist response there was came in a form which has been seen on many other occasions since. Although their fight over the proroguing of Stormont was with the British, they engaged in a spiralling campaign of killings of Catholics. There was not the major backlash that had been threatened, but there were the phenomena of mutilated bodies and "romper room" torture, and it was a very frightening period for many Catholics, marked also by the growth to quite massive numbers of the UDA, which paraded in paramilitary gear and masks. There was also a major confrontation between the UDA and the British army in Woodvale in Belfast. The British army climbed down.

Unionism had depended for so long on its leadership that, when that leadership failed to deliver, unionism was for a period lost – not only because its leadership had proved inadequate, but also because the British government on which it depended, to which it pledged allegiance, to which it felt bound and of which it was a subject, took away Stormont. Their disarray became exacerbated when the British, under direct rule, took more and more of the everyday decisions and there was no real role for unionist politicians. They had no power.

On the nationalist side, Óglaigh na hÉireann enjoyed credibility and popular support, but the republican movement failed to intervene politically, and effectively handed over the role of political representatives of the nationalist people to the SDLP. Many Catholics adopted a pragmatic attitude then of support for the IRA's military struggle and voting for the SDLP. Some elements claiming to be "republican" or "nationalist" made attacks on Protestants. These attacks were quite wrong and, like "feuding" between republican and other groups, did not serve any anti-unionist interest.

Support for the IRA amongst the nationalist population of the Six Counties has been, as the tacticians of guerrilla warfare such as Mao and Che put it, the sea in which the people's army has swum and, like the sea, it has its tides, its ebbs and flows, but it is always there. The nationalist people had withdrawn their consent to being governed by Stormont; they and the IRA had brought Stormont down and proceeded, in succeeding years, to make the Six Counties ungovernable, even in an environment of British military saturation of nationalist areas. However, a situation of deadlock in which Óglaigh na hÉireann were able to block the imposition of a British solution, but were unable to force the British to withdraw, produced a sense of war-weariness. The IRA had succeeded in bringing down Stormont and they had promised victory in the form of British withdrawal. But victory had not come and the troops were still on the streets, still kicking down doors in the night, wrecking nationalists' houses, dragging people off for interrogation, torture and internment. British army patrols were sometimes truculent, sometimes terrified, but they were always there; whether you were going shopping or to work, to the pub or just around the corner to a relative or friend, they were always there. And that operated in many ways: it made people determined to resist, and it made people weary. British soldiers harassed children leaving schools; mothers went down to the schools to bring their children home and prevent them responding to the provocations of the soldiers with stones; mothers saw sons graduating from stones to petrol bombs to membership of the IRA, to Long Kesh internment camp. Hardly a family was untouched by death, internment or imprisonment. Heroically they kept their households going, often holding down a job while their husband and perhaps a son as well were in prison, coping on the barest level of subsistence, visiting Long Kesh regularly. Some became political activists in the Relatives Action Committee or in Sinn Féin; they marched and demonstrated and came to be the heart and soul of popular resistance.

In the face of the suffering of the war of resistance in the nationalist ghettos, it was inevitable that a war-weary opposition to the IRA would surface on occasions. It may well be, as other observers and authors have suggested, that some of these movements of opposition received encouragement and finance from the British government, including British army sources. The appalling disruption of everyday life, the incessant assault on nerves by the tension of wondering whether a son, daughter, wife, husband, brother or sister was going to be lifted, beaten up in interrogation, interned or killed, the frequent dangers of loyalist assassination campaigns – all the strains of the situation inevitably raised the question in people's minds as to whether it was all worth it. No one wanted to go back to the "normality" of rule by Stormont, but with no immediate prospect of a British withdrawal, support for the struggle of the IRA was bound to waver. In particular, the British government exploited every opportunity to increase the sense of war-weariness; and, especially when Óglaigh na hÉireann killed or injured civilians, the British were always, in classical counter-insurgency fashion, cynically prepared to exploit these mistakes or to create the conditions in which they might occur.

There always has been and there always will be a yearning for peace among Irish people. The so-called "Peace People" are the best-known example of an organised movement against the IRA campaign, but there have been other organisations through the years, such as "Women Together" and "Protestant and Catholic Encounter", and there have been occasions when people in nationalist areas have protested against IRA actions without actually forming any organisation. But whenever this understandable and undoubtedly genuine desire for peace manifests itself, it is open to exploitation for one political purpose or another. It is easy to suggest that peace is somehow not political and that peace marches are not political, and then sincere people can be swept along behind a vague and emotional demand.

I have very strong personal feelings about the "Peace People" campaign of 1976. The IRA man, Danny Lennon, who was shot dead in the incident which gave rise to the campaign, had been a particular friend of mine since we had met in Cage Eleven in Long Kesh. It was tragic enough that he and the Maguire children had been killed, but, when the British lie about his death was picked up by the media and gained general acceptance, I found it a great deal more difficult to deal with.

The facts of the incident were that Danny Lennon was shot dead at the wheel of the car he was driving by British soldiers firing from an armour-plated landrover and the car ploughed into the Maguire family at the side of the road. Mrs Maguire was seriously injured and three of her children, the oldest of whom was eight years and the youngest only six weeks, were killed. It was never clear whether they were killed by the car or by bullets fired by British soldiers; unusually, the results of the autopsies and inquest were never published.

No attention was focused on the fact that the British troops had opened fire on a car without regard for the lives of civilians on the street. Instead, the headlines shouted their message that an IRA car had killed three children. And, on BBC TV News that night, Mrs Maguire's sister, Mairead Corrigan, broke down crying and understandably affected millions of viewers deeply.

Danny Lennon had been shot dead, yet he was being held solely responsible for the deaths of the Maguire children. It was bad enough that innocent children had been killed. That was awful. But Danny Lennon, now dead and unable to defend himself, was being blamed. That concern may appear ridiculous to people who have an image of IRA volunteers as terrorists, but the reality is that members of Óglaigh na hÉireann are just ordinary citizens who are forced through difficult circumstances into resistance, and Danny Lennon was an ordinary nationalist youth, a member of a large family in Andersonstown, who had become involved in resistance. The tragedy of the deaths of the children rankled, and, in particular, the way in which the British escaped any responsibility at all, by exploiting the children's deaths, and because of the cynical way in which the incident was manipulated.

The "Peace People" lost credibility in nationalist areas very quickly. In fact, what credibility it had consisted basically of sympathy for the Maguires and, indeed, for the Lennons. Only four days after the deaths of the Maguire children, a twelve-year-old girl, Majella O'Hare, was shot and killed by British soldiers in South Armagh; the "Peace People" offered no criticism of the British army. Two months later, fourteen-year-old Brian Stewart was shot dead by British soldiers in West Belfast; again, the "Peace People" were silent, and when they went to a meeting in Turf Lodge they had to be escorted from the hall because of the fury of local people at the one-sidedness of their condemnation of violence. If that was not enough to seal their fate in Catholic areas, they put the cap on it when they characterised the RUC, UDR and British army as "the only legitimate upholders of the rule of law" and played down what they called "the occasional instances when members of the security forces may have stepped beyond the rule of law".

The movement showed that there is always a hope among people that there can be peace, an element of war-weariness that grabs at straws. The people who marched and prayed and engaged in rallies were expressing perfectly reasonable emotions, but these emotions were exploited. The "Peace People" were not even calling for real and general peace: what they were calling for was an end to the armed struggle of the IRA. And that was at best a partial kind of peace, in both meanings of partial – prejudiced against only one element in a violent conflict and incomplete in that it did not base itself on the elements of social justice without which peace simply cannot grow. It was an attempt to move people away from republican physical force politics, and it failed because it did not even seek to remedy the reasons why people felt compelled to have recourse to physical force.

As soon as they tried to examine what peace was and how it could be attained, the leadership of the "Peace People" began to collapse. The media, perhaps because of their nature, represented the failure as lying in the falling out between Mairead Corrigan, Betty Williams and Ciaran McKeown as they disputed who should get what money. But the real reason was far larger than this merely symptomatic disintegration. Peace rallies and prayer may give succour to people, but they cannot of their own volition bring peace. Peace is a political question and cannot be successfully approached without a commitment to political change.

For a short period, the "Peace People" succeeded in diverting public – and particularly international – attention from the real problem of the political situation in the Six Counties. In the end, it brought into question the credibility not only of its own leaders but also of the Nobel Peace Prize, Joan Baez, and others who associated themselves with it.

The episode – for that is what it was – of the "Peace People" deserves to be regarded as a particularly sad one, because it represented a perversion of what is a very important demand. In practice, people have been demanding peace since long before the IRA became active. In my own area of Ballymurphy, community groups have long demanded employment, decent housing, play centres, facilities for the aged, the handicapped and the young. They have sought freedom from heavy rents on homes they will never own, freedom from the dole queues and freedom from the Assistance Office. At the time of the "Peace People", the facilities of the area were a public house, a row of shops, and a bookmaker's office. One hundred of the six hundred families had more than ten people living in cramped, ill-repaired, misplanned, jerry-built houses. Forty-seven percent of the residents were unemployed. Sixty percent of the population were children and teenagers faced with a future which offered them nothing. Those demands for the kind of peace which is based on justice and equality were made year after year, and year after year they were refused.

We cannot have justice and peace in Ireland, because we do not have a society capable of upholding them. Instead, we have a system based on coercion, violence, sectarianism and exploitation. By its very nature, British rule cannot be just or peaceful and, while this is so, revolutionary struggle will continue to strive to overthrow it in pursuit of true justice, peace and happiness. Violence in Ireland has its roots in the conquest of Ireland by Britain. This conquest has lasted through several stages for many centuries and, whether economic, political, territorial or cultural, it has used violence, coercion, sectarianism and terrorism as its methods and has had power as its objective. While the armed struggle has traditionally dominated republican strategy, in this phase it has involved and depended upon a considerable degree of political support. IRA members do not go to people who provide support without being receptive to their thoughts. They do not constantly ask people to do things for them without being responsive to their needs, being careful about how they deal with them, and taking on board some of the criticisms they might have of aspects of the armed struggle. Not only is that receptiveness and responsiveness correct in political terms, it is also a practical necessity in everyday circumstances. If a person providing support is offended by the actions of Óglaigh na hÉireann, then that person will withdraw his or her support and it will not be possible to continue with the armed activity as before.

Aspects of the nature of the armed struggle can be explored by comparing the British soldier and the IRA volunteer. The British soldier is brought to Ireland; he has all his equipment handed to him, he is put into a garrison, given his transport and pointed at whatever task it is that he has to perform. IRA volunteers first of all have to obtain weapons; these may be given to them by higher command or they may have to procure them themselves. They then have to arrange to be able to dump those weapons, and to do this they have to enlist someone's support. If they are on the run, they have to arrange billets for themselves, they have to go and ask people if they can stay in their house. They have no meal tickets: someone has to agree to feed them. And if they want to get from A to B, they have to get someone to agree to provide transport.

To get through a normal day, an active IRA volunteer is involved in politics all the time, continually enlisting support, going to people and asking them to do this and that for him or her. Even if one could describe the armed struggle of Óglaigh na hÉireann as militaristic, it bears little resemblance to what may be called militarism in terms of a standing army. Despite all the British propaganda stories, it is obvious that the IRA exists and operates with the active consent of a sufficient number of people to finance, arm, clothe, feed, accommodate and transport IRA volunteers and in every way build up around them a voluntary political infrastructure.

The armed struggle requires the development of reflex physical force politics. Even if there were no unarmed political struggle, the armed struggle itself has a significant political dimension to it and involves a significant political relationship with the community. As volunteers develop their politics, their vision of the goal they are aiming for, as they come to understand the politics of their opponents and the way the struggle needs to develop, then comes an understanding that armed struggle itself is a tactic and that one cannot shoot or bomb an independent Ireland into existence. You may be able to bomb and shoot a British connection out of existence, given many other necessary political conditions, but you will not bring anything into existence.

The tactic of armed struggle is of primary importance because it provides a vital cutting edge. Without it, the issue of Ireland would not even be an issue. So, in effect, the armed struggle becomes armed propaganda. There has not been, at least not yet, a classic development from guerrilla action to mass military action registering territorial gains; instead, armed struggle has become an agent of bringing about change. That reality is understood even by middle-class professional people, people who have a stake in the Six Counties. Very many people who disagree absolutely with the IRA nevertheless see it as a very important part of the political equation. They might deplore it, dislike it, have moral objections to it, but still have the feeling that if it did not exist there would be no hope of getting change. At the same time, there is a realisation in republican circles that armed struggle on its own is inadequate and that non-armed forms of political struggle are at least as important. As a means of struggle against the British presence in the Six Counties in pursuance of national independence, armed action represents a necessary form of struggle; it has, however, no role to play in the Twenty-six Counties. The struggle there must be non-armed, complimentary to the struggle in the Six Counties and aimed also at securing national independence.

There are considerable moral problems in relation to armed struggle. I cannot conceive of any thinking person who would not have scruples about inflicting any form of hurt on another living being. The republican carrying out an armed action might be very ruthless, determined and callous, but intellectually and emotionally he or she would have difficulty. That difficulty would rarely lie in any sense of religious morality, but would have to do with the type of struggle involved, because it is close-up and it is nothing like joining a "regular" army with a whole ethos about being trained to kill. IRA volunteers are actually civilians, political people who decide, for short periods in their lives, to take part in armed action. That is different from somebody who wants to join a "regular" army, who wants to be a good shot, who wants a military career. The reality is of people who have consciously decided that armed struggle is a political necessity and that they will, in a fairly haphazard way, train themselves in the rudiments of military capability. There are no careerists in the IRA. Republican volunteers face futures of suffering, imprisonment and death.

What gives many people a problem is the length of the struggle. Even ordinary people who feel reservations might not have the same reservations if they felt it was going to be over in a short space of time – a two- or three-year war after which you start building right away. And it is worth pointing out what has happened in other, analogous situations, that the revolutionaries become the best builders; apart from their political commitment, perhaps because of their previous involvement in the destruction of other human beings.

The morality of the establishment does not concern me at all. It is a case – to borrow a phrase from Seamus Deane's *Civilians and Barbarians* – of a "political code disguised as a moral code". I once heard the then Taoiseach Garret Fitz-Gerald saying that he would not talk to those who would not renounce violence, and then he went to meet Margaret

Thatcher, who was up to her neck in the use of armed force in Ireland and other parts of the world. No republican would have the brass neck to express such blatant double standards.

Obviously, I would prefer a situation where armed struggle was unnecessary or even where armed struggle could be limited completely to what one could awkwardly call "clean" operations, where you had Óglaigh na hÉireann and the British army shooting it out. I do not mean "shooting it out" in some kind of heroic sense. The odds are stacked against the IRA volunteers and they operate at great personal risk against forces which are numerically and technologically superior and much better equipped. I admire the tenacity, determination and self-sacrifice of IRA volunteers, but I do not think that any war should be glamorised. In the Six Counties, armed struggle is a terrible but necessary form of resistance which is engaged in as a means towards an independent Ireland. The assessment in November 1978, by Brigadier J.M. Glover of British army intelligence, concluded that, while the British army remained in Ireland, the IRA would remain in existence to fight them. Most impartial observers and many opponents of republicanism recognise that the British presence is the catalyst for the armed struggle.

There are no material benefits for volunteers. Even a *Sunday Tribune* investigation had to conclude that they could find no evidence of republicans making material gains from their involvement. If the life of an IRA volunteer was a career, one might be able to talk about people who wanted to keep the war going rather than lose their livelihoods, but there is not even that mercenary element. War is a very draining process and, at some time, we are going to have to get on with our own lives and pursue our own private ambitions. After all the years of struggle, I look at the city of Belfast which I admire so much and I feel sick about the way in which it has been turned upside-down and I regret that people throughout the course of this war have suffered so much in so many different ways.

A repeated assertion by past Dublin governments and some other elements opposed to us is that, because republicans are engaged in armed action now, they would continue to use armed action in an independent Ireland. What I think they are really saying is that an independent Ireland poses a threat to them, that getting rid of partition means opening a Pandora's box. They are threatened by the spectre of the working people, Protestant and Catholic, no longer divided by partition or sectarian privilege and as a majority galvanising their political position. They are threatened by the notion of normal class politics developing in an independent Ireland, invigorated and encouraged by an immense feeling of euphoria after the settlement of this long war. And the only people who are threatened by that are those who have a vested interest in maintaining the status quo. These, then, are the people who are loudest in their condemnation of the armed struggle and who nowadays hold up the prospect that the republicans are going to come over the border and visit violence upon the Twenty-six Counties. This is not going to happen.

I meet members of the public constantly in the Twenty-six Counties. I cannot be anywhere in a public place or even walk down the street without people coming over and telling me what they think. Their main concern in relation to the IRA is that the war is going on so long. Some have a particular political attitude, in that they would like to see the British out, some are concerned about the loyalists and the difficulty posed by the strength of loyalism. But, in all my fairly widespread travels in the Twenty-six Counties, the worry about the IRA being habituated to violence has not been expressed.

Even if one looks at the matter from a purely tactical point of view, the ingredients for armed struggle are inherent in the Six County state. But, following the restoration of Irish national independence, there would be no popular support for armed struggle. The handful of people who make up Óglaigh na hÉireann could not hope to win anything by pursuing armed struggle without popular support. In its origins and in its continuing role, the modern IRA is an almost entirely working-class organisation of political militants which enjoys popular support amongst nationalists in the cities, towns and countryside of the Six Counties and a degree of passive support in the Twenty-six Counties. British army Brigadier J.M. Glover was forced to conclude that:

> Our evidence of the calibre of rank and file terrorists [*sic*] does not support the view that they are merely mindless hooligans drawn from the unemployed and unemployable.

A study by lawyers of defendants appearing before the Diplock (non-jury) courts charged with "scheduled" offences produces another outsiders' view of IRA volunteers (though by no means all those charged before the courts were IRA members or even republican activists):

> We are satisfied that the data establishes beyond reasonable doubt that the bulk of the republican offenders are young men and women without criminal records in the ordinary sense, though some have been involved in public disorders of the kind that frequently took place in the areas in which they lived. Both in this respect and in other records of employment and unemployment, they are reasonably representative of the working-class community of which they form a substantial part... They do not fit the stereotype of criminality which the authorities have from time to time attempted to attach to them.

It seems strange to reproduce such sociological comment upon my comrades of the republican movement, but I am aware that there may be readers of this book who are habitual consumers of the British press, the Six Counties press or the Twenty-six Counties press and who are habitual listeners to or viewers of British or Irish television and radio. Given the constant stream of lies which have spewed out over the years, not just from the British and Dublin governments but also from the media, it may be useful to show that even lawyers and a senior figure in British military intelligence are forced to recognise that the IRA are neither hooligans nor criminals.

I find it ridiculous to have to make these points because they have nothing to do with reality; they have instead to do with a crude propaganda war. The very people who originate the propaganda lines that wind up as press headlines know perfectly well that the IRA is not a matter of "godfathers of crime", of "pathological killers", of "mad bombers", of "mindless hooligans"; they know that, in dealing with the IRA, they are dealing with determined political opponents who are using the only means at their disposal to bring home their message in terms that will be understood and taken seriously enough to result in action and movement.

An example today of how far the British government is prepared to go to break republican resistance can be found in their efforts to dehumanise women republican prisoners by the brutal means of forced strip-searching. It is an indication of the courage and resilience of these women that after years of being subjected, sometimes on a daily basis, to this brutal, degrading and inhuman treatment, the women remain unbowed and unbroken. Similarly, there is the plight of long-term prisoners, especially the young prisoners, serving unprecedented sentences at the whim of a British judge or a British government minister. Many of these prisoners started their sentences as juveniles and are now in their thirties. Others were young married men and are now grandfathers. This experience has obviously traumatised their families, and it is a miracle of human endurance and a credit especially to the wives and mothers that their families have survived. It is also remarkable that so many released prisoners return to the struggle, and it is an indication of the durability of resistance that there is still an active struggle to embrace them after ten, twelve or thirteen years of imprisonment.

The IRA is ordinary people facing up against the monster of imperial power. It is part of the long tradition of physical force in Irish politics created by British militarism in Ireland.

Our fervent hope is that today's IRA volunteers will be the last of that long line of fighters for Irish freedom. By removing the causes of conflict in our country we will speed that day.

(1986, revised 1994)

The Politics of Irish Freedom

POLITICAL STATUS

If you strike at, imprison or kill us,
Out of our prisons or graves
We will still evoke a spirit that will thwart you,
And, mayhap, raise a force that will destroy you.
We defy you! Do your worst.
James Connolly, December 1914

THE MOST SUSTAINED British propaganda campaign against the IRA was organised, against the background of a protracted cessation of IRA activity, around the attempt to portray IRA members as "common criminals". Abolishing political status for prisoners charged with "scheduled" (i.e. war-related) offences, the British engaged in an intense and energetic campaign of psychological warfare, or "psy-ops". Press releases, speeches and statements from the administration referred consistently to republican leaders as "godfathers" and suchlike. Stories of corruption and gangsterism in the republican movement were invented and judiciously placed in Fleet Street. The advent of the "Peace People" in August of the same year, 1976, was well-timed to add substantially to the British propaganda effort.

In the nationalist ghettos, popular mobilisations were at an all-time low and the prevailing atmosphere was one of war-weariness. Sinn Féin, its ability to organise constantly undermined by arrest, harassment and imprisonment, was a small protest organisation and support group for the IRA and was only experiencing the first stirrings of a feeling that it needed to develop itself as a political organisation capable of intervening and mobilising on a range of issues. The Relatives Action Committee, comprising almost exclusively women from the ghettos of nationalist West Belfast, stood outside the republican movement and had only a limited capacity to mobilise support for the prisoners. The policy of "criminalisation" struck at the heart of the republican struggle, and it did so at a time when it was politically weak. The resilience of nationalist resistance and the central question of support for the IRA were to be tested over the six years from 1976 to 1981 as never before.

The republican insistence on the importance of political prisoner status has nothing to do with any contempt for the "ordinary criminals" who are so often the victims of social inequality and injustice. From Thomas Ashe to Bobby Sands, the concern has always been to assert the political nature of the struggle in which the IRA has been engaged. In September 1917, eighty-four republican prisoners went on hunger strike for political status; one of them, Thomas Ashe, leader of the Irish Republican Brotherhood, died after force feeding; political status was granted then by the British authorities and Ashe's death proved a turning-point in rallying mass support behind the demand for independence. British governments have from time to time granted and withdrawn political status. In June 1972, a hunger strike in Crumlin Road prison in Belfast led by Billy McKee resulted in the recognition of political status. Republicans were asserting the political nature of their struggle and contradicting the British attempt to suggest to the world that the political crisis in the Six Counties was not a political crisis at all, but was merely a problem with criminal elements.

The contradictions in the British position were enormous, but their access to world media and the resources they could bring to bear in the propaganda war meant that they could achieve considerable success in presenting the struggle in the

Six Counties as a species of "Mafia terrorism". When the contradictions threatened to emerge, they used various means in their continuing psy-ops war to obscure the reality of the situation. And the reality was that special laws had been enacted to counter the armed struggle of the IRA; the law was being used, to repeat Brigadier Kitson's phrase, as "just another weapon in the government's arsenal ... a propaganda cover". Special courts had been established, known as the Diplock courts, to deprive those accused of "special category" or "scheduled" offences of trial by jury. Special concentration camps had been constructed to house those convicted of special category offences, as well as those interned without trial. To turn around then and deny that these were special category prisoners was to fly in the face of logic and reality.

An essential element in Britain's criminalisation strategy was the conveyor-belt system of – to use Kitson's phrase again – "disposal of unwanted members of the public." Juryless courts were not sufficient to secure guaranteed convictions of republicans, but the systematic use of torture, primarily carried out in the purpose-built interrogation centre of Castlereagh in Belfast, ensured that detainees could be forced to sign incriminating statements. Once anyone had signed a statement, it was only a matter of passing them on to the next stage of the conveyor-belt where British judges did the job they were paid for and processed them on to the final stage, the H-Blocks of Long Kesh or the Women's Prison in Armagh.

Republicans faced an uphill battle in trying to reverse the tide of British government propaganda. Even when the facts indicated to any competent journalist that wholesale torture was producing litanies of dubious confessions, the media were determined to avoid reporting anything which might seem to support the republican position. However, when, in June 1978, Amnesty International called for a public inquiry into the "maltreatment" practised at Castlereagh RUC station, the media were at last prepared to admit that something was going on and the first chink appeared in Britain's propaganda war. Giving just seventy-eight cases of maltreatment of suspects, and estimating that between seventy percent and ninety percent of Diplock court convictions were achieved on the sole or main basis of self-incriminating statements, the Amnesty report was far from comprehensive and failed to document the extent and intensity of the torture policy.

However, weak as it was, the Amnesty report posed enough of a threat to Britain's psy-ops for the Independent Broadcasting Authority (IBA) to step in and ban a television programme on it. Later in the same year, Fr Raymond Murray and Fr Denis Faul published a far more extensive report on Castlereagh. Fr Faul was in the habit of making vitriolic attacks on republicans and received considerable media attention for these attacks; on the other hand, his and Fr Murray's collations of British brutality, such as their file on Castlereagh, were either ignored or received with hostility by the media.

However, the success of this British strategy began to falter when a police surgeon, Dr Robert Irwin, came forward to state that he had personal knowledge of at least 150 people who had been seriously injured in RUC custody at Castlereagh. Even Independent Television News could not ignore such authoritative evidence, and the British government were faced with a problem. The busy beavers of the British Army intelligence psy-ops department quickly spread rumours designed to destroy the doctor's credibility, alleging that he was seeking revenge for his wife's rape by a British soldier. The government also rushed out a report, the Bennett Report, which offered the mildest of rebukes to those engaged in the torture in Castlereagh. However, the British had suffered a setback in their propaganda war, and it was probably at this time that they began to lay plans for the use of paid informers to secure convictions.

Attention switched to the H-Blocks of Long Kesh, where republican prisoners developed their own opposition to British policy. Prisoners required under the new conditions, after 1 March 1976, to a wear prison uniform, rejected this badge of criminalisation and, not permitted to wear their own clothing, wore blankets instead. The republican attitude was well captured in Francie Brolly's song:

I'll wear no convict's uniform

Nor meekly serve my time
That England might
Brand Ireland's fight
800 years of crime.

Kieran Nugent, the first person to be sentenced for a "scheduled offence" after the arbitrarily chosen date, was first to refuse, on 14 September 1976, to wear prison clothing. "If they want me to wear a convict's uniform," he said, "they'll have to nail it to my back."

Parallel with their withdrawal of political status, the British government stepped up their propaganda campaign to portray the IRA as "godfathers of terrorism" manipulating naive teenagers into committing robberies so that these same "godfathers" could live in luxury houses and drive luxury cars. In particular, they successfully promoted to sections of the British media the image of Maire Drumm, Vice-President of Sinn Féin, as a "godmother of terrorism" and "grandmother of hate". She was shot dead in bed at the Mater Hospital in Belfast where she was being treated for cataracts.

Prison warders subjected the "blanket men" to constant harassment. In 1978, they attacked prisoners as they went to and from the latrines, kicked over chamber pots in cells and threw the contents of pots on to beds. The prisoners were forced to respond by escalating the "blanket" protest to a "no wash" stage; they refused to shave, wash or empty chamber pots. Conditions rapidly became appalling.

Cardinal Tomás Ó Fiaich visited the H-Blocks in August 1978 and gave the following description:

One could hardly allow an animal to remain in such conditions, let alone a human being. The nearest approach to it that I have ever seen was the spectacle of hundreds of homeless people living in the sewer pipes of the slums of Calcutta. The stench and the filth in some of the cells with the remains of rotten food and human excreta scattered around the walls was almost unbearable.

At the time, the prison authorities, the government and the media portrayed the "no wash" protest as arising simply from a conscious decision by the prisoners. However, I was brought

to Long Kesh, held on remand on a charge of IRA membership, and discovered for myself how the provocation by the
prison officers had brought the situation about.

Relatives – almost all women – of prisoners had, in late
April 1976, set up the Relatives Action Committee to campaign for the restoration of political status. However, within
Sinn Féin we lacked a structured national political response to
the prison crisis. This began to change after the 1978 Sinn
Féin Ard Fheis, at which Ruairi Ó Brádaigh, then President of
Sinn Féin, drew attention to the true nature of the situation
and signposted it as a priority for the movement. From that
point on, we attempted to build support on the outside for the
protest of the prisoners.

The Relatives Action Committee, which was campaigning
energetically, was a Belfast-based organisation and, while we
related to it locally, we were unable to take a national approach to it. But, recognising our considerable shortcomings
in dealing with the question, we held a national conference on
the prison issue in 1979, a conference which involved the
whole membership in detailed consideration. It was the first
time that Sinn Féin had actually sat down and looked at a
single issue, analysed it, discussed it and then embarked on
spreading the knowledge shared and the conclusions come to,
and it marked an important development for us.

We set about creating a proper POW department, which
until then had been simply a service for the prisoners, and we
began to look at the issue in terms of a political campaign. We
produced pamphlets and leaflets and we began to seek ways to
broaden out the campaign to involve other forces apart from
our own members.

The creation of the H-Block/Armagh Committee as a united
front was a very important element of the hunger strike. In
1978, we made a mistake in our approach to a conference
called to discuss the building of a broad anti-unionist front.
Lack of experience and lack of preparation on our part resulted in this Coalisland conference becoming a lost opportunity to build unity, because the price our representatives asked
for that unity was that all within the front should express sup-

port for the armed struggle of the IRA. It was a price that many of those who wished to unite in anti-unionist action were not prepared to pay. One of the problems we suffered from at that time was that we were still emerging from a basically conspiratorial type of organisation. Also, we suffered from the effects of a high rate of attrition: members who had been involved in earlier united action with the Political Hostages Release Committee (1973-74) may well have learned lessons from it, but many or most of them were in jail or for other reasons were not involved in our intervention in the Coalisland conference.

Sinn Féin was a protest movement and a movement of support for the IRA; it was, at that time, only just beginning to discuss strategy and tactics, to assess what our attitudes should be in any given circumstances. Part of the impact of our conspiratorial background was that we were temperamentally and organisationally disinclined to engage in any form of action with elements outside the movement itself. The movement had its origins in armed struggle, which had dominated to the extent of even being considered the only form of struggle; in such circumstances conspiratorial methods were, of course, essential. But what we were slowly and unevenly realising was that one could not build a political intervention on the basis of conspiratorial methods and approaches.

The IRA was constantly being denounced from all quarters and all standpoints. It was understandable that members of the movement had considerable difficulty in accepting the right of people with whom they were involved in joint action to attack the IRA. Members were increasingly coming into contact with organisations that expressed a position of "critical support" for the IRA, and any republican was bound to feel that one either supported the IRA or one did not; "critical support" seemed a contradiction in terms and a dishonest one at that. It took a maturing process on the part of republicans to appreciate that a position of critical support was better than one of not supporting at all.

By October 1979, our attitude to united action had changed dramatically and we had dropped the insistence on support for the armed struggle. At a conference in the Green Briar Hotel in Andersonstown, organised by the Relatives Action Committee, the organisations which set up the H-Block/Armagh Committee included Sinn Féin, the Irish Republican Socialist Party (IRSP), People's Democracy (PD), the Trade Union Campaign Against Repression (TUCAR) and Women Against Imperialism (WAI). There were even representatives present from the "Peace People."

While we were making attempts to organise the political campaign, the protest was continuing inside the prisons, and the IRA, for its part, was carrying out a campaign of shooting prison officers, nine being killed in 1979. To the prisoners themselves it seemed that little headway was being made, and they began to suggest that they should instigate a hunger strike. Brendan Hughes and others wrote from Long Kesh pointing out that the protest had been going on for three years and suggested that, while the older prisoners could take it, the length of the protest placed an intolerable burden on the young prisoners coming into the blocks. Eighteen- and nineteen-year-olds faced the prospect of spending ten years on the blanket and no wash protest. There was an almost parental concern on the part of the older prisoners. And they felt that the onus was on them to achieve a short-term resolution of the prison conflict. This they proposed to pursue by means of a hunger strike. We advised strongly against hunger strike and promised – perhaps somewhat rashly and naively – to achieve movement on the issue by intensifying our efforts on the outside.

Meanwhile, the crisis in the prisons intensified. In February 1980, male guards wrecked the cells of republican women prisoners at Armagh jail and beat up several of the women. Prisoners were allowed to wear their own clothes at Armagh and so there had been no "blanket" protest, but now the women responded to the attacks on them and joined the struggle of their male comrades by embarking on the "no wash" protest. In March, the British government extended the denial of political status to those prisoners who had been sentenced before 1 March 1976; there was no sign that the government was willing to take significant steps to defuse the crisis.

The H-Block/Armagh Committee worked hard to raise public consciousness and bring pressure to bear on the British government. Allied to this campaigning, we engaged in intense lobbying. But the H-Block/Armagh campaign was unable to force the British government into movement on the issue, and, in October 1980, the prisoners decided to go on hunger strike. In Sinn Féin we felt we were in no position to stop them, as a year previously we had said that we would sort it out and now they were saying to us, in the nicest possible way, that we had failed. So, we were under an obligation to support the hunger strike – we had tried our means, now the prisoners were going to try theirs.

In late October, seven H-Block prisoners started a hunger strike; in late November, they were joined by three women prisoners in Armagh and, in December, thirty more H-Block prisoners went on hunger strike. One of the seven weakened physically more rapidly than the rest: he was losing his sight and was on the verge of lapsing into a coma. The British government, despite taking a hard line of "no concessions" in public, indicated that a compromise could be reached and that a document setting out details of a settlement would be presented to the prisoners if they came off hunger strike. The hunger strikers considered the condition of Sean McKenna, who was fast approaching death, and considered the indications of movement by the government. Sean McKenna was too ill to take part in their deliberations. On the fifty-third day of the strike, 18 December, they called off the protest. Later that day, the British presented a document to the prisoners, but, meanwhile, they were presenting the world news with a story of surrender, without giving details of any compromise package. The women in Armagh refused to come off hunger strike until they were assured by us that the men had actually ended their fast.

The document did not represent the kind of settlement that the prisoners would have accepted after negotiations, but Sinn Féin tried very hard, with Bobby Sands who was OC of the

IRA in Long Kesh at the time, to work positively within the confines of this very ambiguous and undefined set of proposals. Had they possessed the political will, the British government could creditably, within the terms of their own document, have found a basis for a step-by-step implementation of the prisoners' demands, but I presume that, when they saw the decline in morale which followed the end of the hunger strike, they decided to obstruct any form of movement within the prisons. Twenty prisoners tested the willingness of the government to implement changes by coming off the "no wash" and blanket protest, and relatives brought clothes to Long Kesh, but, on 20 January 1981, the prison authorities refused to distribute the clothes to the men. The prisoners drew their conclusions and, one week later, a group of them smashed up their cells. Preparation began immediately for a second hunger strike.

Through Bobby Sands, the prisoners conveyed to the republican movement outside the prisons their absolute determination to embark on another hunger strike. In calm, reasoned correspondence, they showed that coldly and clinically they had worked out in great detail exactly how it would proceed. From the outside, we continued to advise the prisoners that their deaths would not necessarily achieve the improvements they sought. They could be dead without any advantages accruing, either in terms of prison conditions or of the overall struggle. Also, we felt that the movement could not stand another defeated hunger strike. I wrote to Bobby Sands: "Bobby, we are tactically, strategically, physically and morally opposed to a hunger strike." But, by the time we had gone through all the arguments in our correspondence, I knew that Bobby Sands was going to die.

The prison conditions could have operated as a safety valve: a sophisticated British government could have defused the situation quite easily and avoided a confrontation between itself, as unyielding colonial power, and a group of defenceless political prisoners, which is how it largely came to be seen internationally. The first hunger strike having ended, they would not have been acting under duress if they had allowed for some new arrangements on the specifics of prison conditions. But, as the prisoners pressed for a second hunger strike, they knew that this time not only would some of them have to die but also that they were engaging in a fight with the British government which now went beyond the issue of prison conditions; they were pitching themselves, with the only weapons at their command, against the imperial power. As they faced the prospect of death, they felt that the spectacle of their deaths in prison was going to be politically productive for the republican cause to which they were committed.

Hunger strike is unlike any other form of struggle. An IRA volunteer does not go out to get killed; if he or she gets killed it is because he or she makes a mistake or some other circumstance arises. But a hunger striker embarks on a process which, from day one, is designed to end in his or her death. However, when people contemplate their own deaths, there can be no guarantee that all will go according to plan, no guarantee that they will go through with it to the end. It takes a very particular kind of person to go all the way, to resist the voices in one's own head, the concern of friends and family, not to mention the pressures of the authorities, and it is extremely difficult to know, until one is staring death right in the face, whether one is that particular kind of person.

Our opposition in Sinn Féin to the hunger strike had to do partly with that difficulty, partly with the fact that close personal relationships existed between the prisoners themselves and between prisoners and republicans on the outside, and we all knew that we were entering a period of intense anguish. But, primarily, we opposed it because we did not believe that it would succeed in moving the British government. It must also be said that, in terms of the political priorities of the movement, we did not want the hunger strike. We were just beginning our attempts to remedy the political underdevelopment of the movement, trying to develop the organisation, engaging in a gradual build-up of new forms of struggle and, in particular, we were working out our strategy in relation to elections. We were well aware that a hunger strike such as was proposed would demand exclusive attention, would, in effect, hijack the struggle, and this conflicted with our sense of the political priorities of the moment.

Bobby Sands started his hunger strike on 1 March 1981, the fifth anniversary of the phasing out of political status. A large demonstration marched down the Falls Road in support of Bobby Sands and the five demands of the prisoners:

1. The right to wear their own clothing at all times.
2. Exemption from all forms of penal labour.
3. Free association with each other at all hours.
4. The right to organise their own recreational and educational programmes.
5. Full restoration of remission.

Francis Hughes joined Bobby on hunger strike on 15 March, Ray McCreesh and Patsy O'Hara a week later.

After the initial march in Belfast, the campaign of support developed slowly. It was difficult to mobilise people after the demoralising effect of the first hunger strike, and we struggled to organise even small-scale actions such as pickets. However, the calling of a by-election in Fermanagh/ South Tyrone, where sitting MP Frank Maguire, an independent nationalist, had died suddenly, provided an immediate and dynamic focus for the campaign.

Young and not so young Sinn Féin members had no experience of organising an electoral campaign, but they had plenty of energy and commitment and they combined well with independent republicans in the constituency, with Bernadette MacAliskey and with big Joe Keohane – up from Kerry to canvass support. On 9 April, Bobby Sands was elected Member of the Westminster Parliament with 30,492 votes. His victory exposed the lie that the hunger strikers – and by extension the IRA and the whole republican movement – had no popular support. The British campaign of "criminalisation," which motivated their removal of political status, had sought to portray republicans as "godfathers" operating by intimidation and as isolated fanatics. Their propaganda had now been dramatically refuted and the election of Bobby Sands resounded internationally. For many in the British Labour movement, it was their road to Damascus. It had a particular impact on British

MPs simply because of the status that the parliament at Westminster enjoys: a man had been elected on a massive popular vote who was, according to their lights, a terrorist and a criminal who was offering the people nothing.

The election victory intensified international interest in the hunger strike and uplifted absolutely the confidence and morale of republicans. There was a feeling amongst some of our members and supporters that surely the British government must yield sufficiently to bring about an end to the hunger strike. We had been challenged for years to submit ourselves to the ballot box and now we had done so. We had demonstrated massive popular support in votes; the hunger strikers had shown immense and awesome determination; we had mobilised mass demonstrations. Yet, whether we played by their rules or not, the British government, as we had feared from the outset, showed no willingness to make concessions.

However, we began to receive a stream of envoys from the Dublin government whose message was that the British would concede. Charles J. Haughey, who had recently succeeded Jack Lynch as Taoiseach and leader of Fianna Fáil, wanted to hold a general election in the Twenty-six Counties, but the hunger strike brought a degree of instability, or at least of unpredictability, which he was at pains to avoid. The envoys were well-known people in public life and they conveyed a uniform conviction that Charles Haughey was about to secure a means of resolving the hunger strike. One of the phrases used more than once was "You're pushing at an open door" – a phrase which seems almost to be his motto, since he is said to have used it in several discussions and in negotiations. All the time, the message was that the British government were about to concede the five demands. Our approach, in consultation with the prisoners, was to say, "All right, we'll believe you, but could we have that in writing, please?" And it seemed that, as soon as we said that, all agreement collapsed, and to this day I do not know how genuinely those envoys believed in the message they brought to us.

In the midst of everything, some light relief was afforded by a spokesperson for the Dublin government. He was on the phone to Owen Carron in our Belfast office, conveying the same line that Haughey's envoys had been repeating one after the other, only more so. I and a number of others were in the office at the time listening to the conversation, and we were saying to Owen to ask him this and ask him that. Eventually the government spokesperson outlined what he said was a very definite offer from the British government, and Owen asked him if he would stand over that.

"No," replied the caller, "as far as I am concerned, I never had this conversation with you."

"Well," said Owen, "you're trying to get this hunger strike stopped. There has to be something more substantial than that."

"Tell him," I said to Owen, "that you have the conversation taped."

Well, Owen did just that and the government spokesperson erupted with the most amazing tirade of bad language in which the politest epithet was "fucking bastard"!

There was something perversely funny, too, about the on-off story of the elections in the Twenty-six Counties. Every time an overture was being made to us, the Dublin media were reporting that an election was almost certain to be announced within days. And, as the overtures faded into thin air, the speculations and predictions about election dates were suddenly being dismissed in the media. The Fianna Fáil leadership understood, of course, the possible effect of the hunger strike, and they were trying to get it defused in order to have a clear run in an electoral contest.

In the course of their efforts they placed great emphasis on the International Red Cross, an organisation that had already expressed its opposition to political status. Members of Bobby Sands's family were sent for with great urgency; as they travelled south they were met at Swords in north County Dublin by a garda escort and rushed in the early hours, in fairly dramatic circumstances, to see the Taoiseach. Enormous pressure was put on them: if the prisoners, it was said, would only see the Red Cross, then the British would give in and Bobby Sands's life would be saved. After such intense pressure, and with great misgivings, Marcella Sands agreed that the Red Cross should see Bobby. But there was never any real substance to the Red Cross intervention, and they were certainly not a vehicle by means of which the five demands were going to be granted.

Margaret Thatcher maintained her inflexible approach and, despite all the earnest assurances of their envoys, the Dublin government did nothing to shift her from it.

Bobby Sands died on 5 May 1981, the sixty-sixth day of his hunger strike.

This book is not the place to record my personal feelings about the death of this friend and comrade, nor about the deaths of the other hunger strikers. Even if I was able to express those feelings adequately, I am probably still too close to them to be able to reflect upon them in tranquillity. I would not like to live through the awful experience of the hunger strike again. Scarcely a day goes by in which I do not think of the lads who died.

One hundred thousand people followed the funeral procession of Bobby Sands through West Belfast. It was an overwhelming outpouring of public grief and of identification with Bobby Sands and the IRA. Masked volunteers fired a ceremonial volley of shots over the coffin.

Francis Hughes died on 12 May.

On 19 May, the IRA killed five British soldiers with a land mine in South Armagh.

Patsy O'Hara and Ray McCreesh died on 21 May.

On 23 May, local elections took place in the Six Counties. Sinn Féin did not participate, but two IRSP and two PD members stood and were elected to Belfast city council, in the process unceremoniously dumping Gerry Fitt from the seat he had occupied for twenty-three years. Fitt had publicly called on Thatcher not to concede the five demands; now the Conservative Party's favourite Irishman, his political life in Ireland was over.

The Dublin government called a general election for 11 June; the hunger strike continued. The National H-Block/ Armagh Committee put up nine republican prisoners – four of them hunger strikers – as candidates.

The media were unanimous in writing off the chances of the prisoner candidates. Political correspondents and editors were so strongly prejudiced against the republican movement that they deserted whatever professional skills, experience and standards they may have possessed and indulged instead in an exercise in wishful thinking. They dismissed the prisoners' campaign as being insignificant and proceeded to ignore it.

So, with no media coverage apart from curt dismissals and condemnations, the campaign had its problems, but we had always received hostile media attention and we knew that there was a layer of potential support which was not dependent for its views on the media mandarins. What posed a more substantial obstacle was the fact that the dominant concerns of voters were economic and social; it was only to be expected that they would cast their ballots according to which parties and candidates seemed to offer the best policies in terms of the matters that affected their everyday lives. Our campaign offered nothing, but asked simply for support for the five demands of the prisoners in the Six Counties. The prisoners were in no position to be able to serve their constituents, so anyone voting for them would have to be content with the notion of not being represented in Leinster House – a consideration of particular significance in a state where politics was so dominated by clientilist concerns and approaches. The National H-Block/ Armagh Committee had no base of constituency workers such as provided the foundation for the electoral campaigns of the political parties; in two weeks and without prior constituency work towards an election, campaigns had to be built up and carried out in nine constituencies.

In the event, two prisoner candidates – Paddy Agnew and Kieran Doherty – were elected; a third, Joe McDonnell, was within 300 votes of being elected, and the nine together ran up a very respectable tally of 40,000 votes. It was a triumphant expression of popular support for the prisoners.

Despite the message of the elections, the new government headed by Garret FitzGerald refused, as had Haughey's government, to take the steps proposed by the National H-Block/Armagh Committee: to recall their ambassador from London; to expel the British ambassador from Dublin; end army and garda collaboration with the RUC and British army. The intransigence of Margaret Thatcher was criticised, but no measure was taken which might have caused her to modify her stance.

In late June, the British parliament changed the rules of its own "democracy" by passing what became known as the "Sands Bill", which prevented convicted felons from standing for Westminster elections. They had long demanded that we submit to the ballot box. We had done so and had been spectacularly successful. Their response was to ignore the results, refuse to recognise the MP and the movement he represented, and to change the rules to prevent a similar candidate being elected again.

Our response was to stand Owen Carron, who had been Bobby's election agent, for the new by-election in Fermanagh/South Tyrone.

Joe McDonnell died on hunger strike on 8 July.

Martin Hurson died on 13 July.

Kevin Lynch died on 1 August.

Kieran Doherty, who had been elected to Leinster House, died on 2 August.

Tom McElwee died on 8 August.

Micky Devine died on 20 August.

On the same day, Owen Carron was elected as MP for Fermanagh/South Tyrone, exceeding Bobby Sands's vote by 800.

On 3 October, the six remaining hunger strikers ended their protest. In the meantime, some of the hunger strikers had taken individual decisions to end their hunger strikes. Ten men had sacrificed their lives and massive popular support for their stand had been shown in demonstrations, funerals and elections. Things would never be the same again.

No republican will ever attach the slightest shadow of blame to those hunger strikers who individually ended their fasts. What the ten who died had done was so extraordinary that one almost needs another language in order to convey it in all its awful reality. Catholic clergy intervened with the relatives of hunger strikers to encourage them to bring about an end to the fasts by requesting medical help. But, even without their intervention, it was inevitable that some hunger strikers would eventually pull back in the face of death. I have no regrets whatsoever that some came off their hunger strikes; my regrets are reserved for those who died. My anger is reserved for the government that could quite easily have reached an honourable compromise in the face of the ultimate in selfless dedication to a cause.

Following the end of the hunger strike, adjustments in the prison regime along the lines of the five demands began to be implemented. In an unprecedented way, the prisoners had insisted on being recognised as prisoners in a war of national liberation, and their identity as such had been accepted throughout the world. Britain had been seen internationally as an intransigent force clinging to its last remnant of colonial control. The political and moral standing of Irish republicanism had never been higher.

As the hunger strikers died and as the H-Block/Armagh campaign had its impact, a process of republicanisation took place. Republicans who had done their time in prison and had subsequently dropped out of the movement – people with valuable experience and maturity – recognised that the hunger strikers were undergoing something far harder than anything they had had to suffer, and they came back to the movement. The hunger strike did away with spectator politics. When the only form of struggle being waged was armed struggle, it only needed a small number of people to engage in it. But, with the hunger strike, people could play an active role which could be as limited or as important as billposting, writing letters, or taking part in numerous forms of protest.

The IRA eased back on operations during the hunger strike. But, by the time a number of hunger strikers had died, there was a considerable popular demand for the IRA to take punitive action. Toleration of the IRA increased very significantly, as did identification with it, and this had some strange consequences. There were occasions when IRA volunteers came out on the Falls to engage in armed action, only to have to withdraw because people were crowding around, applauding and patting them on the back.

Prior to the hunger strike we had been planning a slow build-up of electoral intervention, but we were impelled very rapidly into an instant, ill-prepared electoral strategy. The stunning initial success, with the election of Bobby Sands, the election of two prisoners in the Twenty-six Counties and the increased vote in Owen Carron's election, gave many of our members the impression that elections were all about winning. It was not until our second intervention in the Twenty-six Counties, when we tried to follow up the success of our prisoner candidates, that our members began to gain some kind of perspective.

The hunger strike, and the electoral successes associated with it, changed the course of the relationship between the republican movement and British strategy, and set in train a process which continued through to the Hillsborough treaty. The perceived threat posed by republicanism since the hunger strike had led to the new, open relationship between Dublin and London, whereby the two governments now explicitly engaged in collaboration on a joint policy, the overriding aim of which was to deal with the republican threat.

In 1976, the British government tried to criminalise the republican prisoners. In 1981, the republican prisoners criminalised the British government.

(1986)

The Politics of Irish Freedom

CIVIL WAR

WILLIE SHANNON WAS a quiet man. He lived with his sister, Catherine, in the house they had been born in. Willie was seventy-three; Catherine was seventy-five. Until their retirements they had worked for two of the bigger shops in downtown Belfast.

Willie had been a storeman in Woolworth's, Catherine a buyer for one of Royal Avenue's fashion stores. Catherine could have become the buyer for an entire floor, "Silks and Lace" – Mr Bradshaw himself had offered her the position. She had seriously considered accepting his offer but, as she would conclude primly to whoever she was addressing, it wasn't to be. She also had at that time an enduring but temporary attachment to a young man who had moved to Belfast from Banbridge. He was a Protestant and boarded with friends of Willie and Catherine's mother. He was a real gentleman, Catherine would recall, a little sadly perhaps, as she reflected on what might have been. She still had a photograph upstairs somewhere of herself and Ronnie, taken the day they had gone to the Glens of Antrim.

If Willie had tales of lost love he kept them to himself. He was fond of a drink. That was one of the legacies of Woolworth's. He had learned to drink as part of his apprenticeship. At first it was a bottle of stout, carefully nursed for half an hour on pay-days in one of the snugs in Kelly's before he caught the bus home. Later, as he came out of his teens, he graduated to pints of porter and on special occasions to a half-un of Bushmills. On those nights, in the beginning, dinner was delayed until Catherine bustled in to announce that there was "no point in waiting for our Willie. He's with that crowd in the pub."

Their mother would put Willie's dinner in the oven or between two plates atop a pot of simmering water while Catherine served the rest of the family. There were two more in the family, James and Lily, who were younger than Catherine and Willie. James, to his father's delight, won a place in St Malachy's College. By this time Willie was three years in Woolworth's while Lily, the youngest, was still at St Mary's Primary School for Girls.

Then their father died. He died slowly and painfully the year James started in St Malachy's. In a way Willie became the father figure, the head of the family. He was twenty-three years old. After a while pay nights became his late nights. On those nights the family had their dinner at the normal time without him. When he returned later smelling of tobacco and Guinness and full of good humour his mother fussed around him, serving a freshly cooked dinner on a tray instead of at the table. When he had eaten his fill Willie usually slipped young James and Lily their "pay" before presenting his mother with his weekly subscription to the family's income.

"I'm away up for a wash, Ma," Willie would say, "and then I'm off for a pint. I'll be in early."

"That's all right, son," Mrs Shannon would reply. "There's a clean shirt over the chair in your room."

Willie never gave her any trouble. On Saturdays if he wasn't working he'd be off training or playing for the Rossa hurling club, then back home for a big fry of bacon, eggs, black pudding and sausages served up on a bed of soda and potato farls. If the evening was fine he and his cronies would dander up to Charlie Watter's public house at Hannahstown on the shoulder of Black Mountain. Then, as the dusk slowly settled in on the city below them and sea mists smothered Belfast Lough, they strolled back again, yarning and boasting and laughing as young men do. Sundays were family days. They went to early mass together. They ate well at noontime, a Sunday dinner which was prepared and served by Mrs Shannon and her daughters while Willie enjoyed a leisurely read of the *Sunday Press*. After dinner he and James washed up the dishes and they talked of hurling and football or Willie would quiz James good humouredly about his schoolwork. Then Mrs Shannon and the girls went off visiting their Aunt Anne or cousin Mena, James settled down in the parlour to study and Willie strolled across to the Falls Park to meet his friends. In winter the routine was changed only to suit the weather.

It went on like that for years. In time James progressed through St Malachy's and into teacher training. He got his first position as a trainee teacher in a small school outside Ardboe in County Tyrone. Two years later he married and he and his new wife moved to Strabane and from there to Glasgow in Scotland. Lily also married. She wed a schoolboy sweetheart who grew to abuse her. Their marriage soured as his drinking increased and their relationship degenerated into a behind-doors hell for them both, especially for her. Only Willie and Catherine remained the same. Their neighbours and friends, their workmates, the Rossa team, even Willie's drinking companions eventually settled into marriages, emigration and in one case the priesthood. Willie and Catherine and their mother persisted happily in routines which had constancy and reassurance, and when Mrs Shannon died Willie and Catherine carried on as they had when she was alive. They fitted into the rhythms of each other's lives. In many ways they complemented one another's lifestyles.

Willie was by now a senior storeman at Woolworth's and a committee man at the Rossa club. One of the highlights of his year was the All-Ireland Hurling Final in Dublin. He would spend the weekend there, boarding in a bed-and-breakfast house close to Mountjoy Square. It had been part of his annual pilgrimage for twenty years, and on the Saturday he went there straight from the early train. He was treated like a king and revelled in the attention he received. Then, with a jaunty air he was off to tea in Bewley's, a browse along the bookshops on the quays, a steak dinner in Wynn's before strolling up to the GPO to meet the Rossa crowd at Nelson's Pillar. They all adjourned for a few pints and a sing-song in their hotel. No matter who won the match the weekend was always a triumph, and Catherine got a full blow-by-blow account of the game for nights afterwards. She knew every ween and turn of Willie. Sometimes she would tease him gently as he enthused about a particular action on the field or as he berated some player's incompetence. She, for her part, seemed content with her small circle of friends, an occasional small sherry and a regular trip to the theatre.

She went to the Lough Derg pilgrimage every year; that was her All-Ireland. In 1967 she retired from Bradshaw's. After a month of boredom around the house she got involved with the local Ladies' Co-operative Guild. Soon she was enclosed in its circle of activities.

When Willie retired his workmates did a whip-round and presented him with one of the new black-and-white television sets. Willie was delighted. He spent the first few weeks of his retirement between the television set and the Falls Park. There was some sporadic trouble in Belfast city centre that year. Willie and Catherine paid little heed to it. Indeed, if they hadn't had the television set they might not even have known about it. In the first week of October they went on a parish pilgrimage to Rome. It was there on the night of 6 October that Willie saw television coverage of the RUC's attack on the Civil Rights march in Derry the previous day. He was in a small bar when the strangely familiar uniforms rioted across a news programme. He wasn't sure what it was or where exactly in Ireland it happened. In fact, he was slightly puzzled and then embarrassed when the barman drew his attention to the television in the corner of the room. "You Irish, you zed? Si? Look!" he pointed excitedly at the screen. When Willie returned to their hotel the group was talking about the trouble. One woman had phoned her sister in Derry. Fr Crummey organised the phone call. The news wasn't good, but the slight shadow it cast over their visit evaporated the following morning in the Roman sunshine.

"Isn't it wonderful how warm this place is on an autumn

day?" Catherine remarked to Willie as they lunched in a small restaurant in the Via Flavia, a narrow street behind their hotel.

"Indeed it is," Willie agreed. "The Falls Road was never like this."

"You leave the Falls Road alone," Catherine replied.

The slight hint of an edge on her voice puzzled him but he took it in good part. Only when they were home again days later did he remember that little undercurrent of tension. It came back into her voice as they listened to a television debate between civil rights leaders and a Stormont government minister.

"I think they are only interested in creating trouble. Things aren't as bad as all that," she sniffed.

"Well, they're not that great either," Willie answered. "It's good that somebody's standing up for us."

"They're not standing up for me," Catherine retorted. "I'm quite capable of doing that for myself, thank you very much. There'll be no good come out of it. You mark my words. They are only in it for what they can get out of it for themselves. And the young people have no sense anyway. It'll be long and many a day before I'd need any of that crowd to help me. There'll be no good'll come out of their rabble-rousing."

Willie was surprised by her tone. They had never discussed politics before. He wasn't sure if Catherine even bothered to vote. He always voted but more out of some sense of responsibility than any ideological commitment. Of course he always voted anti-unionist. And, he realised to his surprise as he reflected on Catherine's outburst, he had never told anybody about his voting habits. Now, with time on his hands, he was discovering that his attitudes were more questioning than they had been before. There was so much happening every other day, between protests and counter-protests, statements and counter-statements, all transmitted on the black-and-white television or reported in the morning paper. Willie found himself becoming absorbed in the political excitement of the period. At times he found it difficult to comprehend how Catherine avoided what was happening outside. Whenever he tried to talk to her about whatever issue was dominating that day's headlines she refused to be drawn into conversation. Things came to a head between them one morning. A man had been killed in an RUC baton charge the night before. The first Willie knew of the incident was at breakfast when Catherine flung the *Irish News* across the table at him.

"I suppose you and your friends are satisfied now," she cried at him.

He was dumbfounded at first and then, as he read the lead story, anger replaced his bewilderment. Crumpling the paper in his hand he followed Catherine into the scullery where she had retreated after her outburst.

"What do you mean?" he confronted her. "What do you mean, am I satisfied? Them bastards kill a man and you give off to me? What do you mean, woman? What's in your head? I suppose it was that poor man's fault that they killed him?"

Catherine said nothing. She turned her back to him and adjusted the heat under the teapot on the stove. He flung the newspaper at her in anger.

"Don't ever say anything like that to me ever again as long as you live, Catherine. If that's all you think about the situation then keep your thoughts to yourself. And don't worry about breakfast for me. I'm going out!"

He didn't return until nightfall, and although she had kept a nervous vigil at the parlour window awaiting his return, she said nothing as he stumbled his drunken, hurt, mumbling way upstairs to bed. The following day she told him that it might be better if they didn't discuss politics in the house. He said nothing. The next morning he went to the funeral of the man who had been killed in the baton charge. He said nothing about this to Catherine and soon things in the house returned to the way they had always been, as if nothing had happened. But as their effort to avoid contentious topics of conversation intensified indoors, while the troubles outside continued to escalate, the relationship between brother and sister slowly turned into one of long, lonely silences. They were so much a part of each other's routine that the rituals remained unchanged, but as the awkwardness between them grew so did

Willie's feelings of resentment and Catherine's sense of outrage. Gradually the warmth they felt for each other died. It was, as Willie remarked to himself one day, a bit like the cold war.

Yet he could not bring himself to make the peace: Catherine was demanding too high a price. He was prepared to compromise, to meet her half-way, but he was not prepared to surrender. It was she who was attacking him. Even a careless word from him about some incident or other was greeted by a scornful "You know I don't want to know that" from Catherine. Wounded, he would withdraw and a long, brittle silence would follow.

When he got drunk, which was seldom enough, then the resentment flowed out of him in an ugly, frustrated and angry torrent. He'd arrive home late and stumble noisily and clumsily into the quiet, waiting house. At first she used to scold him, rising from the chair where she waited anxiously for him to return, but his fury was so intense that she became a little frightened of him. She still waited up but now she held her tongue. Even then, in his drunken slyness he realised the power he had over her, and poured out his disgust at her, goaded to louder outbursts by her silent refusal to be drawn by his insults.

The next day he would be like a contrite child and for a while it would be like old times as he tried to please her by doing little things about the house and she slowly thawed, despite herself, in the face of his charm. At these times even the television news failed to divide them as they made a special effort not to let outsiders destroy them, but such was the daily controversy which swirled all around and so entrenched were they both in their views that such respites were not only infrequent, they were also short-lived. It was during just such a period, as they sat beside a roaring fire, watching the Sunday film on television, that a newsflash invaded their cozy contentment. Like the broadcast three years earlier in Rome the news this time, at first vague but becoming clearer and more deadly by the hour, was also about Derry.

They sat, numbed as the enormity of it was broadcast into

their sitting-room. It was Catherine who eventually spoke.

"I'm sorry, Willie."

He made no reply.

"Willie ..."

"I'm surprised you're not applauding," he exclaimed savagely. The wounded shock on her face halted him for a second but even then his pain was too great for him to contain.

"That's what comes from your creeping-Jesus refusal to face up to the way things are. Bloody British soldiers shooting our people down like dogs and all you can say is you're sorry! What are you sorry for? You've done nothing wrong."

He was on his feet, glowering at her. She looked up at him. Pain and disbelief was etched across her face. For a moment their gazes met, bewildered and hurt, an old man and an old woman in their own living-room, brother and sister, spinster and bachelor, life-long friends, and then slowly before his eyes she slumped from her chair with a little sigh and sprawled awkwardly at his feet.

She was buried on the same day as the dead of Bloody Sunday. Willie lived on, on his own after that. He retained his interest in politics. Indeed despite his age he attended the litany of local protests all that spring and early summer, yet he himself knew that the fire inside him had died. His sense of outrage had gone. He was, as he acknowledged to himself, only marking time. He died in August in the Royal Victoria Hospital while being treated for pneumonia. The hospital chaplain anointed him just before he passed away. As he did so the priest thought he heard him whisper something.

"What's that, Willie?" he asked.

"I'm sorry, Catherine," Willie sighed. "I'm sorry."

(1992)

The Street and other stories

THE STREET

CASTLE STREET WAS quiet. Mid-morning sunshine warmed the pavements and the shopfronts and created a pleasant, half-asleep, half-awake spring mood about the street. Sammy McArdle stood at the doorway of the bank. He had started as security man at the bank at the age of sixty; he was now in his second year in the job, the first regular, full-time employment he had ever had. He checked customers' bags and parcels as they entered the bank; it wasn't strenuous work and he enjoyed it.

Castle Street was a short, bustling street of high buildings, pubs, clothes-shops, arcades, a bank, big stores and a fish and poultry shop, and most days street traders hawked their wares on the side of the street. By now the usual opening rush of early morning customers was over. Sammy hadn't checked any of them: after all, they had been coming to the bank for years, since before he had ever graced its portals. On Wednesdays like this there were few strangers or new customers for him to scrutinise.

Jimmy from Eastwood's bookies had given him a tip for the big race and Big Gillen had stood for a minute or two with his bags of loose change, chatting about his bad back and the poor trade. Since then no one else had come Sammy's or the bank's way. Not that he minded: it would have been difficult to mind anything, he mused, on such a fine day. Even the British Army foot-patrols didn't bother him.

From the other side of the street Buster Traynor, the street-sweeper, shouted a greeting to him.

"What about ye?"

"Dead on," Sammy replied, stepping out from the shade of the bank's doorway. "It's a great day, isn't it?"

"Gorgeous," Buster agreed, leaning, arms crossed, on his brush. "It's well for you, nothing to do but to stand about all day enjoying the sunshine."

"Aye," Sammy laughed, "it's desperate isn't it?"

"And you're getting paid for it too," Buster continued. "Some people have all the luck." He started brushing the street again.

"G'wan out of that with you," Sammy chuckled. "You neither work nor want. A day's work would kill you, so it would."

"That's all you know. You and Cloop have a lot in common." Buster gestured down to the corner.

Sammy gave a wry smile: Cloop was the bane of his life. "You really know how to hurt me, don't you?" he chided.

"See you later," Buster smiled. "I can't hang about here all day. I'll send Cloop up to keep you company."

"Well dare ya," Sammy warned.

Buster continued on his way, pushing his brush and little pile of rubbish in front of him.

Sammy gazed down the street towards Cloop, who was sitting on the pavement at the corner of Chapel Lane. Basking in the sun, his back against the wall, face tilted towards the sky, he had one leg beneath him and the other stretched across the pavement so that pedestrians had to make a detour around him and his strategically placed cap. Cloop was a wino and he and Sammy confronted one another whenever Cloop set up his pitch outside the bank. Sammy was under strict orders to shift all loiterers. Usually Cloop complied with his request to move along but occasionally he was abusive, especially if there was anyone watching or if he was egged on. Sammy had given him a few bob once to bribe him to leave: the next day a queue of winos had settled outside the bank. That was the day Sammy's patience with Cloop ran out.

Sammy was a decent man. Life had not been good to him but he tolerated its inadequacies. He was by temperament a patient, pleasant, easy-going Christian. He had learned through a lifetime of little indignities to be dignified, to turn the other cheek, to endure. But he had rarely been satisfied; that had come belatedly to him with his job at the bank. It wasn't the wages: they were meagre, but his needs were humble enough anyway. No, he just liked being employed. He liked the responsibility, the company, the sense of well-being, of belonging; he liked having something to do. He liked Castle Street, especially on mornings like this. But he resented Cloop. And now Buster was going to wind Cloop up and he was going to be tormented for the rest of the day.

Sammy glowered.

"Morning, Mr McArdle." It was Mrs Murphy from the holy shop in Chapel Lane.

"Morning, Mrs Murphy."

"You don't look a bit well," she observed.

"Aw, nawh, I'm grand," he said quickly. "I was just thinking to myself about something. I'm great really."

"That's good," she concluded. "Such a fine morning. It's too good to be wasted worrying, Sammy. I'm glad you're okay." She went into the bank.

"Thanks, Mrs Murphy," Sammy called after her. "She's right you know," he muttered to himself. "Worrying is a waste of time." He peered cautiously down the street.

Buster had gone round the corner without disturbing Cloop. Sammy brightened visibly, so much so that Mrs Murphy remarked on the change as she left the bank.

"I'm glad you're back to yourself," she saluted him. "Keep your chin up."

"Right, Mrs Murphy. Good luck to you."

"And to you too, Sammy. Remember, there's always somebody worse off. Look at poor oul' Cloop."

Sammy's face darkened. He looked towards Cloop, who waved cheerfully back at him. Sammy gazed past him, then averted his head and looked down Royal Avenue. When he looked up Castle Street again Cloop had shifted his position.

He was moving slowly, still seated on one leg, edging himself laboriously down towards the bank. When he saw Sammy looking at him again he stopped and waved.

Sammy's face remained impassive. "It's almost lunchtime," he thought to himself. "The worst possible time." Lunchtime was when Mr Timmons, the manager, left the bank. He would be going out the door just as Cloop arrived. Sammy sighed. It was just his luck, he thought uncharacteristically; it was going to be one of those days. Such a lovely day, too. He glared again at Cloop, who was slowly pushing himself into an upright position. He gestured to Sammy, then resumed his slow passage towards the bank. Sammy clasped his hands together in exasperation; he scowled down at the pavement and swung his hands apart. "Ah well," he thought, "nothing else for it. I'd better head him off."

Cloop was now almost at the bank's front window, but he stopped and leaned against the wall as Sammy walked slowly towards him.

"Mr McArdle," Cloop greeted him. "Mr McArdle, I was just sitting down there enjoying the sun."

Sammy glared sullenly at him.

"I was just relaxing there with not a care in the world."

Sammy stopped before him.

"And I looked up here and here you were all on your own-i-oh. Now don't worry," he said, anticipating Sammy's next move. "Don't worry, Mr McArdle, you won't have to move me today. Nawh, that's not why I came up here. You just looked so alone and so worried lookin'." Cloop shoved his hand into the pocket of his tattered coat. "So I just said to myself: it's not fair me sitting here without a worry in the world and Mr McArdle up there like all belonging to him was dead. So I brought you up a wee smoke, so I did." Cloop drew his hand from his pocket. His fingers clutched the butt of a cigarette and a whole one. He put the butt in his mouth and pointed the other one at Sammy.

"Here you are now. Give's a light and I'll leave you in peace."

Sammy looked at him. He looked past the cigarettes and

Cloop's outstretched hand; he looked beyond his unshaved face. He looked along Castle Street and sighed. In the sunlight a shop window winked at him.

"Okay, Mr McArdle?" Cloop asked. "You really shouldn't let things get you down. Especially on such a nice day. Here, have a smoke."

(1992)

The Street and other stories

DOES HE TAKE SUGAR?

TOM MACAULEY, YOUNGEST son of Martha and Joe Mac-Auley, was nineteen years old. Joe worked in the office of a Derry shirt factory and he, Martha and Tom lived not far from the Strand Road.

Tom, who had Down's Syndrome, had been born ten years after his four brothers and three sisters, and when they had all left home to get married or to seek work abroad Tom had remained to become the centre of his parents' lives. Already in her late forties when Tom had been born, Martha's health was starting to fail by the time he had reached his teens. But when he wasn't at school Tom rarely left his mother's side.

"Poor Mrs MacAuley," the neighbours would say when she and young Tom passed by. "She never gets a minute to herself. That young Tom is a handful, God look to him. Morning, noon and night he's always with his mother. She never gets a break."

Tom attended a special school and when he was sixteen, the year his father retired from the shirt factory, he graduated to a special project at a day centre on Northland Road. A bus collected him each morning at the corner and brought him back each evening. His father escorted him to the bus and was there again in the evening faithfully awaiting his return.

Tom loved the day centre. He called it work and it was work of a sort; each week he was paid £3.52 for framing pictures. He also had many new friends and was constantly falling in and out of love with a number of girls who worked with him. Geraldine was his special favourite but he was forced to admire her from afar; she never gave any indication that she was even aware of his existence. His relationships with the others never really flourished, but at least with them he wasn't as invisible as he was with Geraldine. He could enjoy their company and one of them, Margaret Begley, wasn't a bit backward about letting him know that she had a crush on him. Tom gave her no encouragement: his heart was with Geraldine. Anyway, he was too shy for Margaret's extrovert ways.

Tom's parents knew nothing of all his feelings towards the girls, but they knew that the work was good for him. At times he would return home excited or annoyed by something which had occurred at the day centre, and when this happened Martha knew the instant she saw him. When he was excited, perhaps from having had a trip to the pictures or when his supervisor praised his work in front of everyone, he radiated happiness. When he was annoyed, he stammered furiously.

On these occasions he rarely volunteered information and Martha and Joe soon learned that it was useless to question him. Under interrogation he would remain stubbornly non-committal and if pressed he became resentful and agitated. Left to his own devices, though, he would reveal, in his own time, usually by his own series of questions, the source of his discontent. Tom's questions followed a pattern.

"MMMM Ma," he would say, "DDD Does Mick Mick Mickey BBBBradley know how how how to ddddrive a ca-caacar?"

"No, son, Mickey wouldn't be allowed to drive a car."

"Hhhhehe says he cacacan."

"He's keeping you going, Tom."

"If we had a cacacar could I drdrdrive it?"

"Of course," Martha would smile. "Your Daddy would teach you."

"Right," Tom would say, and that would be that.

Work gave Tom a small but important measure of independence and his experiences at work rarely impinged on his home life. Martha and Joe's relationship with him remained largely as it had been before. They still never permitted him to go off alone, except in his own street. Tom didn't seem to mind. He collected postcards. When he was at home he spent most of his time counting and recounting, sorting and resorting his collection in scrapbooks and old shoeboxes and writing down their serial numbers in jotters which his father bought him.

He also did small chores around the house. It was his job to keep the coal-bucket filled and he always cleared the table after dinner. Occasionally he helped with the dishes and he fetched dusters and polish or things like that for his mother when she did her cleaning. Most mornings he also collected the paper in the corner shop while his mother prepared the breakfast. Seamus Hughes the shopkeeper always delighted him with his greeting.

"Ah, Tom, you'll be wanting to catch up on the news. Here's your paper."

Tom would be especially happy if there was anyone else in the shop to hear Seamus's remarks. He would beam with pleasure and mumble his red-faced and affirmative response.

His father and he went for walks regularly every Saturday and Sunday afternoon and Tom loved these outings. His usual facial expression was blandly benign but when he smiled he smiled with his whole face, and during the walks with his father the smile rarely left him. Everyone knew the pair and had a friendly greeting for them both. Usually they walked out the line where the doggymen exercised their greyhounds, and on one memorable Sunday they took the back road across the border and went the whole way as far as Doherty's Fort at the Grianán of Aileach in Donegal. The following day was the only occasion on which Tom missed work; he was so tired after their outing that Martha couldn't rouse him from the bed. His father joked with him about it afterwards.

At Christmas there was a pantomime at Tom's work. Tom had a small part as Aladdin's servant. All the parents and families along with various agencies and local dignitaries were invited to the centre for an open night. Samples of handicrafts were on display and photographs of their projects adorned the walls. On the night of the performance when the audience were milling around in the main corridor sipping tea and lemonade while they waited for the show to start in the main hall, one of Tom's workmates, a young man from the Brandywell called Hughie, suddenly started yelling and bawling.

At first everyone just looked away and pretended that nothing was amiss but as Hughie's parents failed to pacify him the commotion increased. One of the supervisors intervened but that only seemed to make Hughie worse. Apparently this was the first year that Hughie had not had a part in the pantomime. When rehearsals had begun earlier in the year he had insisted that he didn't want a part. Now when he saw the gathering and the excitement of his friends as they prepared for the evening's performance and when it was too late for him to do anything, he had changed his mind. He wanted to be in the pantomime and nothing would satisfy him except that.

His parents were distracted and as Hughie continued his bad-tempered hysterics their consternation spread to the audience. Some of the pantomime players came from the big hall, where they were nervously finalising last-minute arrangements, to see what the racket was about. Tom was among them, dressed in an oriental-type outfit made by his mother from old curtains and an old dressing-gown.

No one paid much attention when Tom left his costumed friends and made his way through the throng to where Hughie stood bawling in the corner, surrounded by his distraught parents and two of the day centre supervisors. Then to everyone's surprise Tom intervened.

"Excuse me," he said to Hughie's parents, and without waiting for a reply he pushed his way past them before stopping with his face close to Hughie's.

"Shughie, ddddddon't be be ge ge gett-ing on like th th this," he stammered.

Hughie ignored him. Tom looked at his friend beseechingly. Hughie still ignored him and carried on bawling.

Tom leaned over and whispered in Hughie's ear, then stopped and looked at him again. Hughie continued to bawl but less stridently now. Tom leaned over and whispered again in his ear. Hughie stopped. Tom looked at him once more.

"All rrrright?" he asked.

Hughie nodded.

Tom turned and walked back to his friends. As they watched him Martha and Joe were as pleased as Punch, especially when Tom's supervisor came over and shook their hands.

"That's a great lad you have there. He's a credit to the two of you the way he handled Hughie."

After the pantomime Hughie's father was equally lavish in his praise.

"I'm really grateful for the way your Tom quietened down our Hughie. It's wonderful the way they can communicate with each other in a way that the rest of us can't. Your Tom's the proof of that. The way he was able to get through to our Hughie. None of the rest of us could do that. It never fails to amaze me. Tom's a great lad."

On the way home that night Joe asked Tom what he had said to Hughie. Tom was pleased with all the attention he was receiving but he was non-committal about his conversation with Hughie. When Joe pressed the issue Tom got a little edgy. Martha squeezed Joe's arm authoritatively.

"Leave things as they are," she whispered.

Joe nudged Tom.

"I'm not allowed to ask you anything else!" he joked.

Tom smiled at him.

"That's good," he said.

Over the Christmas holidays all Tom's brothers and sisters visited home. Tom especially enjoyed his nephews and nieces and the way they brought the house alive with their shouting and laughing, crying and fighting.

A few days after Christmas Martha's sister Crissie came to visit them as she always did. During her visits Tom spent a lot of time in his room sorting his postcards. He was in the living-room when Aunt Crissie arrived – his mother insisted on that – but after the flurry of greetings had subsided Tom made his

escape. A retired schoolteacher and a spinster, the oldest of
Martha's sisters, Aunt Crissie tended to fuss around him, and
this made him uneasy. Joe shared his son's unease in the presence of Aunt Crissie, thinking her a busy-body but all the
same marvelling at her energy and clearness of mind.

"I hope I'm as sprightly as that when I get to her age," he
would say to whoever was listening.

Crissie hugged Tom and held him at arms' length for a full
inspection. "Tommy's looking great, Martha," she said.

She always called Tom Tommy. He shifted from foot to foot
and gave her his best grin.

"Thhhh tank th thank thank you, Aunt CiciciCrisssssie."

"I've-brought-you-a-little-something-for-your-stocking,
Tommy."

When Aunt Crissie spoke to Tom directly she did so very
slowly. She also raised her voice a little. She always brought
him two pairs of socks.

"Thhhh tank th thank thank you, Aunt CiciciCrisssssie."

"Away you go now, Tom," his mother said.

Tom and his father usually went off together for a while
before their dinner, the highlight of Aunt Crissie's visit. By
that time Crissie and Martha were in full flow on a year of
family gossip. This continued through the dinner of tasty
Christmas Day leftovers until, appetite and curiosity satisfied,
Aunt Crissie turned her attention again to Tom. She had
poured the tea and was handing around the milk and sugar.

"Does he take sugar?" she asked Joe.

"Do you, Tom?" Joe re-directed the question to his son.

"Nnno, Da," Tom replied in surprise.

Martha looked sharply at her husband. Aunt Crissie saw the
glance and apologised quickly.

"I'm-sorry, Tommy. Of-course-you-don't. I-remember-now.
Your-mother-tells-me-you're-getting-on-very-well-at-the-day-
centre."

"Aaayye, I am."

Joe intervened. He was anxious to smooth things over.

"Tom was in the pantomime. It was a great night. They've a
great team of people involved with that centre. And all the

252

kids love it. Tom really likes it down there. And he has plenty
of friends."

"It must be very rewarding work for the people involved,"
Crissie suggested. She, too, was anxious that the awkwardness
be forgotten.

"Tom's supervisor says she wouldn't work with any other
kids," Martha said. "We were talking to her after the pantomime and she said that Downs Syndrome cases are the easi-
est to work with."

"They retain the innocence and trust that the rest of us
lose," said Joe, "and you know something, they are well able
to communicate with one another in a way the rest of us will
probably never understand. Isn't that right, Tom?"

Tom looked up from his tea and smiled blankly at his father.

"Wait till you hear this, Crissie," Joe continued. "Before the
pantomime another lad, Hughie, a friend of Tom's, threw a
tantrum and the only one who could calm him down was
Tom. It just goes to show you. Nobody else could get through
to him; then Tom spoke quietly to him and the next thing
Hughie was as right as rain. Isn't that right, Martha?"

Martha took up the story from there and recounted the pantomime night episode. When she was finished Aunt Crissie
turned to Tom.

"Well done, young man. It's wonderful that you were able
to do that. What did you say, by the way?"

Joe chuckled.

"That's something we'll never know. Eh, Tom?"

"Och, Tommy, you can tell us," Aunt Crissie persisted.

Tom lowered his head and shifted self-consciously in his
chair.

"C'mon, Tom," his mother encouraged him.

He looked up at them. Aunt Crissie was smiling at him.

"Is he going to say something?" she asked.

Tom looked towards her. He was frowning. Then slowly his
face smiled as it was taken over by one of his huge grins. He
looked at his father, as if for encouragement, before turning
again to Aunt Crissie.

"I told him I would knock his balls in if he didn't stop messing about," he said slowly and without a single stutter. "Shughie'sss spoiled. All he needed was a gggood dig. That's all I sa sa said to hhhiim him."

Martha, Joe and Aunt Crissie were speechless. Tom looked at each of them in turn, a little hesitantly at first. Then as his father winked slowly at him the bland, benign expression returned to his face. Joe started to laugh.

Tom's anxiety vanished and his face lit up at the sound. He looked again at his mother and Aunt Crissie and began to laugh also as he watched the looks on their faces. He turned again to his father and winked slowly in return.

(1992)

The Street and other stories

254

A Good Confession

THE CONGREGATION SHUFFLED its feet. An old man spluttered noisily into his handkerchief, his body racked by a spasm of coughing. He wiped his nose wearily and returned to his prayers. A small child cried bad-temperedly in its mother's arms. Embarrassed, she released him into the side aisle of the chapel where, shoes clattering on the marble floor, he ran excitedly back and forth. His mother stared intently at the altar and tried to distance herself from her irreverent infant. He never even noticed her indifference; his attention was consumed by the sheer joy of being free and soon he was trying to cajole another restless child to join him in the aisle. Another wave of coughing wheezed through the adult worshippers. As if encouraged by such solidarity the old man resumed his catarrhal cacophony.

The priest leaned forward in the pulpit and directed himself and his voice towards his congregation. As he spoke they relaxed as he knew they would. Only the children, absorbed in their innocence, continued as before. Even the old man, by some superhuman effort, managed to control his phlegm.

"My dear brothers and sisters," the priest began. "It is a matter of deep distress and worry to me, and I'm sure to you also, that there are some Catholics who have so let the eyes of their soul become darkened that they no longer recognise sin as sin."

He paused for a second or so to let his words sink in. He

was a young man, not bad looking in an ascetic sort of a way, Mrs McCarthy thought, especially when he was intense about something, as he was now. She was in her usual seat at the side of the church and as she waited for Fr Burns to continue his sermon she thought to herself that it was good to have a new young priest in the parish.

Fr Burns cleared his throat and continued.

"I'm talking about the evil presence we have in our midst and I'm asking you, the God-fearing people of this parish, to join with me in this Eucharist in praying that we loosen from the neck of our society the grip which a few have tightened around it and from which we sometimes despair of ever being freed."

He stopped again momentarily. The congregation was silent: he had their attention. Even the sounds from the children were muted.

"I ask you all to pray with me that eyes that have become blind may be given sight, consciences that have become hardened and closed may be touched by God and opened to the light of His truth and love. I am speaking of course of the men of violence." He paused, leant forward on arched arms, and continued.

"I am speaking of the IRA and its fellow-travellers. This community of ours has suffered much in the past. I know that. I do not doubt but that in the IRA organisation there are those who entered the movement for idealistic reasons. They need to ask themselves now where that idealism has led them. We Catholics need to be quite clear about this."

Fr Burns sensed that he was losing the attention of his flock again. The old man had lost or given up the battle to control his coughing. Others shuffled uneasily in their seats. A child shrieked excitedly at the back of the church. Some like Mrs McCarthy still listened intently and he resolved to concentrate on them.

"Membership, participation in or co-operation with the IRA and its military operations is most gravely sinful. Now I know that I am a new priest here and some of you may be wondering if I am being political when I say these things. I am not. I am preaching Catholic moral teaching and I can only say that those who do not listen are cutting themselves off from the community of the Church. They cannot sincerely join with their fellow Catholics who gather at mass and pray in union with the whole Church. Let us all as we pray together, let us all resolve that we will never cut ourselves off from God in this way and let us pray for those who do."

Fr Burns paused for the last time before concluding.

"In the name of the Father and the Son and the Holy Ghost."

Just after Communion and before the end of the mass there was the usual trickling exit of people out of the church. When Fr Burns gave the final blessing the trickle became a flood. Mrs McCarthy stayed in her seat. It was her custom to say a few prayers at Our Lady's altar before going home. She waited for the crowd to clear.

Jinny Blake, a neighbour, stopped on her way up the aisle and leaned confidentially towards her. "Hullo, Mrs McCarthy," she whispered reverently, her tone in keeping with their surroundings.

"Hullo, Jinny. You're looking well, so you are."

"I'm doing grand, thank God. You're looking well yourself. Wasn't that new wee priest just lovely. And he was like lightning too. It makes a change to get out of twelve o'clock mass so quickly."

"Indeed it does," Mrs McCarthy agreed as she and Jinny whispered their goodbyes.

By now the chapel was empty except for a few older people who stayed behind, like Mrs McCarthy, to say their special prayers or to light blessed candles. Mrs McCarthy left her seat and made her way slowly towards the small side altar. She genuflected awkwardly as she passed the sanctuary. As she did so the new priest came out from the sacristy. He had removed his vestments and dressed in his dark suit he looked slighter than she had imagined him to be when he had been saying mass.

"Hullo," he greeted her.

"Hullo, Father, welcome to Saint Jude's."

His boyish smile made her use of the term "father" seem incongruous.

"Thank you," he said.

"By the way, Father ..."

The words were out of her in a rush before she knew it.

"I didn't agree with everything you said in your sermon. Surely if you think those people are sinners you should be welcoming them into the Church and not chasing them out of it."

Fr Burns was taken aback. "I was preaching Church teaching," he replied a little sharply.

It was a beautiful morning. He had been very nervous about the sermon, his first in a new parish. He had put a lot of thought into it and now when it was just over him and his relief had scarcely subsided he was being challenged by an old woman.

Mrs McCarthy could feel his disappointment and resentment. She had never spoken like this before, especially to a priest. She retreated slightly. "I'm sorry, Father," she said uncomfortably, "I just thought you were a bit hard." She sounded apologetic. Indeed, as she looked at the youth of him she regretted that she had opened her mouth at all.

Fr Burns was blushing slightly as he searched around for a response.

"Don't worry," he said finally, "I'm glad you spoke your mind. But you have to remember I was preaching God's word and there's no arguing with that."

They walked slowly up the centre aisle towards the main door. Fr Burns was relaxed now. He had one hand on her elbow and as he spoke he watched her with a faint little smile on his lips. Despite herself she felt herself growing angry at his presence. Who was this young man almost steering her out of the chapel? She hadn't even been at Our Lady's altar yet.

"We have to chose between our politics and our religion," he was saying.

"That's fair enough, Father, as far as it goes, but I think it's wrong to chase people away from the Church," she began.

"They do that themselves," he interrupted her.

She saw that he still had that little smile. They were almost at the end of the aisle. She stopped sharply, surprising the priest as she did, so that he stopped also and stood awkwardly with his hand still on her elbow.

"I'm sorry, Father, I'm not going out yet."

It was his turn to be flustered and she noticed with some satisfaction that his smile had disappeared. Before he could recover she continued, "I still think it's wrong to exclude people. Who are any of us to judge anyone, to say who is or who isn't a good Catholic, or a good Christian for that matter? I know them that lick the altar rails and, God forgive me, they wouldn't give you a drink of water if you were dying of the thirst. No, Father, it's not all black and white. You'll learn that before you're much older."

His face reddened at her last remark.

"The Church is quite clear in its teaching on the issue of illegal organisations. Catholics cannot support or be a part of them."

"And Christ never condemned anyone," Mrs McCarthy told him, as intense now as he was.

"Well, you'll have to choose between your politics and your religion. All I can say is if you don't agree with the Church's teaching, then you have no place in this chapel."

It was his parting shot and with it he knew he had bested her. She looked at him for a long minute in silence so that he blushed again, thinking for a moment that she was going to chide him, maternally perhaps, for being cheeky to his elders. But she didn't. Instead she shook her elbow free of his hand and walked slowly away from him out of the chapel. He stood, until he had recovered his composure, then he too walked outside. To his relief she was nowhere to be seen.

When Mrs McCarthy returned home her son, Harry, knew something was wrong, and when she told him what had happened he was furious. She had to beg him not to go up to the chapel there and then.

"He said what, Ma? Tell me again!"

She started to recount her story.

"No, not that bit. I'm not concerned about all that. It's the end bit I can't take in. The last thing he said to you. Tell me that again?"

"He said if I didn't agree then I had no place in the chapel," she told him again, almost timidly.

"The ignorant-good-for-nothing wee skitter," Harry fumed, pacing the floor. Mrs McCarthy was sorry she had told him anything. "I'll have to learn to bite my tongue," she told herself. "If I'd said nothing to the priest none of this would have happened." Harry's voice burst in on her thoughts.

"What gets me is that you reared nine of us. That's what gets me! You did your duty as a Catholic mother and that's the thanks you get for it. They've no humility, no sense of humanity. Could he not see that you're an old woman."

"That's nothing to do with it," Mrs McCarthy interrupted him sharply.

"Ma, that's everything to do with it! Can you not see that? If he had been talking to me I could see the point, but you? All your life you've did your best and he insults you like that! He must have no mother of his own. That's all they're good for: laying down their petty little rules and lifting their collections and insulting the very people ..."

"Harry, that's enough."

The weariness in her tone stopped him in mid-sentence.

"I've had enough arguing to do me for one day," she said. "You giving off like that is doing me no good. Just forget about it for now. And I don't want you doing anything about it; I'll see Fr Burns again in my own good time. But for now, I'm not going to let it annoy me any more."

But it did. It ate away at her all day and when she retired to bed it was to spend a restless night with Fr Burns' words turning over again and again in her mind.

Choose between your politics and your religion. Politics and religion. If you don't accept the Church's teachings you've no place in the chapel. No place in the chapel.

The next day she went to chapel as was her custom but she didn't go at her usual time and she was nervous and unsettled within herself all the time she was there. Even Our Lady couldn't settle her. She was so worried that Fr Burns would arrive and that they would have another row that she couldn't concentrate on her prayers. Eventually it became too much for her and she left by the side door and made her way home again, agitated and in bad form.

The next few days were the same. She made her way to the chapel as usual but she did so in an almost furtive manner and the solace that she usually got from her daily prayers and contemplation was lost to her. On the Wednesday she walked despondently to the shops; on her way homewards she bumped into Jinny Blake outside McErlean's Home Bakery.

"Ach, Mrs McCarthy, how'ye doing? You look as if everybody belonging t'ye had just died. What ails ye?"

Mrs McCarthy told her what had happened, glad to get talking to someone who, unlike Harry or Fr Burns, would understand her dilemma. Jinny was a sympathetic listener and she waited attentively until Mrs McCarthy had furnished her with every detail of the encounter with the young priest.

"So that's my tale of woe, Jinny," she concluded eventually, "and I don't know what to do. I'm not as young as I used to be ..."

"You're not fit for all that annoyance. The cheek of it!" her friend reassured her. "You shouldn't have to put up with the like of that at your age. You seldom hear them giving off about them ones."

Jinny gestured angrily at a passing convoy of British Army landrovers.

"They bloody well get off too light, God forgive me and pardon me! Imagine saying that to you, or anyone else for that matter."

Jinny was angry, but whereas Harry's rage had unsettled Mrs McCarthy, Jinny's indignation fortified her, so that by the time they finally parted Mrs McCarthy was resolved to confront Fr Burns and, as Jinny had put it, to "stand up for her rights".

The following afternoon she made her way to the chapel. It was her intention to go from there to the Parochial House. She was quite settled in her mind as to what she would say and how she would say it but first she knelt before the statue of Our Lady. For the first time that week she felt at ease in the chapel. But the sound of footsteps coming down the aisle in her direction unnerved her slightly. She couldn't look around to see who it was, which made her even more anxious that it might be Fr Burns. In her plans the confrontation with him was to be on her terms in the Parochial House, not here, on his terms, in the chapel.

"Hullo, Mrs McCarthy, is that you?" With a sigh of relief she recognised Fr Kelly's voice.

"Ah, Father," she exclaimed. "It is indeed. Am I glad to see you!"

Fr Kelly was the parish priest. He was a small, stocky, white-haired man in his late fifties. He and Mrs McCarthy had known each other since he had taken over the parish fifteen years before. As he stood smiling at her, obviously delighted at her welcome for him, she reproached herself for not coming to see him long before this. As she would tell Jinny later, that just went to show how distracted she was by the whole affair.

"Fr Kelly, I'd love a wee word with you, so I would," she rose slowly from her pew. "If you have the time, that is."

"I've always time for you, my dear."

He helped her to her feet.

"Come on and we'll sit ourselves down over here."

They made their way to a secluded row of seats at the side of the church. Fr Kelly sat quietly as Mrs McCarthy recounted the story of her disagreement with Fr Burns. When she was finished he remained silent for some moments, gazing quizzically over at the altar.

"Give up your politics or give up your religion, Mrs Mc-Carthy? That's the quandary, isn't it?"

He spoke so quietly, for a minute she thought he was talking to himself. Then he straightened up in the seat, gave her a smile and asked, "Are you going to give up your politics?"

"No," she replied a little nervously and then, more reso-lutely: "No! Not even for the Pope of Rome."

He nodded in smiling assent and continued, "And are you going to give up your religion?"

"No," she responded quickly, a little surprised at his question.

262

"Not even for the Pope of Rome?" he bantered her.

"No," she smiled, catching his mood.

"Well then, I don't know what you're worrying about. We live in troubled times and it's not easy for any of us, including priests. We all have to make our own choices. That's why God gives us the power to reason and our own free will. You've heard the Church's teaching and you've made your decision. You're not going to give up your religion nor your politics and I don't see why you should. All these other things will pass. And don't bother yourself about seeing Fr Burns. I'll have a wee word with him."

He patted her gently on the back of her hand as he got to his feet.

"Don't be worrying. And don't let anyone put you out of the chapel! It's God's house. Hold on to all your beliefs, Mrs McCarthy, if you're sure that's what you want."

"Thank you, Father." Mrs McCarthy smiled in relief. "God bless you."

"I hope He does," Fr Kelly said, "I hope He does." He turned and walked slowly up the aisle. When he got to the door he turned and looked down the chapel. Mrs McCarthy was back at her favourite seat beside the statue of Our Lady. Apart from her the silent church was empty. Fr Kelly stood reflecting pensively on that. For a moment he was absorbed by the irony of the imagery before him. Then he turned wearily, smiled to himself, and left.

(1992)

The Street and other stories

BRIAN NELSON AND THE RE-ARMING
OF THE LOYALIST DEATH SQUADS

ON 3 FEBRUARY 1992, a senior judge and former Attorney General for the unionist government at Stormont, Basil Kelly, handed down a minimum prison sentence to a British agent, Brian Nelson. Justice Kelly praised Nelson and described him as a man who had shown "the greatest of courage". The DPP also received a letter sent on behalf of British cabinet minister, Tom King, in support of Nelson and saying that he was a valuable agent.

The sentencing of Nelson to ten years' imprisonment on a series of charges relating to killings in the Six Counties was the result of a deal struck between the office of then British Attorney General, Patrick Mayhew, Nelson himself and the North's judiciary.

The deal was to keep Nelson from disclosing embarrassing information about British Intelligence and its deep involvement with loyalist death squads. Fifteen of the 35 charges against Nelson, including two charges of murder, were dropped by the Crown Prosecution at an earlier court appearance in return for guilty pleas on 20 lesser charges, five of which related to conspiracy to murder.

Brian Nelson has since been transferred to a prison in England and is expected to be released in three or four years time.

NELSON IS A 45-year-old native of Belfast, who once served with the notorious Black Watch Regiment of the British Army. He joined the UDA in the 1970s and was later recruited by British Military Intelligence. He worked undercover for British Intelligence in Ireland from within the ranks of the UDA.

In 1973, he and two UDA members kidnapped a half-blind Catholic man. The victim, Gerald Higgins, was abducted as he was walking along North Queen Street in the North Belfast area. Nelson and the other two electrocuted him and burned his hair off. The RUC labelled Nelson the ringleader of the gang and in a subsequent court report the *Belfast News Letter* said:

> The abducted man was taken to a UDA club in Wilton Street off the Shankill Road, searched, punched, had a gun drawn across his head and had his hair set alight.

Mr Higgins had his spectacles taken away from him, leaving him almost blind. The injured man had a heart condition and his assailants refused to let him take pills which gave him relief. The men wet his hands and then put two wires in his hands connected to a generator and sent an electric shock through his body. In a notebook belonging to Mr Higgins were the words:

"This is one, two to follow."

Gerald Higgins died not long afterwards. His family blame his premature death on the effects on his torturous ordeal.

Nelson and his two UDA accomplices were not even charged with attempted murder. They pleaded guilty to charges of false imprisonment of Gerald Higgins and possession of a revolver. Nelson was sentenced to only seven years in jail.

On his release from prison, Nelson, still working for British Intelligence, became active again in the UDA until the mid-1980s when he left Ireland to work in Germany. While in Germany Nelson maintained contact with the UDA and his British Army "handlers".

In early 1987, his former British Army handler and a representative of MI5 met Nelson outside London and asked him to return to Belfast to resume his role as a British agent within the UDA. The UDA, at that time a legal organisation, is the largest loyalist paramilitary force with responsibility for the killings of hundreds of nationalist/Catholic civilians. Nelson became Director of Intelligence for the UDA. He was directly in control of selecting targets for loyalist death squads. He was actively assisted in this by his British Intelligence handlers who directed the reorganisation and the rearming of the UDA.

From the time he returned to Ireland until his arrest:

*Nelson was assisted by British Intelligence in compiling information on people who would be targeted for assassination;

*The British Intelligence/Nelson combination was directly responsible for murders and attempted murders;

*British Intelligence allowed Nelson to organise a huge arms shipment from South Africa, to come into the Six Counties to be used against the nationalist population;

*The Nelson/British Intelligence ring was responsible for the shooting dead of solicitor Patrick Finucane and for the targeting of fellow solicitor, Paddy McCrory, the man who faced the SAS at the Gibraltar inquest;

*A British Intelligence officer suggested that the UDA should bomb the huge Whitegate Oil Refinery in Cork Harbour.

Nelson was arrested in January 1990 as part of investigations into the widespread leakage of British Intelligence documents to loyalists. This investigation, headed by senior British police officer John Stevens, followed increasing public concern about collusion between British Crown Forces and loyalist paramilitaries. It later emerged that Nelson's British Intelligence handlers impeded the Stevens Inquiry by delaying for months the handover of 1,000 Crown Forces photo montages which Nelson had in his possession as the UDA's Director of Intelligence.

In mid-January 1993, British Secretary of State for the North Patrick Mayhew denied that weapons imported by Brian Nelson with the knowledge of British Intelligence, are being used to kill Catholics. This is untrue. Mr Mayhew's denial came in the midst of a sustained loyalist killing campaign.

The modern weapons used in recent killings including the Milltown Cemetery attack, the Ormeau and Oldpark bookmaker's shop attacks, and individual killings, came from the consignment brought in by Nelson with the assistance of British Intelligence.

British Intelligence and the British government were kept fully informed of all Nelson's activities, including those relating to a weapons shipment which came in in January 1988 and included 200 AK47 rifles; 90 Browning pistols; around 500 fragmentation grenades; 30,000 rounds of ammunition and a dozen RPG7 rocket launchers.

At Nelson's trial a "character witness", a Military Intelligence colonel referred to as "J", stated that he was the commander of a Military Intelligence unit in the North between 1986 and 1989 and had been responsible for Nelson.

Colonel "J" admitted that he gave monthly briefings to the British Army GOC in the North and other senior officers. He said that it "would be normal for Nelson's information to be referred to at these briefings. The Secretary of State for Northern Ireland might also be interested in such information".

Evidence given in court and uncovered by journalists since then has revealed the extent of the importing of weapons and that Colonel "J" knew of these events.

Brian Nelson's case reveals the extent to which the British government is prepared to use covert operations and "counter gangs" in order to advance its political objectives in Ireland.

Informal contacts between loyalists and South Africa were first established in the mid-1970s when some former UDR men went there as mercenaries. By 1989 the Pretoria link had been developed into a well-established two-way traffic. The starting point for this new relationship was the visit to Belfast in 1985 of a forty-eight-year-old ex-merchant seaman, originally from Portadown, who had gone to live in South Africa.

Dick Wright's Ulster connections made him a useful intermediary – he was the uncle of Alan Wright, leader of the Ulster Clubs and co-founder of Ulster Resistance. He was also an agent for Armscor, the South African state-owned company which, in defiance of the 1977 United nations arms embargo, set about making South Africa self-sufficient in military hardware.

Within a decade it had made the country one of the world's top ten arms exporters. It was particularly anxious to acquire a missile system for use in Angola and Nambia. Israel (which had given South Africa its start in the arms business, supplying designs for ships, missiles and small arms) was equally keen to get details of the most advanced missile available – the Starstreak being developed by Shorts in Belfast.

Wright visited the home in East Belfast of a senior UDA leader and offered to supply guns; the order would have to be worth at least a quarter of a million pounds, but missile parts or plans would be an acceptable alternative to cash. The offer was taken seriously by the UDA. John McMichael sent UDA intelligence officer Brian Nelson to South Africa to investigate the possibility of a deal.

The crowds travelling from Belfast to London over the weekend of 7/8 June 1985 for the McGuigan/Pedroza boxing match provided cover for the first part of Nelson's journey.

During the two weeks in South Africa, Nelson was shown warehouses full of weapons by Dick Wright, the Armscor agent representing the South African state. The conditions of the deal offered by his host became decidedly more attractive: the loyalists were to supply South African agents with secrets or parts – if possible a complete Shorts missile system – in return for a substantial shipment of arms and finance of up to £1 million.

By 1985, Brian Nelson had been a British agent for at least ten years. Official knowledge of the South African negotiations, however, may have gone far beyond the reports of Nelson on his return. *Private Eye* claimed in February 1992 that Nelson's visit had been cleared not only by the Ministry of Defence but by an unnamed government minister.

The DPP's deal with Nelson at his trial was intended to

ensure that no mention would be made of either the visit or the minister. (In 1987 a US State Department report named Britain as one of the countries which had violated the UN arms embargo.)

In June 1987 the robbing of the Northern Bank in Portadown provided the money for the deal to go ahead – £150,000 of the £300,000 taken in the raid was spent on South African arms. This bought more weaponry than the UDA could handle, so the UVF and Ulster Resistance were made "partners" in the enterprise. A top secret unit responsible for developing channels of communication on behalf of several loyalist paramilitary groups were set up.

Roy Metcalfe, a member of the unit, represented Ulster Resistance in the negotiations. When he and Thomas Gibson were executed by the IRA in October 1989, Ulster Resistance claimed that they had been "set up" by British Intelligence.

The deal was completed and final arrangements were made in December 1987. Military Intelligence had been informed by Brian Nelson of developments at every stage of the proceedings; he passed on all the details, including the method to be used to smuggle in the weapons. No action was taken.

At the end of December 1987 Joseph Fawzi, a Lebanese intermediary employed by a US arms dealer working for the South Africans, dispatched a huge consignment of arms which landed without difficulty in January 1988 somewhere along the County Down coast. Two hundred AK47 automatic rifles, 90 Browning pistols, around 500 fragmentation grenades, 30,000 rounds of ammunition and a dozen RPG7 rocket launches disappeared without trace, the haul having apparently been divided into three parts shortly after its arrival.

If discovered, the arms would not have revealed their true origin; many were Czech-made weapons initially used by the PLO in Lebanon where they had been captured by the Israelis and sold to Armscor.

The shipment had not been let in through negligence, mistake or oversight. The decision to allow it to go ahead had been taken (presumably at the highest levels) months before. Nelson states in a prison journal:

In 1987 I was discussing with my handler Ronnie the South African operation when he told me that because of the deep suspicion the seizure would have aroused, to protect me it had been decided to let the first shipment into the country untouched.

Nelson's involvement in setting up the UDA's transport system meant he, and therefore British Intelligence, knew the location of the farmhouse where the weapons would be stored initially after landing.

In January 1988 Davy Payne, an ex-British paratrooper and a UDA brigadier, was arrested outside Portadown as he transported 60 assault rifles, rockets and handguns – most of the UDA's portion of the shipment. At the time the arrest was attributed to good luck and keen observation. Payne's arrest drew attention to Ulster Resistance – a telephone number written on Payne's hand turned out to be that of Noel Lyttle, a civil servant, former member of the UDR and close associate of Ian Paisley and Peter Robinson. Lyttle had stood for the DUP as a candidate in local government elections.

Lyttle was warned on two or three occasions that he was under surveillance by the Crown forces. Even his questioning and release without charge did not interrupt Ulster Resistance's attempts to renegotiate with the South Africans.

The Starstreak, being developed under a £225 million Ministry of Defence contract at Shorts, was what the South Africans wanted. A fully operational unit had been on display until a few hours before a raid in 1987 in which Ulster Resistance had stolen a Javelin aiming unit. The extraordinary coincidence did not raise any suspicions: Lyttle's questioning and the warnings were ignored and three Ulster Resistance members travelled to Paris to negotiate with the South Africans, who had already made a down payment of £50,000.

They were offering not only the parts (which though not operational could be used for research purposes) but expertise in firing the weapons – one of the three, Samuel Quinn, was a senior NCO in the Ulster Air Defence Regiment of the Territorial Army. Quinn trained recruits in the use of the Blowpipe missile. One of the weapons offered to the South

Africans was a dummy Blowpipe, stolen from Newtownards, where Quinn served.

In April 1989, the three – Noel Lyttle, Samuel Quinn and James King – were arrested in Paris along with arms dealer Douglas Bernhardt and a South African diplomat, Daniel Storm.

Storm claimed diplomatic immunity and was expelled from France. A diplomatic row blew up – but there was more noise than genuine surprise on the part of the British authorities, who were well aware of Bernhardt's activities. A naturalised American citizen, born in South Africa and married to an Englishwoman, he had operated a gun dealership, Field Arms, in Mayfair for three years – it had received assistance from the Department of Employment.

The security services knew of Bernhardt's loyalist connections; they knew he was the US dealer involved in the January 1988 arms shipment. They would also have been aware that Armscor agent Dick Wright had been employed as a marketing executive by Field Arms. Noel Lyttle later admitted that he had known Dick Wright, for Dick Wright as Armscor agent represented the South African state "quite a few years".

No request for the extradition of the three was made. Although the Swiss authorities began an investigation of Bernhardt's Geneva-based container-leasing company Agencia Utica, the British made no request for an examination of Bernhardt or his company. The Ulster Resistance members were released on bail. Following the "revelations" of contacts between the South African government and the Paris trio, the British government expelled the three South African embassy personnel. They were Staff Sergeant Mark Brunwer, who did not appear on the diplomatic list, and was described in the press as a "technical officer"; the First Secretary at the embassy, Jan Castelyn; and Etienne Fourie. Although the foreign Office emphasised that they had been chosen at random, it must have been just another coincidence that one of them, Etienne Fourie, considered the "eyes and ears" of the London embassy, had worked as a journalist in the North in the 1970s.

Two-thirds of the arms shipment landed, with the full

knowledge of British Intelligence, on the County Down coast almost five years ago remains unaccounted for. The other third was seized at a road checkpoint. The results of its arrival, however, are unmistakable. In 1985 the UDA and UVF between them killed only three people. In the five years since January 1988 more than 160 people have been killed by loyalists. The AK47 assault rifles were used in the killing of five people at the Ormeau Road bookmaker's shop in February 1992 and the killings in Murray's bookies on Belfast's Oldpark Road in December 1992. Michael Stone attacked the mourners in Milltown Cemetery in March 1988 with Russian-made RPG5 splinter grenades and a Browning pistol from the same arms consignment.

The weapons created a secure base for a renewed (and sustainable) campaign of sectarian violence by loyalist paramilitary groups. If his handler's explanation is to be believed, Brian Nelson must have been an extraordinarily valuable agent if his safety had to be paid for in hundreds of lives.

The Brian Nelson case is the tip of the iceberg of British covert operations in Ireland. The use of agents is a long established practice and the use of "counter-gangs" is a long standing element in British counter-insurgency strategy. Through Nelson, British Intelligence controlled and directed the UDA. There is nothing to suggest that they have ceased to do this. They obviously have other agents in the UDA and other loyalist paramilitary groups. At the time of writing these groups have threatened the entire nationalist community in the Six Counties as well as the Dublin government. Among the factors involved in the current resurgence of loyalist death squads are:

1. The founding of Ulster Resistance (still a legal organisation) by Ian Paisley, Peter Robinson and others;
2. The use of British Intelligence files, sometimes erroneous, by loyalist death squads to target some of their victims;
3. The arming of the loyalists with the full knowledge of British Intelligence, by Nelson.

There is an urgent need to have the entire Nelson case fully investigated. There are a number of key aspects about which some details have emerged through his trial and from other sources. These are now a matter of public record and include:

The cover-up of the Brian Nelson affair, including the deal at his trial;

Nelson's role as a British Intelligence agent;

British Intelligence involvement with loyalist paramilitaries and their activities;

British Intelligence operations in the Twenty-six Counties;

The arming of loyalist death squads.

The cover-up must be unravelled, all the sordid details revealed to the public, and the British government, the British Army, British Intelligence and their agents in loyalist death squads must be held accountable for the deaths and injuries of nationalists.

(1993)

TOWARDS A LASTING PEACE

And I shall have some peace there, for peace comes dropping slow,
Dropping from the veils of the morning to where the cricket sings;
There midnight's all a glimmer, and noon a purple glow,
And evening full of the linnet's wings
W.B. Yeats, The Lake Isle of Innisfree

WHEN I WROTE *The Politics of Irish Freedom* in 1986, who could have then foreseen Nelson Mandela as the South African President, the re-unification of Germany, or the Palestinian/Israeli peace accord? Although it is a mistake to draw any direct parallels between these and the Irish situation, they prove that even a conflict that appears to be intractable can be brought to an end. Whether or not we agree with what is happening in these individual cases, there is now no doubt that the peace process in these conflicts is in the resolution stage.

One of the common threads running through all of these situations is that the central government in each case (for whatever reason: economic sanctions, domestic or international pressures) was motivated to move, while here in the Six Counties we have the British government which has not been motivated to move in the same way. Secondly, republicans need for a transitional phase in order to reach a settlement.

Although it is a mistake to draw too direct a parallel between conflicts in other parts of the world and the British problem in Ireland, there are lessons for us in these events. And the changes taking place in South Africa, Palestine and other places have an advantageous effect on Ireland and the Anglo-Irish conflict, as they enhance an international climate for conflict resolution. If durable and unjust situations in other countries can move towards a democratic settlement, then why can we not expect similar progress in Ireland?

The early 1990s has been a time of unprecedented political change in Ireland, too, and has seen the far-reaching and historic development of an Irish Peace Initiative. This initiative, which was launched publicly in 1994, represents the culmination of years of work by Irish republicans and nationalists and their supporters abroad. Yet the process of establishing peace in Ireland has in many ways only begun, and it is impossible to know definitively how it will develop. But though we have yet to achieve peace, the political climate has been transformed, not least in terms of the level of political debate which now informs our progress.

The broad evolution of Sinn Féin strategy in recent years has been the catalyst for much of this change. A process of internal discussion, self-examination and renewal proved to be a turning point for Sinn Féin's own development, and our development of a strategy for peace. The first decisive step on this road was taken when we republicans began to engage with our opponents on the need for a peaceful resolution to the conflict in the North of Ireland.

Republicans have always been concerned to embrace a peace settlement. Those who engaged in armed struggle have never dogmatically held it up as the only form of struggle, and on a number of occasions the IRA declared itself willing to examine other means of resistance. It has always been clear to me that those who engaged in armed struggle did so as a last resort, and because from their perspective other forms of action were doomed to failure, not least because alternative forms of struggle had not been taken up; rather they had been ignored

by those institutions which had a moral or national obligation
to deal with them. The deaths of the hunger strikers of 1980-
81 brought this lesson home to Irish people in the harshest
way imaginable.

After the deaths of the prisoners, nationalists reacted with
intense resentment to the anti-republican campaigns of the
British, and more especially the Irish establishment, who
sought to portray the IRA as the cause of every wrong.
Nationalists felt that rhetorical condemnation of IRA action
was a wholly inadequate response in the light of the injustices
they suffered on a daily basis in the occupied area.

In 1982, following a series of particularly anti-IRA remarks
by Dr Cahal Daly, the Catholic bishop of Down and Connor, I
challenged him to outline the hierarchy's attitude to the injustice of partition. I challenged him to give us the benefit of his
views on British occupation and on the methods of pacifica-
tion and repression deployed by the British government in our
country. I called on him to stop condemning the IRA and to
apply himself instead to developing solutions to the problems
which faced us.

A public debate of sorts – the bishop rarely responded directly – continued between us for some months. At this time a
person – I shall call him 'the third party'[1] – who had played a
central role in the efforts made to prevent the hunger strikes,
contacted me privately and on his own initiative to explore
my calls for dialogue. What I wanted to discuss was the need
for the Irish establishment to create real means of securing
justice and the responsibility of those in powerful positions to
encourage and promote a peace settlement in the North. In
the course of a series of discussions with the third party and
later with Fr Des Wilson, a radical community activist, I outlined the republican view that if there was to be peace in
Ireland, a democratic solution to the conflict needed to be
found. In our view this meant an end to British rule.

The third party was conversant with many of the points I
raised, and he was totally committed to peacemaking. He

1. Fr Alec Reid

resolved to pass my views on to others and he arranged for me to meet with Cardinal Ó Fiaich, whom I had known for some time, and we met on a number of occasions to consider these matters. By this time I had made a written submission to the Irish hierarchy in another vain attempt to get a positive engagement on the issues I had put to Bishop Daly.

In the course of my discussions with the third party I indicated Sinn Féin's willingness to open up discussions with the Dublin government and the SDLP. Fr Des Wilson had previously tried to interest the Dublin government in these matters. He now attempted to initiate a dialogue between Mr Haughey and myself, and the third party made strenuous efforts to involve a senior member of the SDLP in these deliberations. All of this took time. By now it was 1985 and three years had passed since first I had challenged Dr Daly. During this period Sinn Féin's electoral mandate had been underpinned in a series of elections, and I had been elected MP for West Belfast.

The Anglo-Irish Treaty at Hillsborough in 1985 marked an historic effort by the Irish and British establishments to defeat Irish republicanism. The essence of the treaty was that Britain formally agreed to permit the Dublin government to assist in running the Six Counties as part of the United Kingdom. It aimed to force a realignment within unionism so that there could be a new internal arrangement in the North which would isolate republicans. In the event, Hillsborough antagonised the unionists without either isolating republicans or accommodating the SDLP. The unionists united and vigorously protested against the Hillsborough agreement, their deep sense of betrayal made all the more acute by the fact that the treaty had been signed by their champion, Margaret Thatcher. The Dublin government, in the mean time, claimed Hillsborough as a great success, and promoted the line that 'the nationalist nightmare was over'. Unfortunately and tragically it was not.

Despite the hype which attended the Hillsborough Treaty, we were satisfied that it would not undermine Sinn Féin electorally. While the growth of our vote was stunted, our electoral base was solid and resilient. At the same time the IRA could not be defeated except by the use of tactics which would clearly have been counter-productive for the London government. British policy instead aimed more and more towards containment, though this strategy was exposed as being inadequate. There was a military and political stalemate. While Irish republicans could prevent a settlement on British government terms, we lacked the political strength to bring the struggle to a decisive conclusion. Military solutions were not an option for either side: this had consistently been the Sinn Féin position. The conflict had been militarised by the British, but it remained essentially political and demanded a political solution.

In these circumstances, the side which broke the stalemate would have the initiative. But how could this be accomplished? We were too small to bring about a settlement on our terms. Republicans could block British strategy, could survive a long stalemate, but the political goals of republicanism meant we needed to do much more than either of these things if our struggle was to be successful. The Hillsborough Treaty had been part of a British offensive, an initiative underwritten by both the London and Dublin governments. We felt that we needed our own initiatives.

As the debate on these topics grew within Sinn Féin, we became increasingly aware that we needed to form broader alliances of nationalist and other progressive forces domestically and abroad. This would only be feasible, of course, if such alliances were based on an agreement, consensus, or understanding of a way forward which reflected a broadly republican or democratic character. We felt there was a need for public debate on these issues, but censorship north and south prevented this debate from taking place or obscured the situation with misinformation. Internationally, however, the political climate was moving towards a new ethos of resolving conflict. Throughout the world other struggles, admittedly most of them more developed than ours, were moving towards a new phase. We needed to internationalise our struggle to capitalise on this international mood, and to learn from the progress that had been made elsewhere in resolving the differences of history.

In Ireland the military stalemate, the war of attrition between Irish republicans and the British, had gone on for more than fifteen years, with little apparent effort being made to settle the conflict. Certainly the British were not interested in finding a democratic solution and needed to be brought to this position. For our part we needed to consider how a negotiated settlement could be secured, and how we could further our objectives in this light. Ever present in our thinking, too, was the need for Sinn Féin to develop as a political party and for us to narrow the gap between ourselves and the layer of political opinion throughout Ireland which is our potential support.

So within Sinn Féin we set about developing a strategy to secure a lasting peace, a strategy which would include political campaigning and agitation as well as diplomatic and publicity initiatives. The search for such a strategy would increasingly become a personal priority for me and others in the leadership, and, as the internal debate widened, would also become Sinn Féin's main political function.

As we searched for the ideas and policies to guide the direction we should take, one thing quickly became apparent. This could not be a debate solely among the members of Sinn Féin. Neither could it be a discussion confined only to the broad republican family. If we were serious in our search for a settlement, we needed to engage our opponents, our rivals and our enemies in debate on these matters, and especially so on the issue of peace.

What is peace: is it merely an absence of war? What causes peace? How can it be achieved? Who is for it, who against? Is peace political? Can the demand for peace create common ground between different political groups? For too long republicans had permitted others to hijack the word 'peace': the Irish establishment, content to attack the IRA as the cause of the problem, while doing nothing to find a solution; the leaders of states and churches, of political parties and the media, continuing to criticise and condemn, but failing completely to create an alternative way forward. They needed to be confronted on their stance. So did the unionists, and the British. This required republican political initiatives and a Sinn Féin offensive in the battle of ideas.

We understood that this would not be easy. In the South Sinn Féin was treated like a pariah by the leaderships of all the other political parties, while in the North relationships between the SDLP and Sinn Féin were extremely polarised. Relations between us and the unionists were non-existent. All these considerations informed the public pronouncements of our senior representatives and their private discussions with a range of political contacts. By 1987 I had met with two Catholic bishops, and the third party was in discussions with Mr Haughey. This contact had been assisted by Tim Pat Coogan, but progress was at a snail's pace, and after much to-ing and froing the SDLP representative had refused our invitation to become involved.

Through all this time senior party members continued, in both private and public, to discuss ways of finding a durable peace with as broad a range of opinion as possible. All of this took place against a background of intensive military activity by both the IRA and the British forces, and threatening noises from their allies within loyalism. Intense efforts were also being made to marginalise Sinn Féin, but despite such actions our support remained solid.

In 1987, Sinn Féin published the discussion paper 'A Scenario For Peace', a document which marked the public launch of our developing peace strategy. We called for an end to British rule, and argued that an enduring peace would only come about as a result of a process which won the support of a wide representation of Irish, British and international opinion. Such a peace process would have to contain the necessary mechanics of a settlement: the framework, timescale, and the dynamic necessary to bring about an inclusive, negotiated and democratic settlement.

That year the third party made direct contact with SDLP leader John Hume and a meeting was agreed between us. It marked the beginning of the most significant discussions in formulating a new peace initiative in the North of Ireland.

Our early talks led to meetings between delegations from our party and the SDLP, which continued from January to September 1988. This series of discussions investigated the possibility of Sinn Féin and the SDLP developing an overall political strategy to establish justice and peace in Ireland. In these meetings Sinn Féin sought a consensus between all Irish nationalist parties on the right of the Irish people to self-determination, and argued that the Dublin government needed to launch a diplomatic offensive to secure this aim. However, Sinn Féin was at odds with the SDLP's position that the British government's role in Ireland was 'neutral'. In our view, if the SDLP's opinion was correct, British neutrality could best be demonstrated by the British 'adopting a policy of ending the union and then actively seeking agreement among the people who share the island of Ireland on how this can be accomplished'. The SDLP refused to take up this option.

The closing Sinn Féin statement, at the end of the delegate meetings, reveals the extent to which the republican peace strategy was already in gestation. It said:

Our discussions with the SDLP elicited the shared political view that the Irish people as a whole have the right to national self-determination and that the Irish people should be defined as those people domiciled on the island of Ireland (and its off-shore islands). In that context it was accepted that an internal Six-County settlement is no solution.

Despite the disagreements between us, valuable work was done in the course of these discussions, and when they ended John Hume and I continued in private with our dialogue.

By 1990 contact had been re-established between Sinn Féin and the British government. A line of contact has existed between Sinn Féin and London for over twenty years, although it has not been in constant use. It has been used extensively during such periods as the bilateral truce of 1974-75 and the hunger strikes of 1980-81. This contact was re-activated by the British government in 1990, leading to a period of protracted dialogue between us. Over three years, outlines of Sinn Féin and British government policies were exchanged and discussed.

Despite the fact that the British government showed little consistent interest in seeking a real settlement, we regarded our contact as a potentially important element in the development of a peace process, even if it was an unsatisfactory form of communication. At all times we proceeded with extreme caution and in the belief that while this contact was direct to the British cabinet, it was also most certainly under the tutelage of MI5.

We were now in communication with the British and had succeeded in establishing contact with our fellow nationalists in the North and South of Ireland; we were also making every effort to open up lines of communication with unionist representatives and Northern Protestants. This sustained dialogue was conducted against a background of intense military activity, and it is to his credit that when Peter Brooke was appointed secretary of state for Northern Ireland he joined the debate with some enthusiasm.

In 1989, after one hundred days in office, Brooke had given an interview in which he acknowledged that it was difficult 'to envisage a military defeat of the IRA'. Mr Brooke also took a more realistic line on talking to Sinn Féin. 'Let me remind you,' he said, 'of the move towards independence in Cyprus and that a British minister stood up in the House of Commons and used the word "never" in a way which, within two years, there had been a retreat from that word.' In November 1990 the secretary of state put forward the view that the British government 'has no selfish, strategic or economic interest in Northern Ireland'.

Brooke initiated talks with the unionists and with the SDLP, and then, tactically and ironically, excluded Sinn Féin. The official talks, and talks about talks, wandered on beyond Mr Brooke's tenure and were picked up by his successor, Patrick Mayhew, but few people had confidence in them. The unionists refused to move from their entrenched position, while the main concern of the British seemed to be to assure international opinion that they were doing something.

While these discussion wandered around the causes of the conflict rather than addressing them directly, the unrelenting disruption of Irish social and economic life continued as it had done for twenty years. The British held the key, but they failed to assert the political will which alone could open the door to the future. Rather they stood in the way of a settlement, underwriting conditions which ensured that the north-east of Ireland should remain a political wasteland. And in this the British government had as its right arm one of the world's most sophisticated war machines, the British army, charged with seeing that 'the supreme authority of the Parliament of the United Kingdom shall remain unaffected and undiminished over all persons, matters and things in Northern Ireland...'.

For over twenty years, repression and manipulation have been the chief means of implementing Britain's authority in the North of Ireland, substituting the power of the state for the consent of the ruled. British rule in Ireland has rested on the twin pillars of division and coercion for even longer. Underpinning the divisions in the Irish nation, which are central to the maintenance of British rule, lies the threat – and use – of British force. Partition was imposed on the Irish people under the threat of 'immediate and total war', and since its creation the Six County statelet has relied for its existence on a system of repressive legislation overseen by a compliant judiciary and enforced by military and paramilitary forces. An abnormal state of 'permanent emergency' has been the norm. Britain's governing of the North of Ireland has won it the worst human rights record in Europe, a fact documented by the European Court of Human Rights. Emergency laws, including seven-day detention without charge or trial, ill-treatment of suspects in custody, convictions on confession evidence alone, and savagely long sentences, have formed the continuing pattern of British 'justice' in Ireland. Numerous travesties of justice have occurred, including the notorious cases of the Guildford Four and the Maguire family, the Birmingham Six, the Winchester Three, Judith Ward, the Ballymurphy Seven, and more.

More than 3,200 people have died in twenty-five years of war, from 1969 to the present. Most of the deaths have been in the Six Counties, but almost one hundred have occurred in the Twenty-six Counties and 118 people have been killed in Britain. The London government and others have blamed all these deaths on the IRA. The IRA is in fact responsible for killing over 1,000 members of the crown forces, over thirty loyalist activists and more than one hundred persons working in direct support of the British crown forces. One hundred and one IRA volunteers have lost their lives in premature bomb explosions. A further 230 civilians have died as a result of premature explosions or in engagements between the crown forces and the IRA.

The British themselves are known to be directly responsible for 370 deaths, and loyalist groups, with or without the assistance of crown forces, have killed 915 people. At least eighty percent of these have been uninvolved Catholic civilians, including eighteen members of Sinn Féin and forty-three civilians in the Twenty-six Counties, thirty-three of whom were killed with the assistance of British Intelligence in the Dublin/Monaghan bombings in 1974, the worst day of atrocities in all of the past twenty-five years. Loyalists have killed twelve members of the crown forces and four times that number of their own membership have died in loyalist feuds. Of the British killings, more than fifty-four percent of the victims have been civilians. One hundred and twenty-one IRA volunteers have been killed by crown forces.

The Six County economy is heavily geared to the war. Military occupation, policing and prisons employ over 34,000 people, more than one-third of the number employed in what is left of the North's manufacturing industry. There is now one member of the crown forces for every 3.5 nationalist males aged sixteen to forty-four, and every year the British spend £9,500 policing each and every one of them. The British government has needed 30,000 armed men and women to maintain its presence in the North. The nationalist people bear the brunt of this military occupation, with harassment on the streets and in their homes, confiscation of their land, and destruction of their property. The British government holds over 700 republican and a few hundred loyalist political prisoners in its jails. None of these men and women would be behind bars if it were not for the political conflict.

The war-related costs of British Intelligence, the British army, the RUC, the juryless courts and the prisons now stand at £1.2 billion a year. This is about the same as the North's education budget, two-and-a-half times what is spent on industry and employment, and five times the amount spent on housing. Fifty thousand jobs in manufacturing may have been lost in the Six Counties because of the war. In many other smaller ways the financial burden of the war is felt in compensation costs, or in financing British propaganda abroad, for example in the fight against the MacBride lobby in the USA which works to counter the North's sectarian employment practices. Extra resources need to be put into promoting tourism and securing inward investment; there are delays at border and other checkpoints, private security costs, health service costs, payments to informers, and money used to contest extraditions and cases brought under the European Convention of Human Rights. In the North alone, the British have spent nearly £18 billion on this war since 1969.

The war has been costly in Britain, too. There is the cost of enforcing the Prevention of Terrorism Act, and other policing costs such as providing security for politicians. Damage to property as a result of the IRA's campaign has led to higher insurance premiums, the proliferation of closed-circuit television and the disruption of commuter traffic. These costs now run into billions each year. Sealing off the City of London in 1993 was priced at £100 million, with recurring costs of £25 million a year.

As well as the political conflict and sectarian divisions which partition reinforced, the social and economic consequences north and south have been disastrous for ordinary people. Partition led to discrimination as unionists sought to shore up their artificial majority in the Six Counties, and the waste of millions of pounds on 'security' every year. The separation of the two economies contributed to the external dependency of both, resulting in levels of industrial underdevelopment, unemployment, emigration and poverty which are significantly higher than European norms. Partition has allowed social backwardness to prevail throughout Ireland. The creation of two states, both of which were dominated by the most conservative elements on the island, set back social progress for decades. The position of women in the two states, the ban on divorce in the Twenty-six Counties, and the degree of clerical control or influence on both sides of the border in the areas of education, health and other public services are further signs of the stagnation which partition helps to sustain.

Recognising the undemocratic reality of the partition of Ireland is the starting-point of the resolution of the conflict. Above all, the pursuit of a democratic solution capable of creating a self-sustaining peace is dependent on the recognition of this fact by the government of Britain. The search for peace in Ireland is everyone's responsibility. In particular, it is the responsibility of the representatives of organised society – the political parties, the churches, trade unions, leaders of industry, the women's movement, cultural organisations and the media. Specifically, it is the responsibility of the two 'sovereign' governments in London and Dublin, who have the power to effect the necessary change, and, in today's 'global village', the resolution of the British-Irish conflict is also an international responsibility. But, fundamentally, it is Britain's responsibility. Britain created the problem in Ireland; for that reason it must play the major role in bringing the conflict to a democratic resolution and a lasting peace.

Britain may assert that, while 'preferring' to keep the Six County statelet within the 'United Kingdom', it has 'no selfish strategic or economic' reasons for doing so. But British preference in relation to matters internal to Ireland holds no validity against the preference of the clear majority of the Irish people for national independence. And since the British have no 'selfish' reasons for maintaining partition, it follows logically that their best interests lie in bringing it to an end.

In the context of Britain's accepting the national rights of the majority of the Irish people, the resolution of the conflict in Northern Ireland must involve the British government's joining the ranks of the persuaders in seeking to obtain the consent of all sections to the constitutional, political and financial arrangements needed to establish a united Ireland. Otherwise unionists are not likely to be influenced and will remain intransigent, confident that the British government will continue to underwrite their contrived majority with force and finance.

Sinn Féin entered into direct contact with the British government in a genuine attempt to develop a dialogue on these fundamental issues. It was right that there should be direct contact between us and the British government; for this reason we sought at all times to protect this contact, believing that the objective of resolving the conflict was far more important than short-term political one-upmanship. This process was not an alternative to the discussions which I was conducting with John Hume. Indeed, on a number of occasions we informed the British side that our talks were dealing with the substantive issues also. They understood that we were engaged in a serious attempt to reach agreement on the principles and dynamic which would bring peace to Ireland.

It is ironic that while the British government was engaged in its propaganda war against us and those we represent, while it was censoring Sinn Féin and preventing me from entering Britain and, through diplomatic pressure, the USA, they were simultaneously engaged with Sinn Féin in prolonged contact and dialogue without preconditions of any kind. In the later stages of this contact, in early 1993, the British proposed that a British government delegation should meet with a Sinn Féin delegation for an intense round of negotiations. The British offered that such round-table talks would result in republicans being convinced that armed struggle was no longer necessary. We were asked to seek a short suspension of IRA operations to facilitate these discussions. Given the importance of this Sinn Féin sought, and was given, a commitment from the leadership of the Irish Republican Army that it would suspend operations for two weeks to enable us to explore the potential of the British government's assertions. This was conveyed to the British government in May 1993.

Although we were informed that this positive response by republicans was the subject of a series of high-level meetings by British ministers and officials, including Prime Minister John Major, the British subsequently backed away from their initial proposal and refused to follow it through.

This was influenced, in part at least, by party political difficulties which overtook the Conservative leadership and led them to depend on unionist support in the House of Commons. The documents we received subsequently avoided the main issues, and the number of leaks and rumours about 'secret talks between London and the IRA' increased quite noticeably. In November 1993 unionist leaks to the British press forced Patrick Mayhew to admit that London had been in contact with Sinn Féin, breaching the confidentiality which we had at all times respected and going on then to misrepresent the content of our exchanges. The bad faith and double dealing involved clearly presented us with serious difficulties in assessing the sincerity of the British government in relation to the growing opportunities for peace.

Notwithstanding the overall responsibility of successive British governments for creating the conditions which have sustained the past years of conflict, Dublin has a clear responsibility and a major role to play in providing the democratic resolution which will bring about a lasting peace. It possesses the resources and has political and diplomatic access to the world centres of power.

For the greater part of the Twenty-six County state's existence, successive Dublin governments have adopted a negative attitude on the question of national democracy. For most of that period, the issue of the British-imposed border has been addressed largely for the purposes of electoral gain. From Hillsborough until recently, Dublin's approach has supported the partition of our country. The North costs the Twenty-six Counties £200 million a year now, and has cost an estimated £2.5 billion over the years of the conflict. It is a sad and expensive irony that taxpayers in Ireland pay two to three times more per capita to maintain the border than their counterparts in Britain.

In our dialogue with Dublin, which continued independently of our talks with the SDLP, we argued that if there was to be peace in Ireland the Dublin government would have to assume its national responsibility. It would have to persuade the British government that the partition of Ireland had been a failure and seek a change in British policy. It should also seek to persuade the unionists of the benefits of a new and agreed Ireland, and seek their consent to the constitutional, political and financial arrangements needed to bring this into being. The international community would also have to be mobilised in support of Irish national rights.

In the interim, we argued, Dublin would have to promote and defend the democratic rights of the population of the Six Counties. There must be equality of treatment for all, and to establish this there must be fundamental political and constitutional change. At all events, the Dublin government should propose no changes in the Irish constitution that would have the effect of leaving Britain's assertion of, and claim to, sovereignty over six Irish counties uncontested, while withdrawing Ireland's rightful claim to sovereignty.

Sinn Féin's recognition of the central role of the Dublin government in the creation of a peace process was a major shift in the traditional republican and northern nationalist attitude to Dublin.

In our view, those parties in Ireland which described themselves as nationalist, including Fianna Fáil and the SDLP, wielded considerable influence, be it on Dublin, London, Brussels or Washington. This, of itself, placed on them a responsibility to represent forcefully and continuously the interests of the nationalist people. If these parties believed that Britain had no selfish, strategic or economic interest in Ireland, they should seek to get Britain to carry this through and formally accept the right of the Irish people to self-determination. Peace in Ireland required such a settlement of the long-standing conflict between Irish nationalism and Irish unionism. We proposed that that often bloody conflict needed to be replaced by a process of national reconciliation, expressed through constructive dialogue and debate. But peace as an aspiration, or expressed only in terms of popular desire, is of only limited use. The achievement of peace requires a peace process. To be achievable and sustainable, peace must have self-determination as its foundation and democracy as its aim. The criteria by which any initiative which claims peace as its end is to be judged is the degree to which it promotes the conditions in which the right to national self-determination can be exercised.

By the early 1990s the Sinn Féin leadership was well advanced in developing and refining its policy and political strategy. Senior party members who had responsibility for developing private contacts in Ireland and abroad were accountable to a small sub-committee of the Árd Chomhairle, and the question of political strategy dominated discussion within the party. The thrust of our policy was debated and agreed on at Árd Fheiseanna, while the broader republican movement supported the direction we took, particularly our objective of building a consensus on the need for a negotiated settlement. As the war and the efforts to marginalise Sinn Féin continued unabated, our internal discussion may at times have seemed unreal to those who were unaware of our private contacts, and especially to the media, whose willingness to demonise us per the instructions of their political masters had distorted their perception, and their reporting, of events in the North. But Sinn Féin has always had a policy which looked for dialogue, and for as long as I can recall we have maintained contact with different elements of Irish and British opinion. In many cases we perhaps conducted such discussion in a responsive mode. Now, however, we took the initiative.

Hindsight or retrospective summary might suggest that we started off with a blueprint. We did not. But we had a confidence in our struggle and its democratic premise which despite everything remained resilient. We had over two decades of commitment behind us, and we were agreed on policy objectives and broad principles. Political strategy was dictated by the needs of the struggle, our engagements and internal discussions, and our ultimate aims. We dealt with the objective reality of the situation. There were the effects of censorship and revisionism in the Twenty-six Counties, as well as the stunted nature of the Sinn Féin organisation. In some areas we had little more than a network, and the isolation, sometimes the self-imposed isolation, of republican activists demanded a major effort to promote the core Irish republican demands in a way which citizens in that state could relate to. Our struggle had to be developed on an all-Ireland basis. At the same time the character of the struggle in the Six Counties demanded an effort to develop a nationalist consensus on the basis of constitutional change. We sought, therefore, to develop an Irish national consensus on the same basis, both in party political and grassroots terms.

The role of the Dublin government was crucial to any effort to move the situation on. At the very least we needed to promote a positive London/Dublin government axis. The involvement of unionists was crucial to solving the problem. They had to be able to give their allegiance to a political settlement: without their participation and agreement there could be none.

There was little indication that any significant section of unionism was prepared to take up such a position, and it was unlikely that this would happen while Britain guaranteed the unionist position. There was a need, therefore, to develop a debate about the separate interests of the British government and the unionist population, and to advance the veto *vs* consent debate on the basis of accepted democratic principles. If possible we needed to build a dialogue with mainstream unionist opinion. As part of this we needed to initiate a meaningful public debate with unionism.

Dialogue was established with a range of Protestant opinion, in most cases with middle class religious or community activists through our local councils. Contact was also established with the main Protestant churches, though not with their leaders. The main breakthrough came in the spring of 1992 when Tom Hartley and I began a dialogue with two former moderators of the Presbyterian church.

Sinn Féin also made contact with working-class unionist representatives. Despite unionist hostility, our councillors followed a strategy which aimed to engage with unionist councillors in a meaningful way. This was difficult, particularly in Belfast City Hall where unionists conducted a campaign of deliberate physical hostility to Sinn Féin councillors, but even here our resilience paid off. Sinn Féin had also developed regular contact with grassroots unionist opinion, which expanded in scope and lasts up to the present time, though the unionist leaderships have not been directly involved.

In 1992 Sinn Féin published *Towards a Lasting Peace in Ireland*, a comprehensive and refined discussion paper which summed up our analysis of how the North's political logjam could be broken. It was officially launched in Ireland, Britain, the United States, Australia, and in several European cities. One of the key sections of the document sets out Sinn Féin's analysis of what is needed for fundamental political change to be achieved:

1. The recognition by the British government that the Irish people have the right to self-determination.
2. That the British government change its current policy to one of ending partition and handing over sovereignty to an all-Ireland government whose selection would be a democratic matter for the Irish people.
3. That the future of the unionists lies in this context and that the British government has a responsibility to influence unionist attitudes to this end.
4. The London and Dublin governments should consult together to seek agreement on the policy objectives of ending partition.

These four propositions, if enacted by the British and Irish governments, would secure for the peace process the maximum national, and international, political and popular support.

Towards a Lasting Peace in Ireland clearly placed the onus on the two governments, but particularly on the British government, to work to secure change. It called on the British government to 'join the persuaders', to use its influence to convince the unionist section of our community that their future did not lie in continuing the link with Britain. It called on the Dublin government to work to persuade the British that partition has failed, to persuade the unionists of the benefits of Irish reunification, and to persuade the international community that it should support a real peace process in Ireland.

Sinn Féin had itself been working to develop the international dimension throughout this time. The Irish diaspora which resulted from British policy in Ireland ensured an ongoing interest, though partition had blurred the purpose and focus of that interest. As a small party we were extremely underdeveloped in Britain and Europe; the USA naturally was a better area for us. Our main support group there, Irish Noraid, recognised the potential value of mainstream outreach work in the States, while other stalwarts like Clan na Gael gave invaluable help as we sought to achieve co-operation and unity among a wide range of Irish-American groups. A new organisation, Americans for a New Irish Agenda, which included prominent Irish Americans and former Congressman Bruce Morrisson among its founding members, made a particularly significant contribution, pressing at all times for all-inclusive dialogue between the parties to the conflict. Irish America gave hugely important support to the peace process at a time when its roots in Ireland and the UK were still extremely fragile. North America offered moral and political support, and the prospect of real aid to help secure a lasting settlement in Ireland. At crucial moments Irish-American organisations spoke out, encouraging communication and dialogue, and acting as honest brokers in a process which was fraught with difficulties for the parties directly involved.

In April 1993 John Hume and I issued the first of several statements outlining the results of our more than five years of dialogue.

As leaders of our respective parties we accept that the most pressing issue facing the people of Ireland and Britain today is the question of lasting peace and how it can best be achieved.

Everyone has a solemn duty to change the political climate away from conflict and towards a process of national reconciliation, which seeks the peaceful accommodation of the differences between the people of Britain and Ireland and the Irish people themselves.

In striving for that end, we accept that an internal settlement is not a solution because it obviously does not deal with all the relationships at the heart of the problem.

We accept that the Irish people as a whole have a right to national self-determination. This is a view shared by a majority of the people of this island, though not by all its people.

The exercise of self-determination is a matter for agreement between the people of Ireland. It is the search for that agreement and the means of achieving it on which we will be concentrating.

We are mindful that not all the people of Ireland share that view or agree on how to give meaningful expression to it. Indeed we cannot disguise the different views held by our own parties.

As leaders of our respective parties, we have told each other that we see the task of reaching agreement on a peaceful and democratic accord for all on this island as our primary challenge.

We both recognise that such a new agreement is only achievable and viable if it can earn and enjoy the allegiance of the different traditions on this island, by accommodating diversity and providing for national reconciliation.

We had reached agreement on a process, based upon a set of principles containing the political dynamic which could create the conditions for a lasting peace and a total demilitarisation of the situation. This was dependent on the adoption of these proposals by the two governments, and on a positive response to them from the leadership of the IRA. The IRA expressed a positive attitude, saying that 'If the political will exists or can be created it could provide the basis for peace.' Both governments were fully informed of these matters at every stage in the discussions and the Dublin government pledged its support. London refused to respond.

Up until this point it appeared on the surface at least that the political landscape in Ireland was frozen over. The public disclosure of our talks was the first sign that this could change and that an Irish peace initiative was a real possibility. The reaction was immediate. At popular level there was a warm welcome, but the entrenched unionists, sections of the Tory right wing, conservative opinion in Ireland and Britain and most political party leaders in the South were hysterical in their opposition. Yet against all predictions, against a background of censorship and other attempts to undermine us, our support remained high; in the May local elections Sinn Féin was confirmed as the second largest party in Belfast.

John Hume had come to realise that the marginalisation and attempted exclusion of Sinn Féin had been futile. During our discussions he had also formed the opinion that republicans were serious and sincere in trying to create the conditions for peace. But years had been spent building a wall behind which republican opinion was to be corralled, and John Hume's meetings with me were seen as having breached that wall. For daring to engage with us, for daring to explore the possibility of peace, he was subjected to the type of vilification usually reserved exlusively for Sinn Féin leaders. In many cases the loudest criticism came from those who were well versed in the rhetoric of peace, but unrehearsed in the practice of dialogue.

Nationalists, and more particularly republican communities or those which were deemed to be so, were equally subjected to insult. Nationalist West Belfast had long been a target for such odium; however, it was also a community which refused to take things lying down. The community was enjoying its own local revitalisation process, and the creativity, resilience and aspirations of its people were reflected in a thriving range of enterprises.

A short time after the disclosure of my talks with John

Hume, in June 1993, Irish President Mary Robinson visited West Belfast. This was an important initiative. Mrs Robinson's election had marked a watershed in Irish politics. Her stated aim was to reach out to the marginalised sections of Irish society. The nationalists of the North certainly fitted into this category and the West Belfast visit was arranged following lengthy contact between community activists and the president's office.

There was extreme opposition to the visit from the British and sections of the Dublin establishment, because I was to be present at a reception for Mrs Robinson in Belfast's Ballymurphy. This opposition reached fever pitch in the days and even in the hours before the visit, and it is to Mary Robinson's credit that she resisted the pressure put on her to abandon it. The West Belfast organisers were also subjected to extreme pressure, and it is a mark of their solidarity that they refused to be browbeaten.

The President's day in West Belfast was an outstanding success. It sent a timely signal of the need to accord people respect. It was also hugely popular throughout Ireland. In this period of rampant McCarthyism in the Twenty-six Counties, the reaction of the plain people of Ireland sent an equally timely message to their political representatives in Dublin.

By June also, Dublin, John Hume and myself had agreed a process to realise the principles we had outlined in our public statement in April. This was forwarded to the British government. In our view this Irish peace initiative contained the political dynamic which could create the conditions for a demilitarisation of the situation and a lasting peace. Everything depended on the British response.

As efforts to find a new political settlement gathered momentum, the loyalist killing campaign accelerated. The loyalists had been re-armed by British Intelligence. With their authority and assistance, British agent Brian Nelson had negotiated a weapons deal with the apartheid South African government, and a weapons shipment was landed in Ireland in January 1988. It included 200 AK47 rifles, 90 Browning pistols, around 500 fragmentation grenades, 30,000 rounds of ammunition and a dozen RPG7 rocket launchers. In March 1988, Michael Stone attacked mourners at the republican plot in Belfast's Milltown Cemetery with Russian-made RPG5 splinter grenades. The AK47 assault rifles were used in the killing of five people at an Ormeau Road bookmaker's shop in February 1992 and the killing of three people in Murray's bookies in Belfast's Oldpark Road in November of that year. From the time they were re-armed until the loyalist ceasefire in 1994, 160 people were killed by loyalist death squads. They were mainly Catholics uninvolved in politics. Thirteen members of Sinn Féin were killed in a two-year period. Seven other people, relatives of Sinn Féin activists, including women and children, died in attacks on our families; scores were injured. There was also a sustained campaign of intimidation against SDLP members, including attacks on their homes. And there was widespread controversy when evidence of collusion between loyalists and elements of the British crown forces, a long-time feature of life and death in the North, was revealed. This had re-emerged after the killing by loyalists of Loughlin Maginn in Rathfriland, Co. Down, in August 1989. His killers released British files as part of their justification for his murder, an event which started a series of revelations of British/loyalist collusion and led to the Stevens Inquiry.

The loyalist killing campaign had already recommenced when news of my talks with John Hume became public. There was always a danger that such a development, however legitimate and pacific in intent, would be seized upon for propagandist reasons by British and unionist elements, north and south. The loyalist killing campaign was mischievously linked to the Hume-Adams talks, as if our dialogue was the cause of the terror. The theme was taken up by unionist politicians who repeatedly spoke of a pan-nationalist alliance, echoing the language of the death squads. As the impetus of the peace process which John Hume and I initiated faltered in the face of political indecision and unionist opposition, a wave of violent reaction spread throughout the North of Ireland. Killings by loyalist death squads outpaced all others, and as summer turned to autumn the scale of killing reached the worst levels seen in twenty years of conflict. In March 1993 the IRA had exploded a bomb in a shopping centre in Warrington which killed two children; republicans, not least because we had also buried our children, understood the agonies of their families. In April the IRA bombed the City of London, causing hundreds of millions of pounds worth of damage. In October twenty-three people were killed in ten days, thirteen by loyalists and ten by the IRA in a premature bomb explosion on the Shankill Road. At this time, throughout the North but particularly in Belfast and some rural areas, Catholics were gripped by fear as the loyalist terror continued. The intentions of the death squads, and their methods, were as old as the statelet itself. Towards the end of 1993 their activity was at an almost unprecedented level, claiming a Catholic life virtually on a daily basis. The IRA operation on the Shankill came in response to this situation. It was wrong. The aim of the IRA was to wipe out the loyalist leaders who were responsible for the terror campaign. The result was the deaths of nine civilians and one IRA volunteer.

In these tense conditions John Hume and I had issued a second public statement, in September 1993, recognising that the broad principles involved in our proposals were for wider consideration between the two governments, and suspending our own discussions for the time being.

The Irish peace initiative received a cool response from the London government, and in the House of Commons the British prime minister told John Hume that his peace plan was not enough. But our talks had by now sparked an explosion of debate and enquiry throughout Ireland, the UK and to an extent the USA, in which the desire for a peaceful settlement was overwhelming. The force and rightness of these popular demands compelled the political establishments in Ireland and the UK to involve themselves in the process which we had outlined.

The political core of the Irish peace initiative emerged out of the Hume-Adams talks. The basic principles underpinning the Hume-Adams statements were that:

1. The Irish people as a whole have the right to national

self-determination.

2. An internal settlement is not a solution.
3. The exercise of self-determination is a matter for agreement between the people of Ireland.
4. The consent and allegiance of unionists are essential ingredients if a lasting peace is to be established.
5. The unionists cannot have a veto over British policy.
6. The British government must join the persuaders.
7. The London and Dublin governments have the major responsibility to secure political progress.

The subsequent emergence of the Downing Street Declaration – or Joint Declaration – between the British and Irish governments in December 1993, after some months of political turmoil, was by and large a response by both governments to the document which we had given them earlier that year.

Within hours of the Downing Street Declaration being launched, Taoiseach Albert Reynolds and Prime Minister John Major returned to their respective legislatures to seek endorsement of the document. Almost immediately, public statements by the two leaders and the members of their cabinets indicated that real differences existed between both governments, not only on the actual meaning of significant and substantial parts of the Declaration, but on its stated objectives. Clarifying the Declaration in the House of Commons for Ulster Unionist Party leader James Molyneaux, the British prime minister said:

'What is not in the Declaration is: any suggestion that the British government should join the ranks of the persuaders of the value or legitimacy of a united Ireland; that is not there. Nor is there any suggestion that the future status of Northern Ireland should be decided by a single act of self-determination by the people of Ireland as a whole; that is not there either. Nor is there any timetable for constitutional change, or any arrangements for joint authority over Northern Ireland. In sum, the Declaration provides that it is and must be for the people of Northern Ireland to determine their own future.'

Albert Reynold's addressed the Dáil with an entirely

different emphasis. The taoiseach asserted that 'for the first time ever, the right to self-determination of the people of Ireland is acknowledged subject only to the question of consent'. He said 'there is no unionist veto, only the requirement for the consent of a majority', and went on to say that 'the door is open on one hand to a united Ireland if it can be achieved by unity and consent'.

The day after the Declaration was launched I asked for clarification of its terms. My request was refused. The British insisted that there was 'nothing more to tell' Sinn Féin, even while they engaged in lengthy discussion with all other political parties about the Declaration's contents.

A few days after the document was published, John Major wrote in a Belfast newspaper that the Declaration 'reaffirms the constitutional guarantee' to unionists that Northern Ireland would remain part of the United Kingdom, while on the same day Albert Reynolds said that there was a 'constitutional onus' on John Major 'to pursue unity'. It seemed to us republicans that, in the circumstances, clarification of some kind was very much in order.

The British, however, continued to stall the pace of the peace process, refusing in particular to clarify issues for Sinn Féin or to give an unambiguous recognition of our democratic mandate. During this period the efforts of the Irish government and our supporters abroad were crucial in moving the process forward. In early September a group of leading Irish-American businessmen and labour leaders led by Bruce Morrisson had arrived in Ireland to see for themselves conditions on the ground. The ANIA delegation met with Sinn Féin and we provided them with our assessment of the situation. They reported directly to the White House, and lobbied for me to be allowed to visit the USA to support the peace process. When in response to British diplomatic pressure President Clinton at first refused me a visa, Bill Flynn, as chairman of the National Committee on Foreign Policy, organised a one-day conference on Northern Ireland in New York, and I was invited to attend along with other political leaders. Flynn also took out a full-page advertisement

in the *New York Times* in which 220 leading Irish-Americans
and heads of eighty-five leading corporations voiced their support for the Irish peace process. After a time President Clinton
granted me a forty-eight hour visa. This was despite intense
lobbying from the British, including John Major. 'The special
relationship,' *The Irish Times* later remarked, 'would never be
the same again.'

While the British government refused to meet Sinn Féin or
to clarify the Declaration formally, Northern Secretary Patrick
Mayhew made several key speeches in the months after
Downing Street. He seemed to directly contradict John
Major's earlier statements when he said in January 1994: 'No
outcome is ruled out. We accept a binding obligation to introduce the necessary legislation to give effect to any measures of
agreement on future relationships in Ireland.' Even though
Mayhew said that 'the outcome cannot be predetermined', he
reiterated the promise of a constitutional guarantee and said
that all depended on 'the democratic wish of a greater number
of people in Northern Ireland.' He went on:

'The British government agrees that it is for the people of
the island alone, by agreement between the two parts respec-
tively, to exercise their right of self-determination on the basis
of consent freely and concurrently given, North and South, to
bring about a united Ireland if that is their wish.' This, he
added, 'is not about coercion, nor any power to impose a
veto. It is about founding a resolution of our troubles upon
the principles of agreement, consent and democracy.'

In the House of Commons he affirmed that the Declaration
offered 'real assurance to unionists' but told nationalists that
Britain no longer had 'any colonial or strategic ambitions' in
the Six Counties, and that 'the peaceful aspiration to a
sovereign and united Ireland was now a fully legitimate one.'
In a major speech to the Association of American correspondents in February, the Secretary of State went a little further.
The British and Irish governments, he said, would 'commit
themselves to be persuaders for peace and persuaders for
agreement on the divided island of Ireland'. He conceded that
'nothing is ruled out', and that 'only the people of Ireland can

decide the form of the agreement'. In the same speech he acknowledged that 'We do not have a blueprint or a master-plan to impose. We do not have some private interest that would lead us to seek to frustrate any particular outcome.' This speech was welcomed by John Hume as 'a significant piece of clarification'.

Two weeks before the Sinn Féin Árd Fheis in February, John Major wrote: 'The Declaration is not a peace plan. It certainly isn't a solution on its own. It is simply the view of the two governments about the principles involved in a process lead-ing to an agreed outcome. Those central principles are democ-racy, and an absence of coercion – in other words consent, no outside interference, and an end to violence.' Patrick Mayhew later responded to criticism of the unionist veto made at the Árd Fheis. He said: 'The two governments agree, and are determined, that it is self-determination, in other words democracy, that shall prevail. It is in democracy that we find the supreme concept in which the ideas of national identity can be accommodated. No one should claim a veto to over-ride that.'

Alongside these official statements issued in speeches and communiqués, debate on the issues involved had began to take hold amongst people in both Ireland and the UK. Section 31 of the Broadcasting Act, which had censored Sinn Féin from Irish television and radio for twenty years, was lifted; Britain later rescinded its broadcasting ban too. In order to consult with the public, Sinn Féin set up a peace commission which organised public hearings in each of the four provinces to discuss the issues involved in the peace process and the Downing Street Declaration, and community activists, trade unionists, women's groups and individuals came forward to offer their views. However, nothing so typified the deeply felt desire to open up communications as the clamour from communities on both sides of the border for the re-opening of roads which for years had been sealed off by the British army.

Finally, in May 1994, Patrick Mayhew responded to a list of questions from Sinn Féin which had been passed to his office by the Irish government. Republicans now had to make some fundamental assessments. Did the Downing Street Declaration represent a genuine movement by the British government in the direction of a lasting peace? Or was it merely a political response by a government under pressure from the Irish peace initiative, aiming to avoid a political confrontation with Dublin and to fragment the nationalist consensus? Even if our assessment was that it did not represent a positive and sincere advance by the British government, Irish republicans did not feel they should allow this is to influence unduly our willingness to take risks. At the end of the day the consideration of any option available to us had to be in the context of Sinn Féin's peace objectives and the strategy for their achievement. Our aim was to eradicate the causes of conflict in Ireland and to bring about the exercise of the right to national self-determination of the Irish people as a whole. We had worked to establish a peace process in order to bring this about.

The issue of self-determination was central to the resolution of the conflict. That fact had been addressed and was firmly on the political agenda. Democracy demanded that Britain recognise the right of the Irish people to determine our own future in our own interests and on our own terms. Any new agreement must respect the diversity of our different traditions and earn their allegiance. Present policies and political structures had prevented this from happening. Partition had deepened the divisions.

The Joint Declaration was described by its authors as 'the first step' towards a peace settlement. Sinn Féin was committed to such a settlement and even if there was a gap between what was required and what was on offer, then it seemed self-evident to me that we should all move to bridge that gap.

In July 1994, at a special delegate conference in Letterkenny, Co. Donegal, Sinn Féin activists gave their response to the Downing Street Declaration. The party concluded that the declaration marked a further stage in the peace process but that it was not a peace process in itself, nor did its authors claim it to be. Sinn Féin stressed, in contrast, that 'the dynamic necessary to move us all out of conflict does not and cannot lie in a public declaration alone. This dynamic must be found in the principles, framework, timescale, procedures and objectives of a peace process and particularly in negotiation.'

The Letterkenny conference was an important consultative meeting for Sinn Féin activists. It reviewed the previous phase of our strategy and gave a mandate to the leadership to continue.

Prior to the Letterkenny conference, I was asked for and I provided the IRA leadership with an assessment of the existing stage of the peace process. Earlier that year, in April, the IRA had called a temporary suspension of its operations in order to demonstrate its 'willingness to be positive and flexible' as the situation evolved. In August I gave another assessment, again at the IRA's request. The IRA are political people. They could read the situation as well as everyone else. There comes a moment in history when one has to take a decision. It was up to the IRA to hold their own consultations and come to their own decisions. I would have respected whatever decision they took.

Between 25 and 27 August, Bruce Morrison led a second ANIA delegation to the North. After meeting Sinn Féin and hearing our detailed assessment, Mr Morrison said: 'We hope the input that we have given will move [the] process forward. We believe that it will, and we are very encouraged by what we heard here today that the process is moving in a very constructive direction.' That meeting with ANIA was an important and significant step.

On 28 August, John Hume and I issued a statement saying in part:

We have publicly acknowledged that the task of seeking agreement on a peaceful and democratic accord for all the people of Ireland is our primary challenge. We are convinced that significant progress has been made in developing the conditions necessary for this to occur. ... We underline that the process in which we are engaged offers no threat to any section of the people on this island. Our objective is agreement among our divided people.

In any new situation there is a heavy onus on the British

government to respond positively, both in terms of the demilitarisation of the situation and in assisting the search for an agreed Ireland by encouraging the process of national reconciliation.

It is our informed opinion that the peace process remains firmly on course. We are, indeed, optimistic that the situation can be moved tangibly forward.

The same day Irish Taoiseach Albert Reynolds said:

I believe that we now have an historic opportunity, the best opportunity [for peace] since partition.

Of course, the British government have a heavy responsibility in all of this. They are committed under the Declaration to play a positive and important role in assisting the Irish people to reach an agreed accommodation for the future and in removing the injustices which have fuelled conflict in the past.

In this context, I hope to see an all-round demilitarisation of the situation and the full participation of all parties, on equal terms, in talks leading to a comprehensive political settlement.

The jigsaw was complete. These three statements represented a package which the IRA leadership responded to in its historic and courageous statement of 31 August 1994:

Recognising the potential of the current situation and in order to enhance the democratic peace process and underline our definitive commitment to its success, the leadership of Óglaigh na hÉireann have decided that as of midnight, Wednesday, 31 August, there will be a complete cessation of military operations. All our units have been instructed accordingly.

At this historic crossroads the leaderships of Óglaigh na hÉireann salutes and commends our Volunteers, other activists, our supporters and the political prisoners who sustained this struggle against all odds for the past 25 years. Your courage, determination and sacrifices have demonstrated that the spirit of freedom and the desire for peace based on a just and lasting settlement cannot be crushed. We remember all those who have died for Irish freedom and we reiterate our commitment to our republican objectives.

Our struggle has seen many gains and advances made by nationalists and for the democratic position. We believe that an opportunity to create a just and lasting settlement has been created. We are therefore entering into a new situation in a spirit of determination and confidence, determined that the injustices which created this conflict will be removed and confident in the strength and justice of our struggle to achieve this.

We note that the Downing Street Declaration is not a solution, nor was it presented as such by its authors. A solution will only be found as a result of inclusive negotiations. Others, not least the British government, have a duty to face up to their responsibilities. It is our desire to significantly contribute to the creation of a climate which will encourage this. We urge everyone to approach this new situation with energy, determination and patience.

(1995)

Free Ireland: Towards a Lasting Peace

FREE IRELAND

Ní Neart go Chur le Chéile
(Unity is Strength)

To sue for peace is a noble thing. The IRA's initiative
was a brave one, and the 31 August commitment was
made by a confident, united and unbroken army.

The IRA's decision placed a heavy responsibility on republicans and on everyone committed to ending conflict in this
country. We must all become guarantors of the peace process
and bring it to a democratic conclusion. That is the implicit
and explicit import of the IRA's statement.

Nationalists gave a wholehearted welcome to the new development and the concrete support it offered the peace process.
Addressing a spontaneous demonstration outside Connolly
House in Belfast on the day of the ceasefire, I saw before me a
section of those who had carried on the struggle in the city
since the late 1960s. All of us felt the same. All of us who had
lived and hoped, who had fought for freedom and justice,
thought of the friends and comrades we had lost along the
way and pledged ourselves to the task of building a just and
lasting peace.

Throughout the world the IRA statement was universally
recognised and applauded. It put the onus on the British and

the loyalists to respond in equal measure, and it put a moral obligation on everyone who had portrayed the IRA operations as the source of our troubles to look again at the fundamental cause of the conflict in the North of Ireland.

The IRA cessation threw both the British and loyalists into some confusion initially. The British government's guarded welcome focused on the precise phrasing of the statement and the fact that the IRA had failed to use the word 'permanent'. The British prime minister urged the IRA to say expressly that it had ceased its campaign 'for good'. There were British calls too for the IRA to disarm unilaterally, even while the loyalist death squads, the RUC and the British army remained fully armed and active. The Irish government, however, played a leading role at this time, fully acknowledging the import of the IRA's decision and launching a successful diplomatic initiative to win worldwide backing for the peace process. Within a week of the ceasefire, I joined Mr Reynolds and John Hume in Dublin, where we reiterated that our objective was to find an equitable and lasting agreement that would command the allegiance of all, including the unionists, without whose participation and agreement the problem could not be resolved. The inaugural meeting of the Forum for Peace and Reconcilia-tion took place in Dublin the following month. The Forum's remit was to examine the conflict in all its aspects, but unionist parties declined to participate. This decision was unfortunate; a forum for reconciliation obviously needs the involvement of unionists if it is to fulfil its function. We cannot make peace without the unionists. New relationships will have to be forged between all the people of our country, and there must be a readiness on the part of all political representatives to engage in inclusive, democratic dialogue in order to bring this about.

On 13 October the Combined Loyalist Military Command – the Ulster Defence Association, the Ulster Volunteer Force and the Red Hand Commandos – announced a ceasefire. Their action followed directly from the IRA's initiative and, significant and welcome though it was, must be seen in this context. Their response was a tactical move largely dictated by pressure from the British government and the Ulster Unionist Party, who saw continuing loyalist violence as a threat to the union and to their political efforts to minimise the impact of a peace process with which they were never happy and to which they had never willingly contributed. The loyalist cessation was nonetheless an historic event which I commended.

In the period which followed the cessation, as a groundswell of public opinion demanded that the process be pushed forward, the British government sought to convince the UUP and the loyalist death squads that there was no threat to the status quo or to the union. It tried to reduce the momentum of the peace process, to deflate its potential, to avoid taking on board the political and constitutional issues which were fundamental to a lasting settlement. At every stage of the process, the British government's attitude to peace proposals from nationalist Ireland, whether presented by the Dublin government, John Hume or Sinn Féin, has been marked by stalling tactics and diversions. At all times the British have sought to insist on their position, to apply pressure, to create and win a contest of wills, to mislead and to demand concessions and one-sided gains. It seeks victory on its own terms, not peace on democratic terms, and it aims at all times to fragment the consensus around the Irish peace initiative.

In consequence of its initial failure to give full recogition to the IRA's cessation of operations, Britain stalled on the question of opening talks with Sinn Féin for several months, and then allowed that, while talks could get underway, Britain would be represented only by civil servants. Thus, though a ban on ministerial contact with Sinn Féin existed, Sinn Féin's elected representatives could deal directly with British government ministers as members of local government delegations, but not as delegates to talks on the most urgent political issues of the day.

Though the IRA had taken the initiative in bringing an end to the cycle of violence in the North, the British pressed for a complete dismantling of IRA armaments as a precondition for opening full dialogue with Sinn Féin. Quite apart from Britain's grudging attitude to Sinn Féin's democratic mandate, which must neccesarily be given equal respect if an all-inclusive settlement is to be worked out, the British have for tactical reasons tried to impose conditions which have generally not been used in resolving conflicts in other areas. Indeed, in the negotiations which preceeded its withdrawal from other colonies, Britain had no difficulty in dealing directly with its armed opponents.

The frequent contradictions of British policy have obliged Britain to retreat and make concessions, slowly but inevitably. The continuation of the ceasefire obliged the British to make a 'working assumption' that it was in fact permanent. The British broadcasting ban and the orders which excluded Sinn Féin leaders from entering Britain were both lifted in the wake of the IRA cessation, and allowed us to put our analysis directly to the British people in a way which had not previously been possible. The peace process was warmly welcomed by the vast majority of people in Britain, and their support helped push it to the top of the political agenda there. And after several months of prevarication as to whether they would talk openly to Sinn Féin and recognise the party's democratic mandate, the British government eventually opened negotiations with us in December 1994. It was the first publicised meeting between Sinn Féin and the British since the Anglo-Irish Treaty of 1922.

While the British have for some time acknowledged that they no longer have any 'selfish, economic or strategic interest' in staying in Ireland, they have failed to say that they have no remaining political interest. The British government does have such an interest, at least for the present. They remain politically committed to the union, and see the weakening of the link with Ireland as potentially the first stage in the disintegration of the United Kingdom. But despite the Conservative Party's long association with, and Prime Minister Major's oft-repeated personal commitment to unionism, and despite the protestations of unionists to the contrary, the Downing Street Declaration marked a stage in the slow and painful process of England's disengagement from her first and last colony,

Ireland. It may have been a small step, as the Hillsborough Agreement of 1985 had been, but it left its mark.

The British establishment is undoubtedly concerned to bring about a settlement in Ireland. It is concerned also that settlement should be on its terms. But the British establishment is not a monolith. It has no bottom line. It is currently re-examining its role in Ireland. Some tendencies favour a continuation of the union; some would end it. All accept the need for a new relationship between these islands, and there is a widespread acceptance that an internal Six County settlement is not a solution.

The secretary of state for Northern Ireland has said plainly that 'we cannot revert to a system of government in Northern Ireland with which only one community can identify'. He acknowledges that the concept of self-determination 'can lead to a range of possible outcomes, one of which could be a united Ireland', and in principle the British government declared itself ready to legislate for this eventuality, once it was the will of a majority in the Six Counties. While the British declined to become 'a persuader for any particular outcome' in the event of change in the North's constitutional status, and instead stood by Britain's constitutional guarantee that the North would remain part of the United Kingdom for as long as a majority in 'the province' wished, the secretary of state made it clear that:

We are, however, persuaders [for] widely based agreement, whatever character it may turn out to bear. We will work with the Irish Government and the Northern Ireland parties to achieve such agreement, among all the people of Ireland and embracing the totality of relationships, in order to bring about peace, stability and reconciliation. ... Only by addressing all the aspects of the relationships between our peoples within Northern Ireland, between North and South and between the two governments, can we achieve a lasting and stable accommodation. ... There is no predetermined outcome envisaged. Nothing is predicated, and nothing will be ruled out either in advance or in the event.

The publication of the Framework Document by the London and Dublin governments in February 1995 should now clear the way for inclusive peace talks and for the next phase of this process.

The Framework Document is a discussion document. Like the Downing Street Declaration, it does not attempt to preclude or predetermine any particular outcome, but its publication by the two governments was a clear recognition that partition has failed, that British rule in Ireland has failed, and that there is no going back to the failed policies and structures of the past. The ethos of the document and the political framework envisaged is clearly an all-Ireland one. It deals with the general concept of one-island social, economic and political structures, and moves the situation closer to an all-Ireland settlement.

Even though we would like to see this more deeply rooted, prescriptive and thoroughgoing, Sinn Féin will judge the document pragmatically, and in the context of our objectives, policy and strategy. Our principles have not and must not change, but our strategy and our tactics must be rooted in objective reality. Great new possibilities have opened up and demand new thinkings, new tactics and a renewed and revitalised struggle.

The present constitutional position of the occupied area is that 'Northern Ireland' is not and never was a separate state. It never had and does not now have any life or existence of its own. The British parliament, in which rests all sovereignty in Britain, created the constitution of 'Northern Ireland' by an act of parliament. By the same means it can be amended or ended. There is thus no impediment, as far as Britain is concerned, to the building of new structures of a radical nature once the British parliament is satisfied that it should be so. The wording of all statutory undertakings by the British is intended to maintain the union. There is scope for debating how committed to the union the British really are, but it is important to note that the current British position does not prevent constitutional change or political advances which fall short of dismantling the union from going ahead without the consent of a majority in the North of Ireland. This is important, for in this political and ultimately constitutional area, the British can be tested.

One of the most significant advances of the past few years has been the growth of a widespread acceptance that an internal Six County settlement is not a solution. Some have come to this conclusion because they recognise the failure of partition, and understand that it is not only the governance of the Six Counties which has been the problem, but the very existence of the statelet itself. Others, who may not share that analysis, have also concluded that an internal settlement is not a solution.

The northern state was founded on and has been sustained by discrimination. It was and is underwritten by policies determined by London. Under the terms of the Framework Document, however, the British must remove all anti-nationalist symbols and appearances from the Six County statelet in order to provide parity of esteem in the North, and by eliminating as far as possible all obvious and visible difference between the North and the rest of the island of Ireland. They are obliged under the Framework to bring about legislative change to improve the position of nationalists while protecting the rights of other citizens.

Until now, British policy has labelled nationalists as inferior, second class. In a literal sense the phrase 'parity of esteem', which informs the Framework Document and binds the British and Irish governments' policies in regard to the peace process, implies an equality of respect, an equality of opportunity. In the current political context it has come to mean an equality of respect and treatment for nationalists in the North. Ultimately it must apply to everyone on the island. But what does it mean in practice? Sinn Féin believes that this term would be better replaced by the more specific term, 'equality of treatment'.

There is a pressing need for physical, legislative and practical action to deliver positive proof that nationalist rights, identities and allegiances are guaranteed equal parity. We need, for example, effective anti-discrimination laws to remove the disparities in employment levels and opportunities between Catholics and Protestants. These have not changed in any real sense since the Fair Employment Act of 1976; in 1995 the Northern Ireland Labour Force Survey confirmed that unemployment among Catholics is more than twice that of Protestants and that it is still significantly more difficult for a Catholic to find work.

There is need for equality of opportunity in employment, equality of treatment for Irish culture and identity, equality of treatment of elected representatives and voters. Proper security provisions for all citizens must be guaranteed. Equality in the provision of education, particularly through the medium of Irish, and equality of treatment as regards economic development are also fundamental. It is in these areas of our daily lives that the quickest changes can occur. These changes do not require negotiation: they should happen as of right.

The achievement of equality of treatment for nationalists in the North will erode the very reason for the existence of that statelet. The unionist leaders know this: that is why they so dogmatically turn their faces against change. Unionists have traditionally supported the union because it gave them a superior status in relation to nationalists. Once they are treated on equal terms with nationalists, no more and no less, this must inevitably reduce their advantage in practice and undermine the rational basis of the unionist doctrine.

Democratic rights include national rights. Nationalists in the occupied area are not an ethnic minority living in a foreign country. We are Irish people living in Ireland. We want to see an end to partition; that is our primary objective at this time. Our strategy between now and the ending of partition must be based on the fact that there can be no internal settlement; that there has to be a more fundamental change. During a transitional phase there must be maximum democracy, guaranteeing equality of treatment – parity of esteem – between nationalist and unionist.

Irrespective of the content of the Framework Document, of how much of it we might like or dislike, the document and the inclusive peace talks which must follow its publication should open the way for new political arrangements agreed through democratic negotiations between all the Irish people. The Framework Document in itself is neither a solution nor a settlement. The next step is to initiate all-party talks. There is an onus on both governments, and particularly the British government, to move the situation quickly to inclusive dialogue.

Clearly these negotiations cannot take place above the heads of our people. There needs to be a transparency in the negotiation process, keeping people informed and reducing the possibility of the heightening and exploiting of fear and uncertainty. Republicans are not afraid of the prospect of inclusive negotiations: we have long argued that a settlement will only be achieved if all involved reach agreement. Such an agreement will be won when all sides can consider their own situation to have been improved.

Sinn Féin will enter these peace talks on the basis of our republican analysis. We will put our view that a lasting peace in Ireland can only be based on the right of the Irish people to national self-determination, an end to British jurisdiction in our country, and the creation of a new agreed Irish jurisdiction.

Peace can only come about when the causes of conflict are addressed. In the case of the Anglo-Irish situation where the conflict is political, peace must come through a political solution. The war in the Six Counties of Ireland is a legacy of the denial for centuries by the British government of the Irish people's right to national independence. The very existence of the conflict shows that the undemocratic political structures imposed on the Irish people by Britain in 1921, and maintained today, are in fact a continuing source of division and instability. The political structures and institutions born out of partition have failed the democratic test.

Shoring up the unionist political majority in the artificially created statelet has come to be the cornerstone of Britian's rationale for its continuing exercise of sovereignty over the Six Counties. This unionist majority is, in fact, solely the

result of the gerrymandering perpetrated by a British government which dictated the size and make-up of the respective
populations of the Six and Twenty-six County states. The historical purpose and effect of that gerrymandering was, and
remains, to erect a barrier against Irish reunification.

Today's advocates of the unionist perspective represent
some twenty percent of the Irish nation. They are a national
minority; a significant one, but a minority nonetheless.

There is much unnecessary confusion, as well as deliberate
misrepresentation, of the republican position on this principle
of unionist consent. We subscribe to the classic, democratic
position of Irish nationalism. Britain's partitioning of Ireland
turned the Irish unionist minority into an artificial majority in
the Six County area. Unionists are not – and do not claim to
be – a nation with a right to national self-determination, as
this is universally recognised in international law. Unionists
are a national minority, a religious/political minority, with
minority rights, not majority ones. Unionists can have no veto
over British government policy, nor over Irish government
policy either.

The unionist position is, in fact, logically and politically an
absurd one, for they in effect claim to possess a unilateral
right to union with the British state, the majority of whose
people do not want them, when there can only be unilateral
rights of separation, never of union.

At the same time, while nationalists deny that unionists have
any right of veto over British or Irish policy directed at seeking to dissolve the union, most nationalists and republicans
recognise as a matter of pragmatism that it is desirable in
practice that the consent, or assent, of as many unionists as
possible should be obtained to the practical steps required to
bring about the ending of partition and establishing of a
united Ireland. But the argument that the consent of the
unionist population is a pre-condition for any political movement is entirely bogus and without democratic basis. Consent,
applied in this absolutist way, effectively becomes a veto, lock-
ing the unionist community into a no-change mind-set. As
long as their present position is guaranteed and underwritten

by Britain, there is no reason for them to reach an accommodation with the rest of the Irish people. We are left in a
situation of political stalemate and ongoing conflict.

The late Catholic primate of all-Ireland, Cardinal Ó Fiaich,
speaking in 1985, four days after the Hillsborough Treaty was
signed, commented that:

> The present policy of the British government – that there
> will be no change in the status of Northern Ireland while
> the majority want British rule to remain – is no policy at
> all. It means you do nothing and it means that the loyalists
> in the north are given no encouragement to make any
> move of any kind.

As unionists themselves have frequently pointed out, most
emphatically since the signing of the Anglo-Irish Agreement in
1985, the British government has, when it sees fit, chosen to
ignore the wishes of the unionist population. The concept of
consent is one applied selectively by the British government
and only when it coincides with its own political interests. It
has never been extended to nationalists and ignores the fact
that 600,000 nationalists have been forcibly coerced into the
Six County state. Where is the principle of democratic consent for nationalists? There are five million people on the
island of Ireland; 900,000 of us are unionists.

It is often said that there are two traditions or cultures in
Ireland. There are not. There are scores, maybe hundreds, all
making up a diverse and rich culture, and all equally valid.
There is female and male, urban and rural, small town and hill
village. There is Gaeltacht and Galltacht, North and South,
East and West. There is literary and oral, labour and artisan,
the orange and the green. In total they represent the sum of
our diversity and our Irishness.

The Siege of Derry and the Battle of the Boyne are as much a
part of Irish history as the Siege of Limerick, the Famine or the
Easter Rising. The slogan 'Brits Out' is not a call, as is often
mischievously suggested, to banish unionists. On the contrary,
we need them, because a peaceful, just and united society must
include all sections of the Irish people. We do not seek to
exclude. The peace process, like the republican philosophy

itself, is founded on inclusiveness – on bringing together people of different opinions with the aim of finding agreement.

I have consistently argued that the consent and allegiance of unionists is needed to secure a peace settlement. But the argument that the consent of a national minority, which has been elevated into a majority in an undemocratic and artificially created state, is necessary before any constitutional change can occur is a nonsense. It ignores the fact that the present constitutional arrangements, based on partition, have led to decades of bloody war and that all attempts to find a solution within these confines have failed. It ignores the reality that in British and international law the British government, if it wishes, can legislate itself out of Ireland.

Unionist allegiance to the British crown is matched by their deep distrust of the British government. Few unionists really trust London. Amongst ordinary Protestants, there is instead an increasing questioning of traditional political positions, and many accept that far-reaching change is inevitable. The unionist leadership, however, looks for an internal settlement which will restore unionist rule, unionist domination. The furore they created over the Framework Document – 'Ulster has been served with an eviction notice to leave the United Kingdom' – is a case in point. When positive and constructive leadership is most required the unionist elite resort to rhetoric.

Republicans recognise that the national interest demands that the consent, or assent, of as many of our unionist fellow countrymen and fellow countrywomen as possible should be obtained to the complex constitutional, economic and legal aspects of a final all-Ireland settlement, and the time-scale of bringing this about. We believe that the consent of the majority of present-day unionists could, in fact, be won, over time, to these steps to reunification, provided that the two governments, and primarily the British government, made that the basis of their policy. That is why nationalists want Britain to 'join the ranks of the persuaders', to base their policy on encouraging the coming together of Protestants and Catholics, not underwriting our continued separation, as has been the case up to now.

My joint statements with John Hume have made very clear that the ultimate objective of the peace process in which we are involved seeks agreement among the divided peoples of Ireland, an agreement that must earn the allegiance, and agreement, of all traditions, and that both governments and all parties must be involved in this process. The underlying assumption of these joint statements is that the only interest to be accommodated and the only problem to be resolved is the division between the two main sections of the people who inhabit this island and that there would be no selfish British interests involved. That is, the Irish people as a whole have the exlusive right to determine their own future without external impediments of any kind.

Self-determination is a nation's exercise of the political freedom to determine its own economic, social and cultural development, without external influence and without partial or total disruption of the nation's unity or territorial integrity. Ireland today clearly does not have this freedom, nor does the pretext for partition hold good against these criteria.

In the words of Sean MacBride, winner of the Nobel Peace Prize:

Ireland's right to sovereignty, independence and unity are inalienable and indefeasible. It is for the Irish people as a whole to determine the future status of Ireland. Neither Britain nor a small minority selected by Britain has any right to partition the ancient island of Ireland, nor to determine its future as a sovereign nation.

The right of the Irish people, as a whole, to self-determination is supported by universally recognised principles of international law.

The partition of Ireland does not only affect the North of Ireland. It affects all Ireland socially and economically. It saps our national morale and consciousness and actively retards our ability as a nation to shape our affairs, to resolve the causes of poverty, emigration and unemployment, as well as the other more obvious causes of death and destruction and the conflict itself.

We Irish are a colonised people. We have endured centuries of colonial domination. But it is to the credit of this nation that we never succumbed entirely to colonial rule. Or at least that the men and women of no property never succumbed. Not in our minds. We refused and refuse yet to have colonised minds.

Republicans are not worried by the Dublin government's agreement to alter Articles Two and Three of the Irish Constitution, which assert Ireland's right to jurisdiction over the whole island. The Irish people will not support a government which proposes constitutional change that in any way recognises Britain's claim to jurisdiction in the North while setting aside Irish national sovereignty. In particular, republicans do not oppose constitutional change in the context of an overall all-Ireland settlement. On the contrary, we fully support the working out of a new national constitution for the island.

The obvious response in Ireland to the continuing division of our country and our people by the British government should be the development of the maximum degree of political unity and action possible in the peaceful pursuit of democracy. Sinn Féin has the potential to join with others in building a mass movement throughout this island. Many of our potential allies have yet to be persuaded as to how British disengagement can be brought about. It is up to us to outline our strategy and our tactics in a manner which is relevant to the mass of the people.

In the event of the British refusing to assist in securing a democratic settlement, the Dublin government must take the initiative. Dublin should strive to mobilise international support – popular and political – for a viable peace process in Ireland. It should utilise every avenue available in international forums, including the UN, in support of a programme to achieve democracy and peace in Ireland. The support of British public opinion should be sought through a diplomatic offensive, and a debate leading to a dialogue with Northern unionists should be initiated. Dublin should reassure the unionist community of a total commitment to their civil and religious rights and persuade them of the need for their participation in building an Irish society based on equality and national reconciliation. A concerted national campaign to mobilise popular support for a process of national reconciliation in every aspect of Irish life should be launched, and a democratic structure by which the peace process can be agreed upon, implemented, and overseen, should be established.

By any objective international standards, the conflict in the North represents a failure of the normal political process. In view of the intolerable consequences which flow from such a failure, a peaceful resolution may entail international co-operation through the agencies of the European Union and the United Nations.

The political and economic transformation of Europe provides a golden opportunity for Ireland to resolve its British problem finally and initiate a process of economic and political reunification to the benefit of all its people. There is a popular consensus in Europe, reflected even by some governments, that Irish reunification is not only inevitable, but a prerequisite to a durable peace. It is essential that the Irish government galvanise that opinion and translate it through the political mechanisms of the European Union into practical proposals.

Today the debate about Irish self-determination and the fight to end partition takes place within a political, social and economic context that has been fundamentally altered by the creation of the European Union. The fight against the Single European Act and the Maastricht Treaty has been lost, and the reality is that Ireland will remain in the European Union for the foreseeable future. We face new challenges as a result, but the fight for national self-determination is, if anything, more urgent, and more relevant, than it has been at any time since partition.

An editorial in the Dublin *Sunday Business Post* which commented on my first visit to New York asked, 'What might be achieved if the Irish government made a coherent attempt to galvanise Irish America in support of national policy?'

This is something that Irish republicans and nationalists need to think about. For the outcome of the visa controversy showed that, for the first time ever in Anglo-American relations, Washington, faced with a choice between Ireland and Britain, chose Ireland. The issue came up again in March 1995 when, in spite of intense British opposition, I was granted the right to raise funds for Sinn Féin in the USA and attend the St Patrick's Day party at the White House. These things would not have happened but for the extraordinary effort of lobbying and campaigning by leading members of the Irish-American community, including political leaders, business leaders, trade unionists and media people. Nor would they have happened without the support of people in Ireland.

What the coming together of progressive political forces over the visa issue demonstrated was the potential and possibilities of what can happen if Irish nationalism unites and wins powerful allies. Obtaining a visa for one Irish republican might seem a relatively minor matter, but what was achieved was of enormous symbolic and political importance. It also illustrated that international interest and concern can play an important and constructive part in the development of a viable peace process. There has consistently been a need for the international community to exercise its good will and influence to help end conflicts worldwide. This is generally recognised and, at times, acted upon. It has not, however, been a factor in the Anglo-Irish conflict until now. This situation needs to be built on further.

There is a widespread interest in and concern about Ireland in the United States, which stems from the historic links between our two countries. The US government can play a significant and positive role in encouraging a climate which moves the situation on. Indeed it has done so, facilitating agreement among the parties to the conflict and pledging economic support for a settlement. President Clinton's decision to convene and chair a conference on investment in Ireland indicates the kind of practical help which has been offered. The British establishment will do everything in its power to limit the influence of progressive US opinion, but they have a difficulty in this: London still believes that it rules the world, though it doesn't. One thing is clear, however; we must apply ourselves to finding ways to enable wider allies to be won, and won more firmly and solidly in the US, in Europe, in Britain and internationally.

Ireland and Britain have much to gain from peace. A lasting peace in Ireland is as much in the interest of the British people as it is in Irish interests. The billions now spent on war can become an investment in peace; an investment in jobs, in housing, childcare, transport, health and education. Britain's subvention to the Six Counties has now reached £4 billion a year, but most, if not all of this could be saved within the North and in Britain if a lasting peace is secured. With no other changes in economic policy, the unification of the economies will generate tens of thousands of jobs. Peace will release a tide of new economic activity and investment.

A proper peace process will involve a plan for economic transition and reconstruction, including an international aid package. The logic of economic and social development lies with Irish unity, not in union with a declining British economy. This is now recognised by even the most conservative elements of Irish society, by the bankers and the business community. The 1983 *Report of the New Ireland Forum* concluded:

The division of the island has been a source of continuing costs, especially for trade and development in border areas, but in general also to the two separate administrations which have been pursuing separate economic policies on a small island with shared problems and resources.

We conclude that partition and its failure to provide political stability have resulted in extra costs in many sectors and have inhibited the socio-economic development of Ireland, especially in the North. Division has had an adverse effect on the general ethos of society and has contributed to a limiting of perspective, north and south. Had the division not taken place, or had the unionist and nationalist traditions in Ireland been encouraged to bring it to an end by reaching a mutual accommodation, the people of the whole island would be in a much better position to benefit from its resources and to meet the common challenges that face Irish society, north and south, towards the end of the 20th century.

The full benefits of integrating the two economies can only be realised by ending partition.

This generation of republicans seeks an end to Anglo-Irish conflict forever. If the British government commits itself to embracing and promoting a policy for a negotiated peace settlement, then we republicans will commit all our energies and resources to reaching such an agreement. And, when such an agreement is reached, we will continue to use all our resources to promote the healing process that will be necessary to unite the Irish people and to protect the democratic dignity, civil rights and heritage of all our people. The compelling logic of our situation and the climate of international opinion demands a democratic and negotiated settlement of the Anglo-Irish conflict. The alternative locks all of us into a perpetuation of conflict. Is this what the British government wants?

The catalyst effect of the Irish Peace Initiative and the effect of the strategies employed by the various parties, have all brought their own influence to bear on the developing situation. This entails a high risk for all involved, but Sinn Féin is taking a greater risk than any of the others. But what is clear is that we need to bring all-Ireland nationalist opinion with us. In all of this, we in Sinn Féin have a responsibility to build on the progress which has been made. Sinn Féin and the SDLP, for example, remain locked in electoral, as well as ideological battles and we have lots of reasons from our respective experiences to be distrustful of each other. John Hume and I have never attempted to disguise the political differences between our parties. But what we have attempted to do is to put the cause of peace and a negotiated settlement before narrower party political considerations.

My republican analysis is, of course, not identical with that of Mr Hume on all the issues of the day. For example, I would not agree with his views on the out-datedness of the nation state, which we regard as the basis of democracy. Republicans do not believe that we are living in a post-nationalist world. But we are at one with him to holding that 'an internal settlement is not a solution' and 'that the Irish people as a whole have the right to national self-determination', and 'it is the search for that agreement and the means of achieving it on which we will be concentrating'.

In essence, Sinn Féin is attempting to reconstruct an Irish political consensus on the basis of the principles, dynamic and process contained in the Irish peace initiative, to reinforce commitment to such a consensus politically and to sustain political action based on it.

To ensure that the demands and interests of nationalists are given maximum weight and brought to bear fully on the British government in the period ahead, it is essential that public opinion all over Ireland, but particularly in the Twenty-six Counties, encourages the government in Dublin to give wholehearted support to the democratic cause, and helps to obtain allies for this cause all over the world. All republicans and nationalist need now to consider how best to advance the basic national demands in the light of the new conditions and possibilities opening up before us. We need particularly to consider how we can appeal to the national sentiment that is strong particularly at the grassroots of Fianna Fáil, among the ordinary members of and voters for that party, but also among many Labour Party people, and more widely among those disenchanted with, or uninvolved in, party politics.

They need a political focus for their aspirations and activity. They need something around which they can build political unity and concrete common action that will appeal to all true Irish patriots. That is why I suggest the need for nationally-minded people to consider the launching of an Irish freedom charter – A Charter for Justice and Peace in Ireland – around which the broadest sections of the Irish people can rally and unite. This would consist of the most fundamental national demands relating to Irish politics, the Irish economy and our society as a whole, which the widest range of nationally-minded Irish people can support and which can provide a rallying point for their aspirations.

The demands of this Freedom Charter should be directed at the British and Irish governments and appeal to international support. I suggest that the first proposition of such a charter should be an adoption of the first principle of the Freedom Charter of the South African National Congress, which guided their long and inspiring freedom struggle which is now coming to fruition in a free South Africa. It would state: *Ireland belongs to all who live in it*, just as South Africa belongs to all who live in it.

For the first time in twenty years, there is tangible evidence throughout Ireland of increasing self-confidence and awareness among nationalists. Every effort must be made to harness this energy, to build upon it, and to direct it in a way which will advance the peace process and secure a negotiated settlement based on democratic principles.

The political reality of this situation is that there can only be advance, continued advance, if we grasp the opportunity of the times. This means working together, even though we are rivals with other parties. It means winning and maintaining the backing of the Dublin government for the northern nationalist people and co-operating together to obtain the powerful international allies the Irish nationalist cause needs.

What is additionally required are narrower, more specific short-term and intermediate objectives to advance the possibilities which our established peace objectives have provided. At the heart of Irish nationalist concerns are fears about loyalist violence and unionist bigotry, the intimidation of nationalist communities by the British army, and social deprivation and job discrimination. There is also the denial of full and equal recognition of Irish cultural rights within the Six Counties.

In the short to medium term, we need to advance the position of northern nationalists in every conceivable way. This means strengthening the nationalist agenda. It means no return to unionist domination of nationalist communities in the Six Counties. What is abundantly clear, and the political representatives of unionism must inform themselves and their supporters of this, is that there is no going back to the days of Stormont and unionist rule.

It means local republican activists being able to represent and speak for their communities in conditions of peace, not being interfered with by the British military or the RUC, free of personal harassment and free from the threat of the death squads.

It means full recognition of the rights of Gaelgeorí and an equality of status for the Irish language, including proper funding.

It means the speedy release of all long-term political prisoners pending a full amnesty for all political prisoners.

It means an end to all repressive legislation and an end to collusion between the British state and loyalist death squads.

Political concessions of this kind from Britain will not be won without a hard and disciplined struggle. It will require unity between republicans and nationalists in the North, such as the Hume-Adams initiative presaged. It will require the support of the government in Dublin. And it will require the support of powerful allies internationally – in the European Union, in Britain itself, and especially in the USA.

In examining the causes of conflict in Ireland or their resolution, it is a mistake to see this only in the context of the Six Counties. A complete transformation of Irish society throughout the island is required. To join six counties to twenty-six counties is insufficient. A new agreed Ireland must be our aim.

Sinn Féin believes that there is a need for the transformation of all Irish society, not only in the occupied area but throughout the entire island. We believe that there must be fundamental changes in the whole structure and nature of Irish political, social, economic and cultural life. Our vision is of a new beginning for all our people. We seek to end conflict and division, to reverse inequality and poverty. We seek to enshrine and guarantee the rights of women in a new and non-sexist society. We demand civil and religious liberties and the separation of church from state. We seek a redistribution of wealth, a new economic democracy to end unemployment and emigration, to guarantee education, houses and jobs. We seek to turn this vision into a reality.

We seek to be part of the building of a society which can reflect and uphold the diversity of all our people. Our vision is of a free Ireland, a peaceful Ireland, a unity of Catholic, Protestant and Dissenter, with all citizens guaranteeing the civil and religious rights of all other citizens. We hold to the words of the 1916 Proclamation which said:

The Republic guarantees religious and civil liberty, equal rights and equal opportunities to all its citizens, and declares its resolve to pursue the happiness and prosperity of the whole nation and of all its parts, cherishing all the children of the nation equally, and oblivious of the differences, carefully fostered by an alien government, which have divided a minority from the majority in the past.

Sinn Féin seeks a new constitution of Ireland with a charter of rights, which would include written guarantees for those presently constituted as 'loyalists'. Their participation would ensure that the new Ireland would accommodate the the Irish people in all their diversity.

1994 marked twenty-five years of the current deployment of British crown forces on Irish soil. They have been traumatic, mind-bending years of human tragedy for all caught up in the conflict. Patrick Galvin, the poet, had this to say:

> When you came to this land
> You said you came to understand.
> Soldier, we are tired of your understanding,
> Tired of British troops on Irish soil
> Tired of your knock on the door
> Tired of the rifle butt on the head.
> Soldier,
> We are tired of the peace you bring to Irish bones,
> Tired of the bombs, exploding in our homes
> Tired of the rubble, growing in the streets
> Tired of the death of old friends
> Tired of the tears and funerals -

Those endless, endless funerals.

In other parts of the world, conflicts which were formerly deemed intractable are moving towards resolution. These struggles may be more politically developed than ours, but what is at the core of all our effort is our will to be free. This makes the impossible possible. We have entered a new and final phase of struggle which will allow us to put the legacy of conflict behind us. It is that time in our history.

> We dream here
> We dream that this land
> Is our land
> That one day
> Catholic and Protestant
> Believer and non-believer
> Will stand here
> And dream as Irish men and women.

> We dream
> Of a green land
> Without death
> A new silence descending
> A silence of peace

We have over two decades of commitment behind us, and we are agreed on policy objectives and broad principles. The republican struggle is strong and confident, and will continue. We have come through the years of vilification and marginalisation. We are never going back to that, and for us there is no standing still. We are moving forward, to a free Ireland and a lasting peace.

(1995)

Free Ireland: Towards A Lasting Peace

REBUILDING THE PEACE PROCESS

T HE COLLAPSE ON Friday, 9 February, of the eighteen-
month-long IRA cessation was a tragic development. It
need not have happened. It was not inevitable. The
reality is that the potential for a negotiated peace settlement
created eighteen months ago was not grasped.

It was the absence of an effective political means of bringing
about the political changes necessary to remove the causes of
conflict and to secure a lasting peace – the inability even to
bring the British government and the unionists to the negotiating table – which caused the recurrence of conflict.

It is important therefore to revisit the basis on which the
IRA cessation was achieved eighteen months ago to understand clearly how we can re-create the potential and to ensure
that if it is re-created it is acted upon.

The IRA decision to call a complete cessation of its military
activity was largely based on the assessment given by the Sinn
Féin leadership and our view that an overall political package
had been developed which, if acted upon in good faith, had
the potential to bring about the political and constitutional
changes necessary to resolve the conflict. In effect, an alternative to the IRA campaign.

Over a period of years an intensive and unprecedented dialogue had been developed within Irish nationalist opinion in
its broad sense. It was a dialogue which required courage,
imagination and a new approach on all sides, not least on the

part of the then taoiseach, Albert Reynolds, and the SDLP leader, John Hume, who, despite intense opposition, turned their backs on the failed policy of isolation and took the risk required in the building of the Irish peace process.

An alternative strategy to bring about political and constitutional change was developed in dialogue, initially between myself and John Hume, and then with the Irish government and with key elements of Irish-American opinion. This political approach involved a democratic consensus to deal with the causes of conflict in the context of a number of clearly defined democratic principles.

From Sinn Féin's perspective these principles are:

a) Peace, to be sustained, must be based on a just and lasting negotiated settlement.

b) Partition has failed.

c) Present structures are therefore inadequate to sustain peace and must be changed.

d) An internal settlement is not a solution.

e) Partition and the British jurisdiction breach the principle of national self-determination.

f) The Irish people as a whole have an absolute right to national self-determination and must be able to exercise this right freely and without external impediment.

g) The exercise of the right to national self-determination is a matter of agreement between the Irish people alone.

h) It is for the Irish and British governments, in consultation with all parties, to co-operate to bring this about in the shortest time possible and to legislate accordingly.

i) The unionists can have no veto over the discussions involved in this, nor over the outcome of these discussions. There is a need to engage northern unionist and Protestant opinion on the democratic principle of national self-determination, assure them of full commitment to their civil and religious rights and to persuade them of the need for their participation in building an Irish society based on equality and national reconciliation.

j) A solution – a negotiated settlement – requires change, political and constitutional. The effect of this change would be to bring about the exercise by the Irish people of our right to national self-determination.

k)   An agreed unitary and independent Ireland is the option desired by us.

l)   An agreed Ireland is only achievable and viable if it can earn and enjoy the allegiance of the different traditions on this island by accommodating diversity and providing national reconciliation.

There were and are, of course, well-documented differences of opinion on how a number of these principles are interpreted, or on how they would be applied in practical terms. But not withstanding these differences, there was sufficient commonality of view on these political principles to allow us to move forward.

The Irish government assured us that it would work in close harmony and consultation with the representatives of the northern nationalist community at all times, and it was accepted that in the context of an IRA cessation, through a peace process of consultation and dialogue, we would collectively seek to advance these common positions in any negotiations so as to build a solid and democratic basis for a negotiated peace settlement.

We also agreed on the need to address a number of areas of immediate and practical concerns of northern nationalists. These would include:

* Equality of opportunity in employment
* Equality of treatment of Irish culture and identity.
* Equality of treatment of elected representatives.
* Proper security provision for all citizens according to their need.
* Equality in the provision of education, particularly through the medium of Irish.
* Equality of treatment in economic development.

The consensus position was that there could be no return to unionist domination and that there must be parity of esteem, equality of opportunity and equality of treatment for the aspirations, values and identities of both communities, not only at an abstract level but in real immediate and practical terms.

These principles would have to apply across the political, cultural, economic, social, legal and security spectrum.

In short, therefore, there was a commitment in the context of a real negotiation to present the British government and the unionists with an agreed Irish democratic agenda. As I have outlined publicly, Sinn Féin characterised this agenda as:

a) Constitutional change – new political arrangements and structures which would be acceptable to and accommodate all the Irish people.

b) Democratic rights – issues of equality and justice which continue to affect the nationalists in the north.

c) Demilitarisation – involving the removal of the apparatus of war and the release of prisoners, north and south.

A determined approach to these three areas by the breadth of Irish nationalist political opinion would, it is argued, represent a viable and effective approach to conflict resolution on the Irish side.

Against the background of intensive private dialogue, the British and Irish governments agreed to the text of the Downing Street Declaration. Despite our profound reservations about the overall content of this document and our publicly stated disagreement with many elements of it, the declaration did contain a clear commitment by the British and Irish governments to initiate inclusive dialogue as a means to a new political settlement among the Irish people, and furthermore, the British government also gave a commitment that it would encourage, facilitate and enable this agreement. These commitments were repeated frequently over the ensuing nine months.

In May 1994 John Major told a press conference, 'There is an opportunity for him [Gerry Adams] to give up violence and then in a short while enter the constitutional talks.'

The British government claimed that any response by it to an end of violence would be 'imaginative' and 'generous' and 'flexible'. The public commitment by both governments to commence the negotiations which, without preconditions, vetoes or any attempt to predetermine the outcome, would address all relevant issues represented the second element in

333

an overall political package. In the context of a good faith engagement, this contained, in our view, the potential to resolve the conflict on the basis of justice and democracy.

With a clear commitment by all the major political players to proactively pursue a new, negotiated and democratic political arrangement, and a publicly given commitment by the British government to convene with the Irish government the necessary peace talks to achieve agreement, the Sinn Féin leadership gave an assessment to the IRA leadership of the prospects for a lasting political settlement.

It was on this basis of clearly stated commitments and agreements that the IRA announced a complete cessation of military operations on 31 August 1994. The reality, however, of the British response to the IRA's historic decision was very different. In the eighteen months following the IRA cessation, political movement was glacial. The British attitude was best summed up as minimalist and begrudging.

At the heart of Britain's refusal to engage with the peace process was a fear of constitutional and political change, as well as a resistance to the necessary improvements in democratic rights and the eradication of discrimination and inequality. The peace process contained that potential. The British government, frightened of fundamental change and wedded to the failed policies of the past, avoided change by not engaging in the process.

The imperative of British policy became the erection of obstacles and the slowing down of the peace process to the point that it was fatally undermined. Patrick Mayhew, in an unguarded moment, admitted that John Major was treating the peace process like a bicycle, merely keeping it upright without falling off. Crucial to this British approach was the continued exclusion of Sinn Féin and our electorate. Sinn Féin was to be, and continues to be, treated as a second-class party and our electorate as second-class citizens.

It was, in fact, 9 December 1994, over three months after the IRA announcement, before the first meeting took place between Sinn Féin and British officials. The Sinn Féin delegation welcomed the reopening of bilateral discussions with the

British and urged speedy progress into inclusive all-party negotiations without preconditions. Over five meetings we presented the officials with three written papers and raised such confidence-building matters as the release of prisoners and the need for a comprehensive demilitarisation.

At the end of that time the British government was still refusing to bring a British government minister into the meeting. The British then created a bogus argument around the word 'demilitarisation', refusing to accept it on the agenda for discussions. This was despite 'demilitarisation' having been raised in two of the three papers Sinn Féin presented at the Stormont talks; it was discussed at all of the five meetings and was an item on the agenda of the 16 January meeting.

Then in March Patrick Mayhew introduced as a new precondition to all-party talks: his government's demand for an IRA surrender of weapons. The prevarication on ministerial meetings continued through March and most of April. The British announced the commencement of ministerial bilateral meetings with all of the parties except Sinn Féin. Meetings with Sinn Féin were kept to officials.

The British government was widely criticised for introducing what was effectively a two-tier political process which discriminated against Sinn Féin. Not until 10 May, more than eight months into the IRA cessation, did the British government agree to allow a government minister to meet Sinn Féin. Two weeks later British Secretary of State Patrick Mayhew was elbowed, with evident reluctance, into a meeting with me at President Clinton's Economic Conference in Washington. The reluctance of the British to concede this meeting was reflected in the content of this and subsequent meetings, with the British refusing to enter into serious discussions.

On his return from the United States in June, I wrote to Mr Mayhew seeking another meeting. He refused, insisting that there could be no substantive political talks unless the IRA surrendered its weapons. The British constantly argued that it was impractical to set a date for all-party talks if the unionists wouldn't turn up. The unionist position, reinforced by British backing, was a useful mechanism for the British to hide behind.

Having already stalled the beginning of all-party talks for over ten months, the British government had now erected an absolute precondition to further movement in the peace process – the demand for decommissioning.

It is important to remember that the surrender of IRA weapons as a precondition to negotiations was never mentioned by the British government before the IRA cessation. Albert Reynolds, speaking on this issue in August 1995, wrote: 'This new precondition they [the British] have introduced was not part of the Downing Street Declaration... . This was not a precondition and there is no point in trying to say now that it was. It certainly was not.'

While stalling on negotiations, the British approach on other fronts was similarly negative and provocative. The summer of 1995 saw the release of Private Lee Clegg, who served just two years for the murder of a seventeen-year-old girl. Following his release he was not only welcomed back into the British army, but was also promoted. British troop levels remained at their 1994 levels, repressive legislation remained in place and the RUC forced a series of provocative Orange marches through Catholic areas. And conditions for Irish political prisoners in England seriously deteriorated.

Sinn Féin warned of the danger to the peace process because of the British government's stalling tactics. I wrote that 'the urgency of the current situation demands that everyone with influence persuade the British government to face up to its responsibility'. We were accused of making threats.

With the peace process on the point of collapse, the imminent visit of President Clinton provided the necessary impetus for London and Dublin to agree a twin-track approach which would tackle the issue of weapons and prepare the ground for all-party talks at the end of February. Although Sinn Féin had serious reservations about John Major's commitment to this twin-track process, the party, in meetings with the International Body and with the two governments, engaged in the twin track positively.

On 16 January the Mitchell Report was published. I welcomed it, saying, 'It provides a basis for moving forward so that all matters can be settled to the satisfaction of all sides as part of the process... . In other words the Mitchell Report points to a possible avenue into all-party talks.' Within hours, John Major unilaterally dumped the report, retaining the old decommissioning precondition which the report had come down against. And he added a new precondition of elections. The date for the commencement of all-party talks, promised for the end of February, was abandoned and movement was again stalled by the actions of the British government.

Throughout the fifteen months in which John Bruton, as taoiseach, played a major part in the peace process, his management of the process was at times flawed and at key points his miscalculations allowed the British to seize control of the process and steadily run it into the sand. On entering office, John Bruton's efforts to appease unionism caused him to declare that there was no nationalist consensus, seriously undermining the basis on which the IRA cessation had been built.

The taoiseach appeared to see his role as a neutral facilitator or arbiter when the process (and the agreements and commitments made by his predecessor Albert Reynolds) required that he play a leading role. The desire to be a neutral referee was clearly seen in October of last year when John Bruton refused to meet with John Hume and myself together, saying that a joint meeting at that time could have caused offence to unionists. The result of this was to cause much concern to nationalists and republicans and to send out the wrong signals in relation to his position on the peace process.

In the face of an ever-present British strategy which attempted to divide Irish nationalist opinion, the situation required that Dublin take a firm stand and act in unison. Instead we had a coalition with no coherent strategy and often contradictory stances in relation to the peace process.

In the spring of last year John Bruton was responsible for breathing life into one of the main obstacles created by the British government. Instead of holding the British government to its commitment to begin inclusive all-party talks, Mr Bruton called for a gesture on decommissioning, giving much-needed credibility to the new British precondition to all-party talks. This precondition alone wasted over fourteen months of the IRA cessation.

Similarly, when Proinsias De Rossa on a visit to Belfast said that elections could play a part in moving the situation forward, the British government once again used Dublin's own words to replace the decommissioning precondition with the election precondition. Despite the united opposition of nationalist opinion, this unionist proposal was subsequently included in the November communiqué from both governments, and was finally conceded in the February communiqué.

The unfortunate reality is that the failure of the Irish government to take a leading, planned and coherent approach to the peace process allowed the British government, working blatantly to a unionist agenda, to dominate, control and manipulate the entire process. The result was that the process failed to deliver in terms of nationalist aspirations and therefore suffered a fatal loss of credibility.

The breaking of the commitment to negotiations by the British government undermined one of the two key elements of the peace process which had led to the cessation. The second element, the commitment on the Irish side to a consensus approach to addressing the causes of conflict, was significantly weakened as a result of the collapse of the Reynolds-led government and the failure of its successor, led by John Bruton, to uphold this commitment. Once the basis of the cessation had been removed, through the breaking of nationalist consensus and the reneging on negotiations by the British, the collapse of the peace process became inevitable. No diplomatic offensive emerged and the Dublin government was perceived to be divided in its approach.

Sinn Féin has approached the proposals in the February joint communiqué positively, as we have done with all other phases of the search for a lasting peace. We are prepared therefore to participate in the consultative talks. I am disappointed, and it is a matter of concern that this process, which was to be jointly sponsored by the two governments, is excluding Sinn Féin's electorate. We are being punished, while those who have refused to engage and are boycotting these consultations are being rewarded with their elections. How can anyone have confidence in a process which discriminates against a party which secures thirty to forty per cent of the nationalist vote in the North? How can anyone suggest that this is an inclusive process when we are quite blatantly excluded?

Sinn Féin has many legitimate concerns regarding the process proposed by the two governments in the joint communiqué of 27 February. We had wished to outline these concerns to the two governments so that the peace process could be restored. The two governments have, however, reverted to the failed policies of isolation and discrimination. These did not work in the past; they will not work now.

Inclusive dialogue led by both governments is the only effective conflict resolution approach. The two governments need to show that there is a real and viable peace process in place. Both governments need to engage pro-actively in the peace process, and the British government, in particular, needs to provide convincing evidence that they are now prepared to engage, in good faith.

In the aftermath of the February summit, the British have again seized, and have been allowed to retain, control of the process – to set the agenda and to prescribe the terms of the engagement. The start of all-party talks has again been delayed from February, as was promised, to June; the proximity talks proposed by the Irish government have been reduced to a charade; the precondition of an election has been built into the process despite universal opposition from nationalist opinion; only those elements of the Mitchell Report which suit the British and unionist positions have been retained, while suggestions regarding prisoners, licensed weapons, policing, repressive legislation and plastic bullets have all been dumped. The Irish government has been excluded from decisions on the elections and on the internal affairs of the Six-County state when the peace process was clearly based on the commitment of the two governments to jointly lead a process to address all issues.

The British government has effectively created a six-month vacuum in which it is possible that no substantive negotiations can take place. June marks the beginning of the Orange marching season, and the summer recess of the British parliament will follow soon after. By stalling, delaying and attempting to micro-manage the peace process, John Major has succeeded in downgrading it and in turning the clock back to the old narrow talks-about-talks process. In doing so he has strangled the hope created in 1993 by the Irish peace process.

Eighteen months ago the IRA acted in good faith to enhance the potential that Irish nationalist opinion had collectively worked to create at that time. The good faith approach by the IRA and their willingness to take risks for peace was misread by the British as a sign of weakness, and they used it as an opportunity to destroy the republican struggle.

On the Irish side, some elements of the coalition government which had inherited the peace process and therefore had not been part of building it failed to measure up to the new situation. They showed themselves unable to break free from their traditional anti-republican mindset and incapable of standing up to the British government in pursuit of a just and lasting settlement.

What is required now to rebuild the peace process is a political package which has the ability to address and resolve the issues which have led to recurring conflict in the past. This involves the honouring of the agreements and commitments which brought about the IRA cessation in 1994. Broad commitments to negotiations, already repeatedly given and in turn repeatedly broken, are clearly not now enough.

What is required are specific, public and unconditional guarantees of: a firm date for the commencement of all-party talks at the earliest possible time; no preconditions to these talks; a fixed time-scale for the commencement and conduct of the negotiations; an open agenda with no attempt to predetermine or preclude any outcome; both governments leading the negotiations process; an effective conflict resolution approach to the negotiations on the Irish side and, as part of this, a pro-active and evident international and diplomatic strategy to advance these positions supplementary to the negotiations.

In other words, there should be no demands that cannot be delivered, such as decommissioning; no commitment to political formulas which are elevated to political principles before negotiations have even begun, as happened in the Forum on the issue of the unionist veto; no further false trails into negotiations which have the effect of providing potential or actual stalls and diversions.

The absence of democratic negotiations, despite the commitments given by the two governments prior to the IRA cessation, and since, most notably in the November communiqué, led to the collapse of the peace process. The British government must bear the primary responsibility for this, but if we are to avoid the mistakes of the past, the Irish government, which was to have been an equal partner in the search for a lasting settlement, must accept its responsibility for the failure also.

The demand for inclusive negotiations as the means to an agreed peace settlement is hardly an unreasonable one. It is a demand which is shared by the vast majority of people on this island and by the majority of the British people also. The refusal to respond to the democratic imperative of negotiations and the rejection of the popular demand for talks to begin was the rock on which the IRA cessation finally broke.

The basis therefore for rebuilding the IRA cessation and the peace process itself must be the honouring of the commitments which led to the IRA decision eighteen months ago. All-party talks should now be convened without preconditions, with an open agenda and with an agreed time frame and, in the context of negotiations, an agreed and democratic Irish consensus approach to these negotiations, to ensure that the causes of the conflict are effectively dealt with, needs to be applied.

The Irish Times
(March 1996)

TRANSFORMING HOPE INTO REALITY: NEGOTIATING A NEW BEGINNING

In elections on 30 May 1996 Sinn Féin received 15.47 per cent of the vote, which was greater than the combined vote of the five smaller parties participating in the talks, and almost three times the Alliance Party vote. The British government stated that these elections would provide a clear, direct and automatic route into all-party talks. Despite this, Sinn Féin was excluded. This is the speech which Gerry Adams planned to make to the plenary session of the all-party talks on 10 June 1996.

IN THE OPENING line from Bobby Sands' diary on the first day of his hunger strike, he wrote, 'I am standing on the threshold of another trembling world.'

Today there are many in Ireland and throughout the world who at this defining moment in our history are fearful of the future. There is an undercurrent of hope, coupled with uncertainty, of optimism combined with apprehension. This is clearly evident as they watch and listen to those of us gathered here.

The people of Ireland, from every corner of our country and from throughout the Irish diaspora across the world, have expressed that hope in their yearning for a lasting peace settlement and new democracy. This gathering represents the historical opportunity to translate that hope into reality.

Today will be indelibly imprinted in the history of our country. We have before us a unique and unprecedented opportunity to forge a peace accord for all the people of the island. If this opportunity is to be translated into reality, we must all respond to it with courage and imagination.

Más féidir linn atá bailithe anseo inniu – daoine as gach aicme agus as gach traidisiún sa tír seo – más féidir linn an dúshlán seo a fhreagairt, beimíd ag cur tús leis an turas ó chomhrac agus aighneas go dtí síocháin agus daonlathas.

If we who are gathered here, representing all sections and strands of opinion on this island, can meet these challenges, today will mark the commencement of the transition from conflict and division to peace and democracy.

Sinn Féin have played a pivotal role in creating today's opportunity. We are here as peacemakers.

It is our collective responsibility to make an outstanding success of the process in which we are engaged. It is our task to build a democracy which will be owned by every woman, man and child on this island. This democracy is one which they must have a part in creating because it is they who must benefit from the political, economic, social and cultural benefits which will inevitably flow form it.

That means removing the causes of conflict. British policy in Ireland has manifestly failed. Partition has failed. The decades of unionist rule in the North were exclusive and partisan. Those days are gone forever. There is no going back to the failed policies and structures of the past, to the domination of a one-party unionist state supported by the British government.

There can be no return to the abuses and bitterness which marked the Stormont period.

We must move forward. How do we do that? How do we fulfil the potential, the ideals and dreams, so that our children and future generations can enjoy peace and justice?

Is é rún daingean Shinn Féin an próiséas síochána seo a athbheochan. Creidimíd gur cóir na fadhbanna atá againn a fhuascailt go daonlathach agus go síochánta chun réiteach cothrom agus buan a bhaint amach – réiteach atá le toil gach duine ar an oileán seo.

Sinn Féin is absolutely committed to democratic and peaceful methods of resolving problems and we are determined to win an equitable and lasting agreement which can command the allegiance of all the people of this island by accommodating diversity and providing for national reconciliation.

This will not be easy. The road ahead will be difficult and dangerous and risky for all of us, but working together I am convinced we can succeed. It is my conviction that we will have a peace settlement. I am convinced that if we are resilient, if we dig deep, we can overcome all obstacles.

I believe that we can put the anguish of the past behind us; we can heal the wounds; we can learn to forgive. We have all suffered over the generations, we have all lost loved ones, and friends and neighbours. We must learn the lessons of the past – not to recriminate, for as William Butler Yeats said: 'We need not feel the bitterness of the past to discover its meaning for the present and future.'

I acknowledge here the hurt which republicans have caused and I pledge Sinn Féin's total commitment to the task of ensuring that that never happens again.

Part of our joint responsibility is to help illuminate the way, to chart the road forward and provide the people of Ireland with beacons or guidelines, based on international experiences, as we traverse this period of transition. We must embark upon this journey from the past, through our transition and into a new future.

If it is to be successful, the process of negotiation must tackle the many issues which lie at the heart of the conflict.

A viable process of negotiation requires a good faith engagement on all sides. That is Sinn Féin's commitment.

These negotiations need to be inclusive and with all relevant issues addressed in a full and comprehensive fashion.

All issues need to be on the agenda, with nothing agreed until everything is agreed.

There can be no preconditions.

None of those engaged in the negotiating process can have a veto and all involved must be committed to reaching agreement.

There can be no attempt to predetermine the outcome, nor to preclude any outcome, to the negotiations.

The negotiations – to have any real momentum – need to be conducted within an agreed time-frame. We all need to work to make significant progress by the September review date.

Sinn Féin is an Irish republican party. Our objective is to end British rule in Ireland. We want to see a society on this island which reflects the diversity of our people. This is not therefore a northern issue only. Partition affects all of us. Irish freedom, democracy and peace are in the interests of all the people on the island. Sinn Féin seeks national self-determination, the unity and independence of Ireland as a sovereign state.

In our view this issue of sovereignty, the claim of the British government to sovereignty in Ireland, is *the* key matter which must be addressed in any negotiation.

The British government have stated that it 'has no selfish strategic or economic interest in Northern Ireland. Our role is to help, enable and encourage.' If this be the case then the London government should join with the Dublin government to help, enable and encourage the transfer of sovereignty to the people of Ireland.

And while a peace settlement may create conditions for peaceful coexistence, the prosperity and well-being of the people of this island rests on the restoration of sovereignty to them.

We know that others hold a different view, but it is our intention to put the issue of the union on the agenda. Negotiations are an area of struggle for Irish republicans. We know there are difficulties for everyone, not least the unionist section of our people, but I think it is fair to say that there is a broad acceptance that these negotiations must bring about substantive and significant change. From Sinn Féin's point of view these changes must be in the following areas:

Constitutional and political;

Demilitarisation;

Democratic rights.

Let us discuss these and other matters in a positive and constructive atmosphere.

There are many issues which fuel the conflict and which need to be tackled and which do not require negotiation. For example: parity of esteem and equality of treatment will have to be dealt with; the imbalance in the employment ratio; equality in economic development; greater and more equally shared prosperity; the Irish language and culture need equality of treatment; there is a long overdue need to bring about the empowerment and inclusion of deprived and marginalised communities. These should be pursued inside and outside negotiations.

The whole issue of demilitarisation needs to be resolved. This includes the release of all political prisoners, disarmament, policing, the administration of justice and an end to repressive legislation.

Tá an méid seo soiléir. Glactar leis go forleathan go bhfuil gá le hathruithe bhunúsacha. Níl eagla ar Sinn Feein roimh an tathrú sin. Ghlac muid go fonnmhar le hathruithe. Is é an tathrú a bhunóidh réiteach buan síochána. Tá sé de dhualgas orainne déanamh cinnte de nach féidir na hathruithe a filleadh ar ais.

Sinn Féin seeks change. We are not afraid of change. We have embraced change. It is the life-blood of political struggle and the basis for a lasting peace agreement. Our task must be to make change irreversible.

Some weeks ago, in a spirit of generosity and of trying to create a space in which progress could be made, I stated Sinn Féin's preparedness, in the context of proper all-party talks and in a situation in which all the other parties sign up to the Mitchell principles and report, that Sinn Féin will do so also.

I welcome the appointment of Senator Mitchell and his colleagues to this negotiating process. Sinn Féin has long argued for an international dimension to the search for peace in Ireland. The international dimension is one which can play a crucial part in maintaining the momentum and dynamic through the negotiations.

Failure through negotiations is inconceivable. There is no room for failure through error. We need to be persistent and pragmatic.

Clearly, there is a huge gap of distrust between nationalists and unionists. It must be bridged. We need to secure an accommodation, based on equality, which rejects the possibility of any individual, or any section of people, irrespective of religion, gender, age, disability or politics, from being discriminated against. No process which excludes any section of opinion can hope to be successful.

Does anyone here doubt that Irish nationalists and unionists together have the ability to govern ourselves better than any British ministers? Do even those here who profess a loyalty to the British connection trust the British government? Would it not be better for us to build trust among ourselves.

I believe that Ian Paisley and David Trimble, with whom I have many disagreements, but who care about their people, can with the rest of us do a much better job of running our economy and looking after our health service, our elderly, our young, our urban and rural communities.

We don't needs British ministers. The people of this island have the right and the ability to govern ourselves.

Theip ar ar tharla go dtí seo. Caithfimíd a thuiscint anois – mar nár thuig muid riamh – gur ar scáth a chéile a mhairimíd. Caithfear tabhairt agus glacadh a bheith ann. Tá sé in am againn na dearcaí claonta a fhágáil ar leataoibh agus aghaidh a thabhairt ar na deacrachtaí atá ann. Caithfimíd ár gcloiginn a ardú os cionn na mbaracáidí – baracáidí na heagla agus an amhrais atá ina gcuid lárnach d'ár stair.

What has gone before has failed all of us. We must realise now, as we never have before, our interdependence on each other; that we must give as well as take.

It is time to set aside our prejudices, to acknowledge the difficulties which exist and to lift our heads above the barricades of fear and suspicion which have been part of our history for much too long.

This is equally true of the relationship between Irish republicans and the British. Mr Major, let each of us put behind us the failures of the past, the lack of confidence, the distrust. We can do business, we can find agreement if we are prepared to take risks and if the political will exists on all sides.

Today I offer the hand of friendship to all our political

opponents. I pledge Sinn Féin's commitment to peace and to negotiations and to agreement. We have the political will to pursue these goals and we ask others to demonstrate that same commitment. That is the only reliable guarantor for all our future.

The imperative of peace demands that we apply ourselves to the enormous task before us. Peace cannot be built unilaterally. Peace cannot be based on inequality or injustice or exclusion. Peace demands justice. It requires freedom. Building peace is a collective responsibility. In setting out the republican position, I also want to stress our willingness to listen to other positions and to see and to uphold the dignity of all sections of our people.

Sinn Féin is committed to a transformation of Irish society. We know that peace is not simply the absence of violence. Our vision sees beyond the present conflict and beyond the present phase of our history. Our vision foresees the unity of the people of this island. East with West, North with South, urban with rural, Catholic with Protestant and dissenter.

Our vision is for the redistribution of wealth, for the well-being of the aged, for the advancement of youth, for the liberation of women and for the protection of our children.

Our vision rejects forced emigration and unemployment, the destruction of the environment, cultural oppression, sexism and inequality.

Our vision embraces education. It embraces democracy. It is economic, as well as political. Our vision is for a free Ireland and for a free people. It is for an end to war.

It foresees the relationship between Britain and Ireland resting upon our mutual independence. It is this vision which sustains our struggle. It demands that we take risks. Negotiations are an area of struggle for us. It demands that we persevere in our efforts to reach agreement and a new accommodation between all our people.

Seo uair na cinniúna inár stair agus caithfimíd an uair a fhreastal. Seo an tam ag muintir an oileáin seo chun seasamh le chéile agus muid ag cur chun bóthar ar turas achrannach a thabharfaidh chun réitigh sinn.

Tá a bhfuil i ndán dúinn feasta – cé acu ann chun tosaigh nó ar gcúl a ghluaisimíd – ag brath ar na cinnidh agus na gníomhartha a dhéanfaimid as seo amach. D'fhág an stair dúshlán ag an doras againn. Tá sé riachtanach go néireoidh linn d'ár muintir uile agus dona glúnta atá fós le teacht.

This is a watershed moment in our history which must be seized. Now is the time for all the people of this island to stand together as we embark on this difficult journey toward agreement.

Our decisions and actions will determine whether we move forward. History has placed a challenge at all our doors. We must succeed in this for all our people and for generations yet to be born.

Nobel laureate Seamus Heaney put it well: 'Once in a lifetime the longed for tidal wave of justice can rise up and hope and history rhyme.'

Let us make hope and history rhyme.

(10 June 1996)

349

Glossary

ar mhaith leat dul ag siúl?: would you like to go for a walk?
arís: again
bígí ciúin: be quiet
blimp: look
blirt: fool
bogging: dirty
broo, bureau: Labour Exchange
boul: walk
cage-car: open military lorry with a wire cage to ward off
  grenades
ceart: right
champ: potatoes mashed with scallions and butter
cheeser: chestnut
Chi-Chi: James Chichester-Clark, prime minister of Northern
  Ireland, 1969-71
clár: agenda
cog ecker: copy homework
crabbit: cranky, bad-tempered
cratur: creature, fellow
Cumann na mBan: republican women's organisation
dander: stroll
deoch don dorais: one for the road
dia dhuit: hello, good day
doffer: linen-worker
dunt: shoulder-charge
Eire Nua: New Ireland, political manifesto of Sinn Féin
falourie: the origin of falourie is obscure. David Hammond
  suggests it may mean 'forlorn' or be a variant of 'Gable'oury
  man', which in English ballads means Gabriel, holy man
fenians: generic term used to describe Catholics; the name
  comes from the Fenian movement, the Irish Republican
  Brotherhood, a secret society founded in 1858 to fight for
  Irish independence
geg: joke
glyp: giddy person

gravy-ring: doughnut
grip-work: piece-work
gulder: shout
gurn: complain
hallion: rogue
jawbox: big washtub or sink
knollered: caught
latchiko: oddball
Lazy K: Long Kesh
lumber: kissing session
maidin mhaith: good morning
marley: marble
Mick: Catholic
mixed-ups: assorted sweets
Nollaig shona (dhuit/dhaoibh): Happy Christmas (to you)
Oíche Chiúin: Silent Night
Omeath: being just over the border, Omeath was one of the
    nearest spots where Northerners could avail of the South's
    more liberal licensing laws, especially Sunday opening;
    Omeath's pubs reputedly never closed
Paisley Amnesty: in May 1968 after the ousting of Captain
    Terence O'Neill, the Northern prime minister, his successor,
    Major Chichester-Clark, announced an amnesty for public
    order offences. Its primary purpose was to release Rev Ian
    Paisley, who was serving a jail sentence for obstructing a
    civil rights march. As a spin-off charges were also dropped
    against a number of civil rights activists
peeler: policeman
Penal Days: 18th century suppression of Roman Catholics in
    Ireland
picker: instrument used for picking or cutting the ends of
    linen threads
pigging: smelly, dirty
pockel: awkward person
poitín: poteen, illicit spirits
poke: twisted paper cone
Prod: Protestant
Ralioh: street game

reddener: blushing face
rubber: rubber apron
scoutsie: lift
sean nós: old style
sevens: Irish dancing
simmet: net vest or undershirt
sin é: that's it
sláinte: (your) health
slagging: teasing
sleekit: cunning, sly
snout: tobacco
Specials: the Ulster Special Constabulary set up in November 1920 by the British government. It was the main arm of the Northern government until the Royal Ulster Constabulary (RUC) was established in mid-1922. The Specials included a full-time section, the A force, and two part-time sections, the B and C forces. The A and C Specials were disbanded at the end of 1925. The B Specials were retained until 1970.
spondooliks: money
stumer: fool
Taig: Catholic
wackey: watchman
whack: prison sentence, time